THE END
OF THE
POSTWAR ERA

THE END OF THE POSTWAR ERA

A New Balance of World Power

ALASTAIR BUCHAN

Saturday Review Press
E. P. Dutton & Co., Inc.
New York

327
B918e

ISBN: 0-8415-0338-9
Library of Congress Catalog Number: 74-10476

To David and Benjamin

Contents

Preface

Since 1962 the Ditchley Foundation near Oxford has been an active centre for the international discussion of different aspects of public policy, principally between American and British scholars and officials. In 1971, the Foundation's Council, responsive to the multiple processes of change taking place in international politics, wisely decided to organize a series of five related international conferences over a period of some fifteen months on 'The Bases of Foreign Policy'. Unwisely, I accepted the invitation of the Director, Sir Michael Stewart, to write a book that would attempt to analyse the more significant aspects of the changing international system, using the discussions at these conferences as a foundation.

I say 'unwisely' because as the process of drafting advanced, it became increasingly apparent how difficult it is at this very moment to find firm footing on which to analyse the process of change, still more to make predictions about its course; for, quite apart from the dramatic intervention of such events as Watergate, or the fourth Arab-Israel war, we are in an era of negotiations on several planes of international activity, whose outcome cannot be judged with any certainty. I nearly abandoned the attempt, and persuaded myself to continue only from a belief in the value of an effort by someone to try and draw together the multiple threads of change, however tentative are the conclusions that one can offer at present.

I am very grateful to the participants in these Ditchley conferences—many of whom sacrificed valuable weekends involving trans-Atlantic flights—for stimulating my own thoughts and focussing my own perspective. I also owe especial thanks to friends on both sides of the Atlantic, in particular to Percy Cradock, James Fawcett (who served as the rapporteur of the five conferences), Bayless Manning (President of the Council on Foreign Relations in New York) and Michael Stewart himself for reading and criticizing my draft. Its judgements are entirely my own, but I should like to draw attention to the date that stands at the foot of this page. After it was well into the process of publication, the constitutional crisis in the United States began to deepen, and conflict erupted between the Arab States and Israel with consequences not only for the Middle East, but for the Soviet-American relationship, European-American relations, and energy relationships in a way which neither I—nor, as far as I know, anyone else—had foreseen. I was able to rescue it for long enough to make certain corrections, but anyone who attempts to write about the immediate past and the immediate future is inevitably the victim of the present. I hope, therefore, the reader will accept this book for what it is, not only one man's judgements, but those made at a particular point in time.

I am most grateful to Jessie Doughtery and Joanna Barry for typing and organizing my illegible manuscript and to Benjamin Buchan for assistance in editing it.

A.F.B.

September 1973
Oxford

PART ONE

Introduction

I

As the last quarter of this century approaches, anyone who is concerned with the public interest, national or international, has a curious sense of having lost old landmarks and of being confronted with a new and unfamiliar landscape. True, every mature person born in this century is inured to a rapid and insistent pace of technological and social change: anyone in their mid-twenties, for instance, can remember the world before manned space flight or polio vaccine: anyone over thirty-five can recall what it was like before television or penicillin or the welfare state: those over sixty-five can recall the world not only before radio but before women's suffrage.

And the pace of change has been no less rapid in the political relations of mankind. The rise of two states to the position of super-powers is a phenomenon unknown in modern history. The number of sovereign states has more than doubled in the past fifteen years, as the difficult process of decolonization has substantially been accomplished. The impact of one civilization upon another, the speed and distance over which it is possible to transmit ideas and comprehension, to project power or resentments, has steadily increased throughout the past quarter century. The volume and value of world trade has risen by 250 per cent in the last ten years alone.

Yet for just over twenty-five years, for roughly a generation, we have lived within a broadly unaltered structure of international power, a system dominated by the antagonism of two diverse coalitions that aggregated around the United States and Soviet Union in the decade after the close of the Second World War. This bipolar balance, clamped on the world by mutual fear and antagonism before there had been any comprehensive settlement of the unfinished business of the Second World War, began to fracture some time ago. But it is only in the last three or four years that the end of what one may call the post-war era, a period longer than that of active Cold War, has become palpable, under the impetus of two forces in particular: the Soviet Union's attainment of full strategic parity with the United States and the latter's acceptance of the limitations of American power; and a deepening of hostility, that has both national and ideological roots, between the Soviet Union and China to a point just short of open conflict.

As a consequence of these and other subsidiary causes, the developed and semi-developed world is now no longer rigidly divided into hierarchically organized coalitions, but appears to be resolving itself into a different pattern in which there are a number of power centres of different strengths and interests, and in which ideological differences can, within limits, be over-ridden by other considerations. China has re-emerged as a full member of the United Nations and of international society in general; the European Community has been successfully enlarged; and Japan has been for several years the world's third strongest economic power. The President of the United States has accepted, indeed praised, the greater stability of such a 'multipolar world'.[1]

At the beginning of 1973 the ordinary citizen, recalling China's admission to the UN in 1971 and her recognition by almost every significant country,* having read of the strategic arms limitation and other agreements between the Soviet Union and the United States in May 1972, remembering the signing of the intra-German treaty and the electoral victory of the West German government that signed it in November, and witnessing the final withdrawal of the United States from Vietnam early in 1973, might pardonably feel that for the first time in forty years (that is, since the Japanese invasion of Manchuria or Hitler's reoccupation of the Rhineland) something that could be called peace has descended on the world. Men must have felt like this when learning of the Treaty of Westphalia. True, there is still blood being shed in parts of Africa and Asia; true, the nations of the world continue to spend nearly $200 billion on armaments and armed forces; true, there are areas of continuing high tension such as the Middle East and South East Asia. But the objectives, the preoccupations and the assumptions of governments have changed profoundly in the past few years.

* The United States and China have not yet granted each other formal diplomatic recognition but have sent distinguished permanent emissaries to each other's capitals.

In the industrial democracies, and many semi-industrial ones as well, the level of personal affluence in terms of housing, warmth, nourishment, freedom from disease, physical mobility and access to information has increased beyond the best expectation of the reformers even of the 1940s. The spread of both education and information has created greater social mobility and equality. The gifts of science may not be inherently beneficent, but the great discoveries of the mid-century years laid the basis of strategies of deterrence, which despite their risks enabled an international system cleft by an ideological rift to survive without another global war; a quarter of a century later the major scientific advances are now primarily in the beneficent field of the life sciences which has led among other things to the Green Revolution in tropical agriculture. Indeed one well-known student of the future, Dr Herman Kahn, has suggested that we are in the midst of *une belle époque* like that at the end of the last century, though if we are vigilant it need have no such disastrous ending.[2]

Yet the problems created by the continued existence of two quite antithetical conceptions of domestic and world order, of nuclear and other weapons of mass destruction, of poverty and anger, of gross disparities of affluence or of national power, by the emergence of a large number of unstable states, have not in any sense been solved: they have merely been altered or modified, while new problems are rising up to join them.

Moreover, these developments reflect only one side of the balance sheet and there is much in the other column. Within the industrial democratic societies, the complexity of economic and social planning has forced governments to acquire powers of decision and enforcement which would have been considered draconian a generation ago; yet few comparable advances have been made in the power of the citizen to protect his own rights, still less to participate in or influence these decisions. Hence the familiar phenomenon of alienation, with all its social consequences, compounded by the development of mass communications which themselves now set the agenda of popular debate and make the task of political leadership increasingly difficult. We do not, therefore, know whether our western societies possess the internal coherence, the fidelity to their own ideals, to confront those societies that are led from the top downwards in a prolonged test of wills, if our own assumptions about coexistence and a stable balance prove wrong.

Nor can we assume that because the extremes of ideological competition have been modified, because the Sino–Soviet alliance has now been fractured for some years, because there is now a certain agenda of Soviet–American cooperation, because China is no longer completely shuttered from the outside world, we are now returning to anything resembling the kind of multilateral balance of power which preserved stability in Europe for long periods in the eighteenth and nineteenth centuries. Limited wars or mutual compensation in distant continents are no longer accepted as conventional instruments of great-power adjustments. Sino–Soviet hostility, though ideological in expression, partly derives from the existence of a long land border on which full-scale conflict could easily arise, and from which one can not say for certain that the non-Communist powers could divorce themselves. Japan, though a powerful and dynamic trading nation, is strategically vulnerable by reason of her geographic position, her population density and her dependence on imported raw materials; she has a period of difficult debate ahead to decide whether and how she should attempt to translate her remarkable economic power into political influence in the world, or to determine what her settled national interests should be.

Western Europe, where the aspirations of the founders of the Economic Community in 1957 to create a central focus of political authority as well as of economic coordination were thwarted for nearly a decade by President de Gaulle's insistence on a *Europe des Patries*, enters the new era with none of the attributes of a single powerful actor in world politics, and at best will need the whole of the coming decade and more to acquire them. Her constituent countries are strategically vulnerable like Japan and like Japan have become accustomed to American strategic protection for the inner confidence to expand and progress. Yet the credibility of such protection in a crisis may now be in doubt.

The United States enters the post-war era in a similar mood of uncertainty. While it is mistaken, or at any rate premature, to talk of a new mood of isolationism, there is no doubt that a combination of events, the bitterness and frustration engendered by the Vietnam War, pressing domestic problems including racial conflict and urban regeneration, and serious deficits in overseas trade and payments, has destroyed the domestic alliance of business, organized labour and the universities that was the political basis of an active American foreign policy in the post-war era. Already the years of the first Nixon Administration have witnessed a more careful definition of American overseas interests. Yet too narrow a definition risks a shift in the balance of global power and the isolation of the United States at a time when she is becoming economically more dependent on the outside world.

Nor does the monolithic character of both Soviet and Chinese society, the fact that both have less need to worry about domestic support for external policy, mean that they are free from similar constraints and choices. The Soviet Union, now in most significant senses the equal of the United States in long-range strategic power, with an increasing ability to project its influence to distant areas, less dependent on the fortunes of overseas Communist parties, may appear to be becoming more assertive and more influential at a time when the United States and its allies are becoming introspective or uncertain of their interests. But she too faces uncomfortable domestic pressures, as the non-Russian minorities increase faster than the Russian, as the maintenance of strategic parity creates strains on her still limited technological base, and as her agricultural productivity fails to keep pace with both expectations and with population growth so that she must rely on the United States and other western countries to help feed her people in a bad year. Is she as self-sufficient and as powerful as she seems? Indeed is her conception of state power a modern or an antiquated one, and to what extent can she impose her own conceptions on the rest of the international community? Can she pursue a new relationship with the United States without intensifying Chinese hostility to her? Can she contain Chinese influence in the developing world without an increasingly onerous range of new commitments?

As for China, she too must make choices soon. Despite the vast size of her population she is still only 'the largest village' in terms of per capita income, and the expansion of her technological base has been seriously constricted by the disorganization of the Cultural Revolution and the requirements of defence. She may not be an aggressive power but she is a vulnerable one. Moreover, she is a proud and an ambitious one in terms of influence and she must soon decide where, and in what frame of reference, such influence is to be exerted. Are her interests, for instance, primarily regional or are they more extensive? Again, are they to be advanced by traditional techniques of exerting power and influence or by other means?

Moreover, although these five power centres include all the states that possess nuclear weapons, comprise 44 per cent of the world's present population, produce three quarters of its wealth and account for about 65 per cent of its trade, they dwell in the midst of a large constellation of middle and lesser states. Some, notably developed or semi-developed countries such as Canada, Australia, Iran, and Brazil have clearly much to gain from the end of a tight bipolar structure of world politics, as affording them greater freedom of action without jeopardizing their security. In certain areas, notably the Middle East, tension and conflict are beginning to be affected by changes in the nature of the central balance and other factors. But in certain areas where the interests of two or more of the major power centres conflict or overlap – the Mediterranean, the Indian sub-continent, South East Asia, East Africa – the relationships of the local states seems likely to be complicated by the development of multipolarity.

This differentiation in the involvement of different parts of the developing world in the competition or conflicts of the great powers coincides with an increasing distinction in their economic and social prospects. The Third World, *le tiers monde*, has ceased to have much meaning as an accurate description of the new or non-industrial states of the world, all supposedly with common problems, objectives and affiliations. Some, like the oil states, are on their way to becoming rich and even powerful, at least in regional terms; some, like the states of the Pacific littoral, are prosperous; new middle powers like Brazil, Iran and Nigeria are emerging. But many, in Asia, Latin America and Africa, are stagnating politically under military regimes, while in some countries, notably in Latin America, population growth is continuously eroding economic growth, creating a destitute peasantry and vast urban slums with the attendant evils of disease, terrorism and violence.

At the same time, the conscience of the rich, the readiness of the industrial states to sustain a high level of aid to the developing world in general, is becoming blunted. They are becoming increasingly concerned with the problems of their own social and physical environment, and there is some disillusionment with the achievements of earlier assistance programmes. Neither the Western nor the Communist powers any longer regard the developing world as one large amphitheatre in which each side contends for influence; each of the major powers has become more selective in its dealings with different parts of it; and in the Western

countries that have used military intervention either to preserve their own interests or in pursuance of some general conception of order, there is an even stronger disillusionment with its
utility.

Yet, although the major powers may be becoming increasingly
preoccupied with their own affairs or their mutual relationships,
they do not in any sense form a closed system. For one thing,
given even cautious estimates of industrial growth rates over the
next decade, their competitive demands on finite sources of certain
raw materials are creating new patterns of trade, dependence and
competition in the developing world. For another, the conflict
between nationalism and transnationalism, of which the multinational company is simply one aspect, is creating a new dimension
in the relations of the developed and the developing world.

Just over a hundred years ago, after the American Civil War and
the Franco-Prussian War, the preoccupations of the major powers
– even in countries like Britain which had been largely unaffected
by either war – underwent the same sort of change as we have been
experiencing in recent years. One of the most acute observers of
his day, Walter Bagehot, the Editor of *The Economist* wrote then.

> 'A political country is like an American forest; you have only to
> cut down the old trees, and immediately new trees come up to
> replace them: the seeds were waiting in the ground, and they
> began to grow as soon as the withdrawal of the old ones brought
> in new light and air. These new questions of themselves would
> have made a new atmosphere, new parties, new debates.'[3]

II

If we live in a high civilization and, for the moment, a relatively
war-free world, it is also an anxious one, and no politician or citizen in any field of activity could now accept, even in jest, Salis-
bury's famous description of the conduct of British foreign policy
(even though he said it partly in exasperation at his colleagues),
'English policy is to float lazily down stream, occasionally putting
out a diplomatic boat-hook to avoid collision.'[4] It is not merely that
a much higher proportion of a much larger intellectual population
is professionally concerned with the analysis of political, scientific
and economic trends than was the case in the last *belle époque*; it is
not only that capital-intensive societies must plan much further

into the future than earlier and simpler ones; it is also that the historical experience of this century makes us continuously aware of the disastrous consequences of empty confidence – the Wall Street crash of 1929, the failure of appeasement in the 1930s, the endemic failure of Soviet agriculture, the unsaleability of the Anglo-French *Concorde*, to take examples from four different fields and two epochs. Being secular, interdependent societies in a world of diminishing distances we have lost what J.H.Plumb has called the 'sanction of the past'.* We know that neither the gods, the Royal Navy, nor the broad oceans offer us salvation; only our own foresight and alertness can provide it.

In an era where the consequences of errors of judgement, in the policies of individual nations, in the assessment of economic or scientific developments, can have such serious consequences, it is not surprising that increasing attention should be devoted to the study of the future. Thinkers have always been concerned with the study of the present as a possible key to the future; but as the century has progressed, governments also have had to project their forecasting further ahead, originally because of the increasing complexity of military equipment (the first *Dreadnought* was in the water a year after its keel was laid in 1906: a comparable ship now takes between seven and ten years to design, build and fit). Official forecasting in many other fields than defence, in transport, civil aviation, energy, housing, and education, now runs a number of years ahead, and what was once a bold innovation, the Soviet five-year plan, now seems for many purposes to cover too brief a span of time. Despite the unpredictability of international politics, Foreign Offices now have planning staffs. Great corporations whose investment plans take many years to mature must also attempt to assess as accurately as they can what will be the economic, political and social climate in which their projects will reach maturity, and, as with governments, the decisions they make today help condition the future.

The study of the future can be pursued along two lines. On the one hand, it can take the form of projections to some future point, say, ten years hence, of those developments or trends in economic, social or technological activity for which a firm statistical basis in the recent past, say the preceding twenty years, exists. Thus if a wide enough range of factors can be comprehended it is possible

* 'The strength of the past is far, far weaker than it was a generation ago, indeed few societies have ever had a past in such galloping dissolution as this.' (*The Death of the Past*, London: Macmillan, 1969.)

to achieve a rough sketch of a society or the world a decade hence; or rather a number of alternative sketches, since straight-line projections of past trends into the future are, in most fields, almost always wrong.* One may call this descriptive forecasting, and much effort is devoted to it even though its evident limitations are sufficiently apparent to induce caution: economic forecasting, both short and long term, has acquired no infallibility, even though it has greatly advanced in recent years: in technico-economic forecasting most estimates made fifteen years or so ago about the competitiveness of civil nuclear energy with fossil fuels, for instance, proved premature by a decade or more. Even demographic forecasting, despite recent refinements, has often proved wide of the mark; Britain and France were judged a generation ago to be in for an inevitable period of falling birth rates; even the apparently more calculable estimates of rapid population growth for the developing world or of the exponential growth in the demand for oil may prove overdrawn, though they are unlikely to prove wholly wrong.

In addition to the prediction of developments in spheres of activity that lend themselves readily to quantification, interesting attempts have been made, particularly in France and the United States, to attempt descriptive projections of more imponderable factors such as relative national dynamism or political climate; by studying trends or patterns of social and cultural factors, such as education, voting, political participation, industrial disputes, personal savings and so on. In the hands of skilled and cautious political scientists like Bertrand de Jouvenel or Karl Deutsch who are always conscious of the element of the incalculable in political affairs, this provides some stimulating insights into our possible futures, even though Herman Kahn's sweeping conjectures about the long, or even the mid-term, future may lack credibility.[5]

The other approach to 'futurology' relies only partly on quantitative extrapolations, and is concerned to help provide the basis of judgements about the kind of international or other situations that we wish to see develop. It is concerned with values and with

* The danger in straight-line projections has perhaps its most famous example in Condorcet's essay of 1784 when he spoke of 'the great probability that we have fewer great changes and fewer large revolutions to expect from the future than from the past. The progress of enlightenment in all the sciences throughout every part of Europe, the prevailing spirit of moderation and peace, the sort of disrepute into which Machiavellism is beginning to fall, seem to assure us that henceforth wars and revolutions will be less frequent.'

choice within the framework of such quantitative predictions as we can reasonably rely upon. Its technique is to use our knowledge of the present and the recent past to construct two or more models or scenarios of an aspect of future relationships, in order to determine what are their advantages and disadvantages, either from the standpoint of one's own interests or that of the community in general, and what are the key variables that will produce different results.*

Though much may be said here of choices, I should make it clear that this brief study does not attempt a systematic study of the future of the international system, nor to evolve fully developed models of it. For one thing it would require a team of experts in many different fields to produce the different quantitative assessments or to construct the comprehensive models for either descriptive or normative forecasting.

Moreover, this is not an opportune moment to undertake such an essay in conjecture, for the reason that although the post-war international system has profoundly altered over recent years, we are still in the midst of the subsequent 'era of negotiations'. Until its outcome is clearer, the firm basis for an examination of the more distant future, of 1984 and beyond, does not yet exist. Over the next few years, for instance, seven significant international negotiations will be in train: the second round of strategic arms limitation negotiations (SALT) between the Soviet Union and the United States (and possibly involving other powers as well); the thirty-four-nation Conference on European Security and Co-operation; a negotiation between the members of NATO and the Warsaw Pact on mutual and balanced force reductions in Europe; intensive discussions and negotiations on the adaptation of the international monetary system; the Tokyo negotiations on the reduction of trade barriers under the auspices of GATT; a new conference on the Law of the Sea which will have important

* This is a technique originally adapted from economics, and now often used in the analysis of international relations. I attempted, for instance, with a small team of European colleagues during the Gaullist 'ice age' of the late 1960s, to construct a series of alternative Western Europes in the 1970s with a view of seeing what kind of Community structure might emerge, given different sets of assumptions about external and internal factors. It has now been partly over-taken by actual decisions and developments, but I hope it played a modest role in helping Europeans make up their minds about the kinds of Community different factors and decisions would produce. *Europe's Futures, Europe's Choices: Models of Western Europe in the 1970s* (London: Chatto & Windus for ISS 1969).

political and economic implications; and further negotiations between the oil producing states and the principal oil-importing
countries.

In addition, of course, even if one can make reasonably firm
assumptions about the political climate in the industrial democracies, there are important developments impending within
several major governments which may occur at any time in the
next five or so years, the death and succession of Mao and Chou
En-lai in China, the death of Chiang Kai-shek, the replacement of
some of the significant members of the Soviet Praesidium. In
addition the Watergate scandal has cast doubt not only on the
future of President Nixon but on the authority of the Presidency.

My purpose is first to analyse whether, why, and to what extent,
the nature of international politics, and in particular the structure
of great-power relationships, had in fact altered by the early 1970s
from the pattern imposed by the events of the second half of the
1940s, which persisted with various modifications throughout
much of the ensuing two decades. Is one right in assuming that
the international system is undergoing an identifiable change?
Even if this is the case, we know that no historical epoch is self-
contained; many of the characteristics of the old European states
system, for instance, survived even the French Revolution and
the Napoleonic Wars; despite the growing power and influence of
the United States, Japan and China from the end of the last century onwards, despite the stature and influence of Sun Yat-sen,
Lenin, and later Roosevelt, the international system was still
fundamentally Euro-centric, in the sense that the issues of war
and peace were decided there, as late as 1940. Despite the evidence
that the world of the 1970s is no longer dominated by the United
States and Soviet Union and their strategic relationship to an
extent that was undeniable ten years ago, they remain countries
with a combination of strategic, political and economic strength
which no other countries possess. How great in reality is the extent
of change? Is China's importance as a new great power justified or
overrated? Will the alliances of the Cold War years, especially that
between the United States and Japan and the Atlantic Alliance
buckle under the strains of rising economic or other discord or
still be maintained, though possibly on a different basis, by a sense
of wider political interests as in the past?

My second purpose is to attempt to examine those aspects of
change that are palpable and undeniable, those decisions that must

be confronted in the next few years and which will condition the future, as well as certain novel problems which were scarcely on our horizon a few years ago. 'We are in the position' says de Jouvenel, 'of a tourist who is planning a journey with the help of a guidebook that is already out of date.'[6] I hope I can at least trace some of the new arterial roads that are under construction.

Two final words by way of introduction. My personal field of competence is limited. Though I was trained as a historian and have attempted to educate myself as a political scientist, I have only a concerned layman's knowledge of economics and finance, sociology and technology. Consequently I shall tend to concentrate on those aspects of world politics, of change and continuity, with which I am most familiar, hoping to make clear where my judgement in other fields is derivative. I am, moreover, a middle-aged, white, northern European, and I claim no divine powers of objectivity. I can produce no comprehensive map even of the present that will be accepted as the product of aerial photography by men in every society or continent.

Second, this book is concerned with the structure of international politics, with the interactions, past, present, and perhaps future, of nations and important transnational forces and institutions. It is neither a judgement on, nor a guide to, the policies of individual countries or the decisions of individual statesmen. It points to problems and to certain possible solutions. It is an attempt at analysis, and neither a blueprint for policy nor a philosophical discourse on the nature of political change.

The present emerges from the past, and to achieve even a rough perception of the terrain around us, we must bear in mind the path we have already trodden. So I have started with a brief reminder of the way in which the structure of international relations developed in the post-war years and of the extent to which it became primarily bipolar in character. Then I have explored the reasons why this bipolar structure began rapidly to erode as the last decade progressed, ending Part One with some preliminary consideration of what are the constituents of the contemporary balance of power, bearing in mind that this is a world of nations that generate increasing and increasingly diverse forms of power, yet have made only limited headway in achieving means of reconciling and controlling them.

Part Two opens with a chapter that attempts to analyse the climate, the opportunities or constraints, in which a successor structure of international power and politics must be considered, the direction in which changes of strategic, economic, social and ideological considerations point. I have then sought to view the present and the immediate future through the perspective of the five major actors, the United States, the Soviet Union, China, Japan, and Western Europe. This is not because I believe that we are creating an international structure dominated solely by a five power balance. Nevertheless, the way in which these five centres now conceive their interests, or express their hopes and their anxieties, can not fail to have a profound effect upon the nature of world politics in general, at several different planes or levels of interaction, strategic, political, and economic. Then I looked at their political relationships in the world's greatest continent, Asia. Finally, I have concluded with a sketch of different possible outcomes of the 'era of negotiations' and some brief reflections on approaches that might protect the gains we have made while modifying the dangers that we see ahead of us.

2
The Bipolar World

The beginning and the end of the post-war era have been characterized by a structure of power between nations that was in many
ways alike, certainly more similar than that of the intervening
years. In the early 1970's there are two 'super-powers', but much
of the power they generate does not translate into political influence
and there are at least three other major power centres in the world,
as well as many secondary ones, though all deploy different kinds
of strength. In the second half of the 1940s the situation was
analogous: there were no super-powers, though the phrase itself
had already been coined; there was one power of undiminished
economic strength, the United States, with a monopoly of a new
form of strategic weapon, the atom bomb, but which was engaged
in the rapid reduction of its military forces; there was one strong
military power on the Eurasian mainland, with universal pretensions, but whose economic disarray made its real interests
regional only; one shattered and divided Asian power, China; one
European power with a still world-wide Empire though with a
weak domestic economic base, Britain; and three other European
countries with overseas imperial interests. It was a plural world as
ours is a plural world: one difference is that the cast of major
powers has changed, as has the nature of power itself; another is
that the stage itself has become crowded.

The intervening years have been ones of radical change in the
structure of the international system, the aggregation of two great
alliance systems around the United States and the Soviet Union,
the elevation of these two from great powers to super-powers, their
dominance of the international system for a span of five years or so,

and the decline of that dominance in the past decade, the rise of a 'third world' of non-aligned states and its fragmentation. I have no intention of chronicling this period in any detail, but simply of calling attention to certain salient features of it which continue to affect our judgement about the present and the future.

Was the Cold War, whose origins are now a matter of intensive study, simply an action and reaction process between two ideologically antithetical groups of powers, who until a decade ago could identify hardly any common interests, or was it a product of the internal dynamics of the United States, the Soviet Union and their allies? Surely it was both. Stalin's preoccupations in the postwar years were, as Louis Halle has put it, 'those of an illegitimate czar',[1] namely, to fortify Soviet safety by the consolidation of a sphere of influence in Eastern Europe – although the Marxist framework of reference made him justify this in universalist terms. Similarly when the Truman administration saw Greece and Turkey foundering politically and Europe as a whole stagnating economically in 1947, the decision to offer unilateral measures of support implied such a fundamental change in American peacetime diplomacy and such a departure from the principles upon which the UN Charter had been based that it had to be justified not in pragmatic terms but by reference to doctrinal principles. Thus a contest that was classical in character, for security and relative influence in Europe and East Asia, became ideological in character and eventually universal.

But it was not originally a military confrontation, for the North Atlantic Treaty, signed in April 1949, largely in response to the Prague coup of 1948 and the Soviet blockade of Berlin, was originally envisaged as much as an instrument of Western political solidarity as of collective or integrated defence. What largely militarized the political confrontation was, apart from the continuing presence of strong Soviet forces in central Europe, the Korean war which broke out in June 1950, and which was represented as the prelude to a similar act of Soviet aggression against Western Europe.

Yet in retrospect the outbreak of war in Korea seems to have been caused by a series of accidents and crossed signals of a kind that have caused many past wars. The United States, dominant in the Pacific, had assumed unilateral responsibility for the postwar occupation of Japan, yet by 1950 was finding the cost a heavy one and had concluded that Japan, politically democratized and socially docile, could reassume the mantle of a responsible sovereign power. She began to canvass the possibility of a Japanese peace treaty, anchored by an American security guarantee, at almost exactly the same time as the new People's Republic of China was about to enter into an alliance with the Soviet Union. It is probable that the prospect of an independent Japan convinced Mao and Stalin, meeting in Moscow in February 1950, that Korea, divided by the accident of Soviet and American dispositions at the war's end, but which had been the springboard of earlier Japanese activities on the mainland, must be consolidated under Communist rule before Japan – assumed to be as potentially martial and irredentist as before – recovered both her independence and American strategic protection into the bargain.

The Korean war marked the beginning of the bipolar era. By the time it was over the United States was more than *primus inter pares* among her allies: she had developed thermonuclear as well as atomic weapons, and was now an operational nuclear power, her general defence expenditure had more than tripled, her economy was ten times the size of that of any ally and the basis of the whole Western system of trade and payments; and she had a global conception of her own responsibilities. Soviet industrial production was approaching its pre-war level, she had developed atomic and was developing thermonuclear weapons, and to her sphere of influence in Eastern Europe she had added alliance with the world's largest power. And the allies of both were reasonably contented with such dominance. Soviet military strength kept new Communist regimes in power in Eastern Europe, though Yugoslavia had revolted against her suzerainty. China was acutely aware of her vulnerability and of American ground, sea and air power, in Acheson's words 'on the very edge of the Western Pacific'.[2] In Europe, France's twin fears of Soviet pressure and of a Germany rearmed to meet that pressure were impelling the government of the Fourth Republic to press for the strongest commitment of American military power to Europe, for a forward strategy and an integrated command system.[3] The British government felt that half a century of diplomatic effort had been successfully crowned by the permanent commitment of American power to the defence of Western Europe. Moreover, if the Sino-Soviet alliance was born only of necessity, the United States brought more intangible assets than strategic and economic power to her new position of leadership. Not only had she a sufficient margin of strength to be generous in the application of it, but her society was widely admired; the achievements of the New Deal and its influence upon European intellectuals, the home she had given to the Jews, the appeal of Hollywood, made the United States seem in a hundred ways a freer and more liberal society than a shabby Europe, still restricted by rationing or scarred by recriminations about wartime 'collaboration' and the black market.

Yet in its early years, the confrontation and expansion of the new super-powers by no means extended to the whole world. It was confined primarily to Europe and North East Asia, though the United States, partly for domestic reasons, partly as an aspect of her strategy of containing Soviet power, had developed an independent interest in the integrity of Iran and of Israel. Her mediation in the conflicts between Holland and Indonesia was partly an extension of her Pacific policy, mostly an expression of her anti-colonialist views. However, the beginning of involvement in Indochina, with the decision in 1948 to support France's effort to assert control over the Vietminh, was a sign of the leverage that France could exert on the United States by reason of her central position in Europe.

Eisenhower entered the White House and Stalin died in early 1952, and in the ensuing five years or so, the two alliance systems were less dominated by their core powers than they had been in the first period of the Cold War or were to become again, though these core powers had now become super-powers. The countries of Eastern Europe, Poland, East Germany and Hungary in particular, were restless throughout these years; and the foundation of the Warsaw Pact in 1955 which multilateralized what had hitherto been bilateral security arrangements with the Soviet Union, and the dissolution of the Cominform in 1956, were concessions to their desire for greater autonomy. The Western alliance system was less Americocentric, despite the creation of an integrated military command system in NATO under an American supreme commander. The American relationship occupied only part of the British horizon, for, after the absorption of India, Pakistan and Ceylon under a new style Commonwealth, this gained for a while a vitality which gave it many of the characteristics of alliance. Moreover, as American strategy became transformed from one of defence into deterrence, she was dependent on her allies in both Europe and Asia for bases, since her bombers were of medium range only. The first attempt at the rearmament of

Germany depended on French popular as well as official agreement, and, although Dulles might threaten an 'agonizing reappraisal' of American commitments in Europe if France failed to satisfy the European Defence Community, he was too deeply committed to the survival of Western Germany for such a threat to have much credibility. When EDC was rejected, it was Eden not Dulles who took the diplomatic initiative that enabled Germany to enter the Atlantic Alliance by converting the earlier Brussels treaty into Western European Union, endowed with custodial powers over German rearmament. The British and French positions on disarmament were different from the American, and London and Washington disagreed violently on the question of trade with China. The creation of the European Coal and Steel Community in 1952 showed that, in addition to recovering economically, the continental powers were acquiring objectives of their own.

Super-power dominance 1957–63

The mid-1950s were a period of marked diversity in the policies of the members of both alliances, partly because they were a period of relative détente in East–West relations – the Eisenhower 'atoms for peace initiative', the Austrian Peace Treaty, the Geneva summit conference of 1955 which, though it failed to find an answer to the problem of German reunification, did furnish a chance for the two super-powers to communicate their unreadiness to face the prospect of war with each other. What led to the assertion of super-power dominance was not so much the Suez crisis and the Hungarian revolt of 1956 as two developments that had been gathering force throughout the decade. The first was the successful development of the long-range ballistic missile, and the other was the extension of super-power conflict to new areas. The orbiting of *Sputnik* in the autumn of 1957 dramatized not only the advent of the missile but an apparent Soviet lead in this field. Though these fears proved alarmist, the missile created real uncertainty as to how a stable policy of deterrence, which had become mutual with Soviet development of long-range bombers in 1954, was to be maintained. The basis of deterrence on either side consisted of a force of bombers which now could be virtually eliminated by a relatively small force of missiles, leaving the adversary without riposte in a crisis; there would therefore be a high temptation to be the first to strike.[4]

Though the focus of Western public debate in the late 1950s on a non-existent Soviet numerical superiority in ICBMs was wrong, it is possible to see from this perspective that the strategic relationship between the two super-powers was bound to traverse a period of considerable uncertainty, not only until sufficient ICBMs had been constructed on each side to make the bomber a deterrent weapon of only secondary importance, but also until advances in fuel and guidance technologies made it possible to 'harden' missiles, underground or under water, in a manner that would enable them to survive an adversary's first strike and still be capable of delivering an unacceptable riposte against his cities – until, that is, the technological basis of second-strike strategies had been laid. This was a process that was not completed on the American side until 1963 and not until the later 1960s on the Soviet side. I do not mean to suggest that every aspect of the technological arms race was inevitable, least of all that a relationship of parity or 'sufficiency' could only have been achieved at the level which it was, some 2,000 missiles with thermonuclear warheads on each side. But I believe it is the kind of fruitless 'arguing with history' of which Lewis Namier used to warn his students, to suggest that the sort of arms control agreements that proved negotiable between 1963 and 1972, or that can be envisaged now, could have been negotiated in the late 1950s. To do so is to overlook not only the degree of mistrust of Soviet intentions in the Republican Congresses of that period, but also the personality of Khrushchev and the gambler's streak in it.

Be that as it may, the period of conceptual and technological flux in strategic relationships which lasted from 1957 until at least 1963 not only revived the tensions of the earlier period of the Cold War, but also made each alliance system more hierarchical in character, for a mixture of political and strategic reasons. On the Communist side one of Khrushchev's first priorities after the Hungarian Revolution was to stamp out revisionism, and he used the fortieth anniversary of the Soviet Union in November 1957 to get a declaration signed by twelve ruling communist parties which referred to 'the invincible camp of socialist countries headed by the Soviet Union'. These were years of Soviet confidence in its strategic prowess, its economic growth and its appeal to the developing countries. But it led also to a highly uncertain reaction to Anglo-American intervention in the Lebanon and Jordan after it appeared that the Soviet Union might be about to extend its influence in the Middle East to a formal alliance with Syria.

It was relations with China that first demonstrated the real problems of maintaining Soviet dominance within the Socialist camp. The Chinese leaders might talk at party congresses about the Soviet Union as the head of the coalition but in terms of state policy they were determined to exert their autonomy just as much as the Soviet Union was determined to circumscribe it. The 1955 attack on Quemoy and the offshore islands had received minimal Soviet support, and when the Chinese re-opened the attack in the summer of 1958, after a visit by Khrushchev to Peking, there was no expression of Soviet solidarity with China until after the latter had unilaterally begun to de-escalate the crisis. In the summer of 1959 the Soviet Union rescinded an agreement of two years earlier on nuclear cooperation, including, so the Chinese asserted, the provision of a sample atomic bomb.[5] It seems probable that the agreement was instituted in the first place because the Soviet Union hoped to forestall an independent Chinese nuclear capability and broke down because Peking would not agree to a unified system of command and control such as the United States was in process of achieving in NATO.

That Khrushchev's concern that his large eastern ally might entangle the Soviet Union in war with the United States, as Austria could be said to have entangled Germany in 1914, was evidenced also by Soviet criticism of Peking during the first round of the Sino-Indian border dispute in 1959. It was possibly influenced by the American view, expressed during and after his visit to Washington in September 1959 that though differences in Soviet and Chinese policy were now discernible on international questions, the Soviet Union must assume, in the words of Christian Herter, the Secretary of State, 'a great degree of responsibility' for Chinese actions. Khrushchev might repudiate any such responsibility but it was an essential characteristic of this period of extreme bipolarity that each super-power did in fact hold the other responsible for the acts of its allies.

The first, acute phase of the Sino-Soviet conflict, the withdrawal of Soviet experts from China in 1960 and the beginnings of overt ideological polemics, Chinese fury with Soviet weakness in the Cuban missile crisis and Soviet criticism of the Sino-Indian war of 1962, and the open breach after the signing of the Test Ban Treaty in 1963, has been skilfully analysed elsewhere.[6] The essential point affecting a consideration of the structure of international power is to note that the period when the Communist coalition was fully hierarchical began earlier, and ended sooner, than the period of American dominance within the Western coalition.

For the process of centralization in the American alliance system had different causes. First, the debacle of Suez had greatly diminished the prestige and influence of Britain and France, not only in the developing world but with their European and Commonwealth allies as well. This, combined with the fact that their control over their colonial empires was rapidly diminishing and that the virtual dissolution of these was now foreseeable, further diminished their value as coalition partners to an American administration who now increasingly saw the struggle with China and the Soviet Union in global terms. De Gaulle's proposal of 1958 for a tripartite direction of Western policy on a world-wide basis had by then no attraction for the United States. Another factor making for centralized American control of both political and strategic decision-making was the introduction of tactical nuclear weapons into the European theatre after 1957, to redress the imbalance of deployed Warsaw Pact and NATO conventional forces, under a double-key arrangement which effectively made the United States government the sole arbiter of the military response to a European crisis involving force or the threat of force.

It is true that the United States had shown every encouragement to the development of European economic and political integration, welcoming the foundation of the ECSC in 1951, saddened by the demise of EDC in 1954, welcoming again the Treaty of Rome which created the EEC and Euratom in 1952. But Khrushchev's decision to capitalize on Soviet post-*Sputnik* prestige, and perhaps to offset his declining relationship with China by attempting to demoralize the Western alliance and if possible detach the Federal Republic from it, led to a period in which security considerations were paramount. In November 1958 he announced his intention to cure the Berlin 'tumour' within six months by denouncing the Potsdam agreements and handing the whole city over to the DDR. The Berlin crisis smouldered on for four years at various degrees of intensity, and was not finally resolved until the collapse of Khrushchev's domestic and international prestige after the Cuban missile crisis. It led to a carefully institutionalized form of crisis planning among the three Western victor powers, the German government and the Supreme Commander, part of it undertaken in Washington, part of it in Europe.[7] There were times, particularly in 1959 when Khrushchev visited Washington and Macmillan visited Moscow, when the allies appeared to be divided, as Khrushchev intended, between the Anglo-Saxons who seemed ready to contemplate a new negotiation on Berlin, and de Gaulle and Adenauer for whom these years laid the foundations of mutual respect and who regarded any such talk as appeasement of Soviet blackmail. But this did not affect relations at the working level where a large number of alternative responses to a possible East German attempt to occupy West Berlin, or a Soviet Union initiation of a new Berlin blockade, had to be carefully evaluated. Nevertheless it was American actions in 1961 and 1962 both on the local and the strategic plane which finally resolved the crisis.

The Cuban missile crisis of October 1962, the careful way in which President Kennedy handled it, his successful use of the right level of duress, and his sensitivity to the relationship between crises in the Caribbean and in Europe, enhanced American prestige in her alliances. Cuba lies outside the area of the North Atlantic Alliance and neither Macmillan, de Gaulle nor Adenauer felt that the United States had acted beyond the interests of the alliance in dealing with the matter unilaterally. Nevertheless, both Cuba and its sequels, the Atmospheric Test Ban Treaty of 1963 (to which Britain was also a signatory) and the installation of a 'hot line' between Moscow and Washington, clarified what had been implicit since the Geneva Conference of 1955, namely that the two super-powers had a relationship with each other, whether of conflict or cooperation, which they did not have with their own coalition partners: the words 'collusion' and 'dual hegemony' entered the polemic debate, most notably in Peking where the rift between the two great mainland powers was now an open one.

With the end of the Soviet threat to Berlin, the surmounting of the Cuban crisis and the beginnings of a serious Soviet-American dialogue about arms control (though the Test Ban was really a measure of environmental protection not disarmament) the chilliest years of the second period of the Cold War were over. There began to be discussion in Western academic circles and foreign offices about a return to a more normal phase of great-power relations, motivated more by rational calculations of self-interest than by either ideology or mutual fear and even discussion of a natural evolution of a polycentric world as the economic strength of first Europe and then Japan advanced, and more and more powers acquired the ability to manufacture nuclear weapons.

But this view ignored a number of difficult questions. In the first place the Soviet Union had suffered a major diplomatic reverse over Cuba and was now engaged in bitter ideological polemics with its one large ally, China. The only way she could hope to restore her position was by expanding her influence in certain key areas of the developing world and by sowing dissension in Western Europe and between it and the United States until such time as she could augment her strategic power. But China was in no mood for a rapprochement with a United States with whom she had been at war only a decade earlier and who was now building up armed forces near her southern border, even had an olive branch been proffered. The frustration of China's external policy, growing Soviet support for her Asian rival, India, declining Chinese influence in Indonesia after 1965, her failure to rally the developing world in a successor conference to Bandung, coupled with fears of American intervention in South East Asia, contributed to the conflicts in Peking which led to the Cultural Revolution in 1966. However the conviction that the Soviet Union was becoming bourgeois in its ideology and imperialist in its interests was more important. And the Cultural Revolution with its xenophobia, its withdrawal of ambassadors from overseas posts, its virtual closure of the Ministry of External Affairs, made China between 1966 and 1969 a power with whom it was impossible to develop relations at all.

As far as the Western coalition was concerned, the United States, it was true, occupied a more dominant position than even during the Cold War years. The development of a second strike force of *Minuteman* ICBMs and *Polaris* submarine-launched missiles had been set at the high figure of 1,054 ICBMs and 41 *Polaris* submarines to be reached by about 1966, which gave the United States in 1964, for instance, a numerical superiority in missiles over the Soviet Union of three and a half to one. More than that, the United States shared certain geopolitical advantages with the Soviet Union, the technological and economic resources for major military research and development programmes, and a metropolitan area that included large areas of very low population density which no other serious aspirant to strategic power (except perhaps eventually China) could match: in addition the United

States had the advantage of ready access to the world's two great oceans. Consequently, although Britain had re-established a co-operative relationship with the United States on the development of nuclear weapons in 1958, and had become an operational nuclear power a year earlier, the basic vulnerability of the British Isles, the small size of her deterrent force, and the fact that it consisted of bombers, gave it small strategic value in American, or presumably in Soviet, eyes. And when in 1962 the Pentagon decided to abandon the *Skybolt* air-to-ground missile which was to enhance the operational effectiveness of the V-Bomber force, the ensuing crisis in Anglo-American relations (the Nassau Conference of January, 1963) led to an agreement that placed Britain in a largely dependent relationship to the United States on nuclear weapons. France's decision in 1956 to embark on the develop-ment of an entirely independent nuclear force met with no offer of American cooperation and became one source among many of Franco-American discord.

One of the consequences of the dangerous years in which the Kennedy Administration had assumed power was to strengthen the conviction of many serious students of strategy and security that the Western alliance ran a serious possibility of having either to risk the use of nuclear weapons or else back down in another crisis, if greater flexibility in meeting a Soviet challenge could not be created: this meant, on the one hand, the need for a highly centralized control of decision-making in a crisis, and, on the other, the provision of larger and better trained European con-ventional forces. The State Department, it was true, had been a consistent supporter not merely of the economic integration of Western Europe but of the evolution by the European Economic Community of techniques of political coordination and eventually of integration; and on 4 July 1962 President Kennedy imparted a dramatic emphasis to these American aspirations

> 'I will say . . . that we will be prepared to discuss with a United Europe the ways and means of forming a concrete Atlantic partnership, a mutually beneficial partnership between the new union now emerging in Europe and the old American Union founded here 175 years ago.'

But his 'grand design' of Atlantic relationship conflicted with an equally strong American insistence on centralized strategic control of any crisis that implied resort to force, an insistence which was spelt out by Mr Robert McNamara in a speech in his home town in Michigan the month before Kennedy spoke in Philadelphia. The conflict between the two conceptions was not then, and never has been, reconciled.

Moreover, there were other counterpoints to the firm belief that the American foreign policy establishment of the early 1960s had inherited from its predecessors of the 1940s and 1950s, namely that a dominant position for the United States in world politics was neither desirable nor would command the support of American public opinion indefinitely. For one thing, the men who surrounded first Kennedy and then Johnson suffered from a not unnatural hubris about the *mission civilatrice* of the United States. Ever since the New Deal and, later, the war and its aftermath had shown that this country could rise to meet its challenges more successfully than older or more *dirigiste* ones, there had been a growing degree of confidence among American intellectuals, businessmen and officials about the superiority of American techniques of organization, progress and consensus; this, when added to her formidable technological prowess, the way in which she overcame the depression of 1957, or her pioneering of new methods of social and economic analysis, made American elites see their country as the prime source both of change and order. The sense that the United States could not easily devolve major political responsibilities on her allies derived only partly from the gradual evolution of a special relationship with the Soviet Union, or from anxieties about the dangers of confused signals in a crisis; it came also from a conviction that she handled them better than anyone else.

Britain's first attempt to join the EEC had been vetoed by President de Gaulle in 1963, so that 'Europe' was not the comprehensive grouping that the proponents of the 'dumb-bell' theory had in mind. Moreover, there were few signs before the late 1960s that the United States was prepared to accept a European partner in any field of relations except trade; the development of British and French nuclear weapons created an anxiety, accelerated by a growing rapprochement between France and Germany which assumed treaty form in 1962, that Germany might either aspire to follow suit, or drift into a mood of neutralism or even accommodation with the Soviet Union. Hence the unfortunate proposal for a multilateral force of nuclear weapons. This was an initiative which bedevilled alliance politics from 1960 until 1964 when it was dropped in favour of a political solution, a Nuclear Planning Group within NATO, a solution which satisfied German anxieties about how American and British nuclear weapons would be targeted and employed in a European conflict – which had been the central German anxiety throughout the years of Adenauer's chancellorship – without breaking an implicit American promise to the Soviet Union to restrict their ownership. Ambivalence about the character of the European partnership had its parallel in the trade field as the Common Agricultural Policy and the creation of non-tariff barriers in Europe came under scrutiny in the Kennedy Round of tariff negotiations between 1963 and 1967.

And the major arms control negotiation of the Johnson years, to provide institutionalized safeguards against the spread of nuclear weapons which culminated in the Non-Proliferation Treaty of 1968 and in which the principal negotiations were conducted by the United States and the Soviet Union, seemed to many countries, France, the Federal Republic, Japan, India, Italy and above all China, designed to stamp a permanent imprint of super-power dominance upon the structure of world politics.

The diffusion of power 1963–8

But what made the years between 1963 and 1972 the most confused since the outbreak of the Second World War was not solely the Sino-Soviet dispute, nor the ambivalence of the American conception of European–American partnership nor the identification of a certain identity of interest between the two super-powers – 'the adversary partners'. It was also a consequence of the political flux caused by the doubling of the number of sovereign states in the world, largely between 1957 and 1962, and the actions and reactions of the super-powers in this totally new environment.

The situation may be different today, but a decade or more ago many of the new countries regarded themselves as potential beneficiaries of the bipolar balance between the developed powers, hoping to gain maximum assistance by playing the one side off against the other, sometimes with considerable success, as in Ghana, Egypt, Indonesia, India, and initially Cuba. Conversely, they were seen in Moscow as areas where, on the one hand, the Soviet Union might hope to profit from the ejection of the old

European colonial powers and to apply some of Lenin's precepts which had not proved particularly relevant to Europe. The United States both feared Soviet encroachment in the developing world and hoped by its own record of opposition to colonialism (including its withdrawal from control of the Phillipines in 1946 before any European power had made a similar gesture) both to counter such encroachment and to stand in a different and more beneficent relationship to the new states than the old metropolitan powers.

This process of widening the area of adversary competition had begun in the mid-1950s when economic as well as military aid first became a serious tool of great-power diplomacy. In certain areas and countries it appeared to create so large a risk of great-power confrontation as to invoke the anxiety and therefore the activity of the rest of the international community through the medium of the United Nations, especially during the great Secretary-Generalship of Dag Hammarsköld (1953–61): Sinai in 1956, the Congo between 1960 and 1964, Cyprus from 1963 onwards (as well as problems such as Kashmir and West Irian which did not involve the great powers directly). But it also converted the endemic state of tension between Israel and the Arab states into a vicarious confrontation of the super-powers, in which a resounding victory by Israel in the Six Day War of 1967 merely had the effect of entrenching Moscow and the United States in their policies. The extension of Soviet military aid to the Mahgreb countries and the gradual increase of her naval power in the Mediterranean gave rise to a fear that she was turning the southern flank of NATO just at a time when East–West relations in Europe were becoming more stable. Elsewhere, in Latin America, in India, in parts of East Africa, Soviet aid and diplomatic activity created a belief that the 'free world' was being undermined.

However, the area of greatest confusion, and direct American involvement, was in South East Asia. American concern with Indochina and Indonesia, the gateway between the Pacific and the Indian Ocean, the bridge between Asia and Australasia, arose originally from Japanese designs on the area and antedated the Second World War. It had a genuine strategic basis, and it was accentuated throughout the 1950s and much of the ensuing decade by the instability of Indonesia and by Sukharno's confrontation with Malaysia and Singapore. For this reason there had been a series of contingency plans from 1954 onwards for direct

American intervention in the area. It also had an ideological foundation, namely a belief that a new situation of confrontation between the two halves of the bipolar world had been created along the line of the seventeenth parallel which was the Asian equivalent of Berlin; below this, free societies must be protected.

The story of deepening American involvement in the politics of Saigon during Kennedy's presidency and the rising level of American involvement from 1964 onwards has been fully documented elsewhere.[8] Its most important effect was the way in which it distorted both popular and official perceptions in the United States and elsewhere in the West of the way in which the international system was changing, giving rise to a 'devil theory' of Chinese imperialism in South East Asia as a rationale of American frustration there, demanding of the new American relationship of détente with the Soviet Union more than the latter had the power to deliver and creating a sense of American unilateralism in world politics when in other areas she was seeking to limit her commitments. Far from upholding American credibility in the rest of the world, Vietnam had led by 1968 to a bitter cleft in American society, particularly between the rising generation and that which had known the rigours of the Cold War or had been sustained by pride in American power, a cleft which put the future cohesion of the country itself in question, as well as isolating the Administration from former friends in Europe and Asia. The race riots of the mid-1960s, the student unrest, the evidence of urban decay, the growth of the drug problem, made it seem that the United States was no longer the world's great experimental society but in a state of decay more closely resembling Rome in the fourth century.

The structure of international power and politics at the end of the 1960s was confused partly because the perceptions of the major actors were themselves confused. The breakdown in Sino-Soviet relations in 1963 should by the traditional rules of international behaviour have led, as it did much later, to a triangular relationship between Moscow, Peking and Washington. It did not do so, in part because of the American attitude – a legacy of the broken love affair which had bedevilled Sino-American relations since the 1940s – which made the liberals around Kennedy and Johnson, just as much as the conservatives around Eisenhower, able to put only sinister constructions on the policy of 'Red China', and in part because of the coincidental rise in the fortunes of North Vietnam which appeared to be a product of Chinese expansionism.* It was also a consequence of Chinese suspicion of what she took to be Soviet–American collusion in the pursuit of arms control and other agreements, while, as I have mentioned, the feedback to Peking from the American escalation in Vietnam accentuated even if it did not cause the Cultural Revolution which in turn made discourse with China virtually impossible until 1969. As Richard Löwenthal has put it, it was 'the continuing domestic momentum of outdated ideological concepts that delayed the full impact of the new triangular constellation on the foreign policies of the powers.'[9]

In the Soviet Union, the elderly conservatives who had ousted Khrushchev in 1964 became as fearful of ideological subversion within their old sphere of influence, Eastern Europe, as the successive American administrations tended to be about the extension of Soviet influence in the Middle East or elsewhere in the developing world. Events forced them to intervene in 1968 in Czechoslovakia against a regime that was unorthodox only in its domestic policy; in so doing they destroyed their own campaign which had been launched two years earlier in Bucharest for the dissolution of the two opposing alliances in Europe, and were forced back on to the secondary objective of seeking to obtain general recognition of the *status quo* in Europe. At the same time the Soviet Union had become a global power in the traditional sense, whereas in Stalin's day she had been a regional power overwhelmingly preoccupied with the question of her own safety in every field except the ideological. As a consequence of decisions taken in Moscow in the years of humiliation after Cuba, she now had a growing fleet of ocean-going ships in addition to her considerable submarine force. Far more important she was by 1968 approaching equality with the United States in land-based ICBMs, overturning Secretary McNamara's judgement of 1965 that they 'have decided they lost the quantitative race and that they are not seeking to engage us in conflict'.[10] In China four years of effort since her first explosion of a nuclear device in 1964 had not yet provided her with an operational capability.

Thus on the strategic plane the structure of power not only remained bipolar but the balance was becoming an even one. But for all but a relatively small number of experts in governments, in

* The full edition of the Pentagon Papers shows that the American intelligence community was dubious, whenever its advice was sought, about the connection between Peking and Hanoi.

legislatures and in research institutes in the West, strategic relationships were by 1969 ceasing to be the prime motive force of
international politics, as resort to nuclear war became year by year
a more remote contingency. Throughout the 1960s the greater
safety of the bipolar balance had been making other considerations,
national autonomy, economic strength and stability, civil order, as
significant as national security in terms of public perceptions of
world politics. Japan's GNP and her external trade had more than
quadrupled during the decade; she was now the world's third
strongest economic power. In Europe, the only great figure of the
1960s who did not think in ideological terms, de Gaulle, had such
an antique frame of reference that he had decelerated the development of the European Community in 1965 almost to the point of
collapse, so that viewed from Washington there was still no
'Europe' with whom to do business on any level except trade.
Britain's second attempt to join the EEC was thwarted by de
Gaulle in 1967. Thus to the American preference for dealing with
Western Europe as a group of individual countries on questions of
security and of international finance was added Europe's lack of
coherence, its inability to find common ground, beyond the relatively narrow confines of its common commercial policy. And yet
among the people of Europe, most particularly those under thirty,
the days of unquestioned respect for American political, intellectual and social leadership were over.

3
The Seeds of Change

Leadership under strain

The distribution of power and influence and the objectives of the major capitals did not appear to be radically different in 1969 – the year in which President Nixon came to office, President de Gaulle left it and in which Mao and Chou En-lai succeeded in getting the Cultural Revolution under control – from what they had been five or six years earlier when Kennedy and Khrushchev appeared to dominate much of world politics. The central balance of power still appeared to resemble that of a pair of scales, in which the relative weight of each super-power was expressed primarily in terms of military strength and political influence, although their achievements in other fields such as the exploration of space, or the relative coherence of their societies and the fidelity of their own allies were also factors. Crises even in the relations of smaller powers tended to be settled at super-power level; thus the Indo-Pakistan war of 1965 was ended by an armistice negotiated by the Soviet Union with, according to his National Security Advisor, the active support and indeed the invisible presence of Lyndon Johnson.[1] The Arab–Israel war of 1967 led to a personal negotiation between the Soviet and American leaders at Glassboro in June, 1967, at which, however, they were only able to clarify their continuing support of opposing sides rather than find a basis for a settlement. It was only in areas which they had long made clear were to be regarded as their own spheres of influence that each felt able to act with no reference to the reaction of the other – the United States in the Dominican Republic in 1965, the Soviet Union in Czechoslovakia in 1968.

In one respect only had the situation clearly changed from that of the second period of the Cold War, from the years of what an eminent American systems theorist has called 'tight bipolarity'.[2] Soviet–American competition, if still world-wide, was now conducted with greater caution. Each, for instance, narrowed its interests in Africa, and the outbreak of civil war in Nigeria in 1967 found both on the side of legitimacy. The United States had disinterested itself, though the Soviet Union had not, in the outcome of civil war in the Yemen. Neither power attempted seriously to influence either the complex series of steps involved in Britain's disengagement from over a half century of political responsibility in the Persian Gulf or her attempt to construct a system of defence cooperation among the Commonwealth countries of South East Asia in which her own share would be considerably diminished.* Neither super-power made any serious move to exploit the downfall of Sukharno, with his Sinophile leanings, or to arrest the large-scale massacre of the Indonesian Communist Party in 1966. True, both powers were the principal source of arms and development aid in the developing world; true, Soviet naval power was beginning to carry the flag into new areas of the world. But their existing involvements and commitments, the implications of their mutual relationships, the extent of their own domestic problems, meant that they no longer had a symbiotic relationship of hostility and competition from one pole of the universe to the other (in fact agreement on the non-militarization of Antarctica in 1959 was one of the earliest post-war arms control agreements).

There were thoughtful men in many countries, and not only in the United States and the Soviet Union, who considered not just that this situation of super-power dominance *would* continue but that it *should*; primarily on the grounds that it made the handling of inevitable political or inter-state crises more manageable (especially after the introduction in 1963 of the 'hot line' between Moscow and Washington which, for instance, was used throughout the Arab–Israel War) without the confusing intervention of third parties; partly on the grounds that super-power dominance made easier the process of absorbing a rapid pace of political, economic and technological change.[3] The emergence of two contiguous German states out of the old Reich, ideologically antithetical, economically powerful, fully armed, but restrained from conflict and moving towards an explicit relationship of coexistence,

* In striking contrast to Robert McNamara's insistence earlier in the 1960s that Britain's role East of Suez was essential to the security of the West.

could be cited as a case in point. So also could the resurgence of Japan as a powerful economic centre, though so far without clear political goals. The technological basis of strategic deterrence had undergone a period of rapid change in the decade before 1969 and appeared to be on the verge of yet another revolutionary change as the anti-ballistic missile became operational and the technique of providing the ICBM with multiple warheads was mastered by the United States.

But beneath the level of formal or strategic relations, other processes, which had been gathering momentum throughout the 1960s, were beginning to have an increasing influence. One was the normal process of generational change which had many facets (some of which I shall attempt to discuss later) but which in its political aspect was sharpened, and acquired at times the characteristics of civil conflict in the democratic societies, for a variety of reasons. It was sharpest in the United States after Johnson's decision to intervene with considerable military force in Vietnam, and, since he would not risk his social legislation by confronting the American public with the likelihood of prolonged war, by his decision to find the men by means of the draft, selective two year conscription. In Japan it was partly a consequence of the breakdown in traditional Japanese familial values as a result of affluence and industrialization, in part a product of the very rapid expansion of the universities. In most European countries student unrest was also a mixture of the impact of American restlessness plus the failure of European educational systems to adjust their structure to both expansion and a diminishing acceptance of the dictates of authority. In China there was a contemporary period of turbulence with the rampancy of the Red Guards during the Cultural Revolution, though these were manipulated by their elders. But there was no similar process apparent in the Soviet Union; the only signs of resistance came from a handful of brave, mature intellectuals.

There were also other social aspects of change than the 'generation gap'. Rising social consciousness made Western societies look again at the vast cities in which a high and increasing proportion of their citizens now lived. In the United States the racial problem was now primarily an urban one. All governments and many societies began to become increasingly aware of the finite nature of the resources at their disposal, land, water, energy, whether from domestic or foreign sources, and in some cases food and pure air. It was about 1968 or 1969 that widespread discussion on the problems of the environment began.

The economic balance of power within the Western system was altering also. When President Eisenhower assumed office the United States generated half the world's wealth; by the time President Johnson left it she generated less than a third. The gains had not been made primarily by her adversaries, though the Soviet Union had sustained a fair rate of growth, but by her allies, notably Germany, France and Japan, and through a dramatic rise in the level of trade within the developed West. The United States had started to run an overall balance of payments deficit (including trade, investment and government expenditures) as early as 1958 but the strength of her trade balance kept it to manageable proportions throughout the first half of the 1960s. However, government expenditure abroad inevitably grew during the peak years of the Vietnam war, and in both 1968 and 1969 her balance of trade and investment which had been favourable to the tune of nearly $5 billion* in 1967 dropped sharply (though it recovered somewhat in 1970 owing to domestic recession in Europe), to less than $650 million. Moreover, it became clear that though she still had a clear dominance in world markets for high technology products such as aircraft or computers, she was now either a major importer or a frustrated competitor in the field of low technology goods, television sets, automobiles, and the like; so that there was no immediate redress from this situation. (In 1967 Japan sold 1·5 million television sets in the United States; in 1969, 3·1 million.)

Ever since the 1880s the United States has been largely self-sufficient economically, both in terms of goods and capital. Hence the invasion of the American consumer market by European and Japanese producers and their successful competition in fields such as cars, electronics, and textiles, that are domestically sensitive because American production of them is concentrated in only a few places, was bound to lead to a sense of xenophobia and of frustration with rich and selfish allies who were contributing proportionately much less to the overall defence of the West or 'the free world'.

To make matters worse, a large part of the outflow of dollars in the 1960s (which had reduced the American share of the world's reserves from nearly 60 per cent in 1946 to 20 per cent in 1966)

* Note: throughout the book a billion (whether of currency or barrels of oil) equals a thousand million.

had taken the form of direct investment by American companies in Europe and Canada and to a lesser extent Japan – the so-called multi-national company – so that by the end of the decade a substantial amount of the European car, electronic and computer industries were American owned. Consequently, to the resentment of the American entrepreneur or workman that his country's allies were robbing him of his livelihood was added the fear of the same sort of man in other Western countries – and their governments – that he was losing his ability to take his own decisions.

The Nixon Doctrine

One of the prime concerns of the new American administration was, therefore, to begin the process of reducing the external commitments of the United States to a level that was supportable domestically and of defining its national interests in less ambitious or universal terms than during the years of 'tight bipolarity' and its aftermath. President Nixon, though he had been an ardent anti-Communist as a Congressman and a keen protagonist of strategic containment of the Communist bloc during his years as Vice President, was a conservative in fiscal matters and also had stood outside the agonizing frustrations of the Kennedy and Johnson years. It looked as if he might assume the Presidency of a nation in an advanced state of internal strife, but the impression which he managed to convey once in office that he intended to liquidate the Vietnam War as rapidly as it could honourably be done, and to reduce the burden of defence expenditure, in fact defused a good deal of this conflict.

But although he had inherited a long agenda of unfinished business the principal focus of American external policy during the first two years of his first Administration was on the bipolar relationship with the Soviet Union. By 1969 the Soviet Union had overtaken the United States in the number of ICBMs she deployed (most of them in hardened silos) and was steadily building up a force of submarine-launched missiles; both forces were still growing. She had also deployed a small force of anti-ballistic missiles (ABMs) around Moscow: more important, among her inventory of ICBMs there were 270 of a type with a very large warhead, the SS9 (20–25 megatons) each of which, it was calculated, could knock out a triangle of American *Minuteman* ICBMs and thus give the Soviet Union the potential ability to disarm all but the *Polaris* force of the United States in a first strike. It could be argued the strategic stability achieved at so much cost earlier in the 1960s was now in jeopardy. A new debate was raging in Congress and among academic strategists as to whether the United States should respond to this new situation by the widespread development of American ABMs or by increasing the number of warheads the United States could deploy against Soviet targets by accelerating the development of MIRVs (multiple independently targetable re-entry vehicles).

Such might have been the American reaction in an earlier period when domestic pressures were less constricting. But several factors operated in favour of constraint. The first was the calculation that, though the Soviet Union had achieved parity in long-range missiles, the United States still possessed a margin of more than two to one in the number of nuclear warheads that could be delivered upon the adversary. Though the President-elect had rejected 'the peculiar unprecedented doctrine called parity' before he entered the White House, he found it relatively easy to accept under the rubric of 'sufficiency' once he had access to the facts. The second was the calculation that the country and the Congress would not stand for an increase in defence expenditure, and Mr Nixon's first defence budget was in fact four billion dollars lower for the fiscal year 1970 (that is July 1969 to June 1970) than his predecessor's.

The third factor was that the framework of a negotiation with the Soviet Union on strategic arms limitations (SALT) already existed in desultory discussions between Moscow and Washington that dated back to the mid-1960s. The initial Soviet response to American suggestions about negotiations had been tepid, because they seemed an attempt to freeze an American numerical superiority in missiles and as late as June 1967 when the ratio of missiles was beginning to equalize McNamara got little response when he raised the issue with Kosygin at Glassboro. 1968 was the year negotiations should have started but Lyndon Johnson's pre-occupation with Vietnam made it difficult to prepare an American position and by the time it was prepared Soviet behaviour over Czechoslovakia made it difficult to pursue it. It is possible to argue, therefore, that SALT, on which serious preparatory negotiation did not in fact start until November 1969, could, if both sides had been prepared to give higher priority to the stability of the central balance, have been initiated before the development of

MIRV which, as we shall see later, complicates any prospect of achieving a formula for the positive reduction of strategic armaments.

Be that as it may, by the beginning of 1969 the Soviet Union seemed as anxious as the United States for negotiation, and on 20 January 1969, the day of President Nixon's inauguration, the Soviet Foreign Ministry convened a special press conference to emphasize that the Soviet Union was ready to begin a serious exchange of views with her adversary partner in the 'mutual limitation and subsequent reduction of strategic delivery vehicles, including defensive systems'. A week later the United States reciprocated.

The reason why SALT was so slow in starting was partly a consequence of bureaucratic problems in Moscow, diplomats and military strategists having hitherto worked largely in separate compartments with little dialogue and much mutual suspicion between them. It was also partly a consequence of the American Administration's difficulty in deciding whether progress in SALT should be linked to the alleviation of other sources of super-power tension, in Europe, the Middle East, and South East Asia. In the end it was decided that the arms control negotiations were intrinsically too important to be made dependent on the settlement of other questions.

The motives for the Soviet acceptance of negotiations on strategic weapons are not fully apparent. True, she was having to divert increasing defence resources to the Far East; true, both powers had pledged themselves to the international community in the Non-Proliferation Treaty to reduce their armaments, and in 1969 several significant countries – Japan, Australia, Brazil – had not yet signed it (in addition to France, China, Israel, and India, who were unlikely to do so in any case). But in terms of *raison d'état* the Soviet economy was in better health in 1969–70 than earlier or later, and the maturing of the boys of the post-war 'baby bulge', combined with an earlier tightening in the loopholes of the conscription laws, had made military manpower readily available. It is probable that the Soviet motive was a dual one; on the one hand, SALT publicly ratified the achievement of full strategic equality with the United States and the bipolar character of the balance of power, a consideration of importance in Moscow in view of the sharpening of the Sino-Soviet dispute; on the other, her scientists, economists, and planners, already bedevilled by the demands of the missile and other defence programmes on her limited technological resources, saw the same sharply rising ladder of costs as did their American counterparts, if strategic planning continued to be based on assumptions of the worst case and if the products of research were automatically and indefinitely converted first into development and then into production.

SALT was, and is, a serious negotiation on both sides.[4] But with its deliberations proceeding behind locked doors in Helsinki and Vienna for two and a half years, with the NATO allies of the United States informed on its progress rather than consulted on its strategy (including Britain who had been a founder member of the negotiations on the Test Ban and Non-Proliferation Treaties), it emphasized the continuing bipolarity of the international system at the plane of strategic relationships. Yet SALT had no clear influence on East–West relations as a whole, on the build-up, for instance, of Soviet naval power in the Mediterranean and the Indian Ocean, her equipping Egypt with ground-to-air missiles which nearly precipitated a fourth Arab–Israel war in 1970, or her demands for a European Security Conference on which the American (and the British and French) response was at that stage hesitant. The super-powers were, however, identifying certain limited common interests, evidenced by mutual restraint of the flare-up of violence in Jordan in October 1970, and the Soviet willingness to desist from acquiring naval facilities in Cuba in that year in the face of strong American objections.

The Nixon administration had other legacies of the period of universal competition with the Communist bloc to liquidate as well as getting the strategic arms race under control. The principal one was, of course, Vietnam where the level of conflict and casualties was still high, even though not on the murderous scale of 1968; where Hanoi had reverted to a successful strategy of protracted war; and where the revelation of the My Lai massacre had further alienated American public opinion from the war. By the end of 1969 President Nixon had announced the actual or impending withdrawal of about a fifth of the American troops deployed in Vietnam when he took office (119,000 out of 550,000); and the 'Vietnamization' of the conflict, that is to say improving the equipment, training and organization of South Vietnamese forces as American units were withdrawn, continued at broadly the same rate over the ensuing three years.

But the course of the war did not pursue such an even pattern, for the level of conflict in Laos heightened in the early part of 1970, and after a military coup deposed the absent Prince Sihanouk in March of that year, the President, at the end of April, sanctioned both South Vietnamese invasion of Cambodia and a limited American operation there designed to destroy Communist bases and sanctuaries along the Ho Chi Minh trail. The peace negotiations in Paris had made little headway in the eighteen months since they had started; and when, on 2 May, American aircraft began, under the rubric of 'protective reaction' attacks on reconnaissance planes, again to bomb North Vietnam, there was a widespread sense of public alarm that the war might spread both vertically and horizontally despite the President's earlier declarations of intent.

These had included his statement at Guam in November 1969 that the United States, while honouring its treaty commitments, especially in their strategic aspect, would expect its Asian allies to assume a larger share of the burdens of local defence, which became generalized in his message to Congress of February 1970, 'A New Strategy for Peace', into what is loosely called 'The Nixon Doctrine', namely, defined partnership with, rather than unlimited commitment to, the Asian allies of the United States. To give substance to this objective plans were announced during 1970 to withdraw 20,000 American troops from South Korea (nearly half the American forces there), 12,000 from Japan, 5,000 from Okinawa, 6,000 from the Philippines and about 10,000 from Thailand by mid-1971. American electronic installations in Pakistan had already been withdrawn, and in November 1969, the President and the then Prime Minister of Japan, Mr Sato, reached agreement on the reversion of Okinawa to Japanese administration (she had never lost formal sovereignty over the Ryukus) in 1972; this seemed to be the popular, as contrasted with the official, Japanese price for continuation of the US–Japan Mutual Security Treaty, as well as being consistent with the Nixon doctrine. The Sato government agreed, however, to American retention of certain base facilities in Okinawa.

The return of China

SALT and the Vietnam peace negotiations proceeded without overt signs of progress throughout 1971, though the American position in the latter now offered complete American withdrawal in return for a complete cease-fire. But by that year the ramifications of an even more important development than the American retreat from dominance in Asia – and potentially elsewhere – even more influential than the super-power negotiations on arms control, were beginning to affect the climate of world politics. The Sino–Soviet conflict in its first phase, discernible after 1958, shrill between 1961 and 1963, had been largely a war of words, harsh and bitter words to be sure and involving the tearing up of agreements. But it had not escalated into military hostility, partly because at that time the Soviet Union was preoccupied with her confrontation with the West, and with her strategic inferiority; partly because China in the wake of the Greap Leap Forward was a weak state militarily. And Sino–Soviet relations had not degenerated seriously between 1964 and 1969, in part because Vietnam created some identity of interest between Moscow and Peking, partly because between the end of 1965 and the end of 1968 China was not only living in a kind of self-imposed purdah, but was economically, and probably militarily, weaker than five years earlier. (Industrial production, for instance, had in some sectors dropped by 25 per cent.)

But by late 1968, Mao had clearly triumphed over his rivals, Liu Shao-chi had been cast out and anathematized, regional committees were being reorganized and China had successfully detonated a thermonuclear device. And as China resurfaced as a coherent state all the latent hostility in the Sino–Soviet relationship resurfaced also. It now took a more sinister form than verbal polemics, namely armed confrontation along the 4,150 miles of common border. The Soviet Union had been gradually augmenting its forces in the Far East since the early 1960s, though China, with a hostile Taiwan to the east and large American deployments around its south and eastern borders, had followed suit only later. The first armed clash, at Damansky Island on the Ussuri River on 2 March 1969, was apparently a Chinese provocation, possibly to stimulate domestic unity by asserting the image of an external adversary; but the skirmishing that continued sporadically from April to August on the border between Sinkiang and Kazakhstan was unmistakably of Soviet instigation. By August *Pravda* was hinting at the possible use of nuclear weapons by the Soviet Union, and Eastern Europe was full of rumours of an imminent Soviet air strike on Chinese nuclear installations. A visit by Kosygin to Chou En-lai in September after the funeral of Ho Chi Minh, and possibly as a consequence of North Vietnamese diplomacy, led to an agreement to open Sino–Soviet talks on the border dispute (though not on the border's adjustment, despite the fact that all Chinese have for a century regarded it as an unfair and illegitimate one); but by December the talks had adjourned and the level of mutual recrimination was beginning to rise again. Talks opened again in January 1970 only to be declared stalemated by Kosygin in June, opened again in October and broke down in December. On 9 May 1969 Marshal Grechko ranked China with Germany and the United States as a major foe of the Soviet Union.

The Chinese position was now both a perilous and a promising one. It was perilous in that she had not (and does not yet have) a strategic retaliatory force against a Soviet nuclear attack, while the superior fire-power of Soviet ground and air forces in the Far East, already estimated to be over thirty divisions and a thousand aircraft by the end of 1970, implied that the Soviet Union could disrupt the People's Republic and defeat the PLA, even if she could not conquer the whole vast country. It was promising in that China was entering into normal diplomatic relations with an increasing number of significant countries – Italy, Canada, Ethiopa, Yugoslavia, Austria – and when the question of her membership of the UN came up in the autumn of 1970 it received a majority vote of fifty-one to forty-nine, though this was still short of the two thirds votes necessary for entry. The question which the Chinese leaders had now to decide was whether to continue branding both the super-powers as collusive imperialists, engaged in arms control negotiations merely to strengthen the Soviet–American dominance of the international system, or whether, as had happened often in the classical European balance of power system, she must now distinguish between her principal and her secondary adversary and seek accommodation with the latter.

The thread of Sino–American contact had been a tenuous one throughout most of the decade, consisting of sporadic meetings between the Chinese and American ambassadors in Warsaw, which were rendered largely sterile by the opposing positions of the two powers on the future and status of Taiwan. Then, thirteen months after a Chinese statement in November 1968 that they were prepared to live on terms of peaceful coexistence with the United States, they were resumed on 11 December 1969, apparently at Chinese instigation. Throughout 1970 the United States government made the minimum of references to the Sino–Soviet dispute and American polemics against 'Red' China as an aggressive power were now a thing of the past. In his foreign policy statement of February 1970 the President had merely noted that 'the success of our Asian policy depends not only on the strength of our partnership with our Asian friends, but also on our relations with Mainland China and the Soviet Union. We have no desire to impose our prescriptions for relationships in Asia.'[5]

But the change in the Sino–American relationship was not a *volte-face* on the part of either power, for it was preceded by a period of intense calculation of the relative costs and benefits to each of moving towards rapprochement. For the Chinese leadership it involved a calculation as to whether the Sino–Soviet rift, which would certainly be deepened by Sino–American détente, was now unbridgeable, and if China's position in the developing world would be damaged by such a move. It involved calculations about the extent to which the unity of the Chinese state could stand such a change of course and in particular whether it might strengthen the hand of those, especially among the military, who wished to re-establish a liaison with the Soviet Union: it involved a judgement as to whether Nixon was really sincere in his determination to extricate the United States from Vietnam (by the end of 1970 about 350,000 troops had been withdrawn) and to reduce American military power around the periphery of China. But probably security, the fear of Soviet attack, was the dominant motive.

On the American side it involved a calculation, not only about public acceptance of a change in Sino–American relations, of which there was by then little doubt, but also whether SALT, whose success was becoming increasingly important to the Administration, had reached a point where a change from a bipolar to a triangular political relationship would destroy or improve American leverage in the bilateral negotiation: it involved a calculation as to the effect on the Asian alliances of the United States of rapprochement with the country against which most of them had been, implicitly or explicitly, constructed; and finally, it involved a judgement on whether the United States might not find herself, rather than China, the more isolated of the two powers as more and more countries normalized their relations with Peking. It also involved consigning to the files some of the official and academic analysis of five or ten years earlier about the greater stability of a bipolar world.

By the beginning of 1971 this cost-benefit analysis had been substantially completed in both capitals, and when discreet feelers were put out from Peking the United States started to reciprocate. On 15 March (the same day that a crucial phase of SALT was resumed), the United States lifted the final restrictions on the travel of American nationals to China, and three months later ended the last embargoes on the export of non-strategic goods to it. In April came a Chinese invitation to an American and a British ping-pong team to visit Peking, which Chou En-lai used as an opportunity to speak of 'a new stage in the relations between the Chinese and American peoples'. This was followed in mid-July by one of the most dramatic moves in current diplomatic history, the arrival in Peking of Henry Kissinger, the President's Adviser on National Security Affairs, who had travelled through Europe and Pakistan, leaving a trail of different cover stories behind him in the various capitals (in London he was said to be there to study the organization of the British Cabinet Office system). On the same day it was announced that the President had accepted Chou En-lai's invitation to visit Peking by May 1972, although the President wisely ensured that this remarkable decision would not sever the thread of Soviet–American communication and negotiation by simultaneously declaring his intention to visit Moscow thereafter.

On 2 August, Secretary of State Rogers expressed support for China's entry into the United Nations, provided it did not prejudice the status of Taiwan. But in fact the breaking of the Sino–American log-jam precipitated a more rapid pace of events than Washington could control. On 25 October, while Dr Kissinger was paying a second visit to Peking, and after two weeks of American rearguard action in the United Nations to protect Taiwan, the General Assembly voted by a large majority, with only Japan, Australia, and a number of small Asian and Latin American states supporting the US, to accord the Chinese seat in the UN to the government of Peking, and the delegation from Taiwan then withdrew. In November the representative of Peking took his seat in both the Security Council and the General Assembly; a chapter of history spanning nearly a generation had been closed.

There was one immediate outcome of the re-emergence of China as a great power and her entry into the international community as a full and legitimate member. The Soviet Union had for some years feared a Sino–American rapprochement, and had been laying the foundations of a policy that would at least contain the expansion of Chinese influence in Asia. North Korea had partly slipped into the Chinese political orbit though dependent on the Soviet Union for arms, but North Vietnam was dismayed by the events of July and was more ready to strengthen her links with the Soviet Union. Yet this was merely support from an existing ally and what was more important was to broaden the range of Soviet allies. Brezhnev had talked cryptically once or twice about a collective security system for Asia; he now sought to strengthen the Soviet position in the Middle East by despatching Podgorny to Cairo in May to sign a fifteen year Treaty of Friendship with Egypt, and in Asia generally by sending Gromyko to Delhi in August to sign a twenty year Treaty of Peace, Friendship, and Cooperation with India – treaties which contained arrangements about military aid and imposed an obligation to consult in a crisis. These were the first treaties of alliance that the Soviet Union had made with non-Communist states since the Second World War.

The first consequence of the new triangular relationship was conflict in the Indian sub-continent. The formalization of Soviet support for India, which had been increasing informally for a number of years, had the effect of fortifying the Indian government in its support for the breakaway of East Pakistan as the new state of Bangla Desh, which had started in March 1971, and which the government of Rawalpindi was attempting to suppress by force. In October India refused the mediation of the UN or the intervention of a peace-keeping force, and in early December recognized Bangla Desh and invaded the area. Unlike her attitude in 1965, the Soviet Union vetoed two cease-fire resolutions in the Security Council and took an openly anti-Pakistan line. Mr Bhutto, who became President of Pakistan at the height of the conflict, had earlier secured a vague assurance of aid from China, though less specific or effective than those that Mrs Gandhi had received from the Soviet Union. President Nixon had merely inflamed Indian opinion by sending a large carrier into the Bay of Bengal at the height of the conflict, leaving Indian opinion convinced that there had been Sino–American collusion, while in Pakistan opinion was indignant at the impotence of her western friends (which shortly led to Pakistan's withdrawal from the Commonwealth and from SEATO), though in truth it was the relative impotence of China that the conflict revealed.

Sino–American rapprochement caused, by reason of its timing, political as well as military casualties. The Nixon administration had not made a practice of consulting allies on Asian questions for some time (except for some association of France with the Vietnam peace negotiations and some use of British and Canadian diplomatic channels in dealing with China). But the President's decision to enter into relations with China was taken, largely it must be said either through diplomatic incompetence or contempt for the diplomatic process, without any consultation with, or even information to, the Pacific allies of the United States – Australia, who had played the loyal ally throughout the Vietnam War, the SEATO powers, or above all Japan, economically the second most powerful country in the whole Western alliance system. Consequently it shook the authority of governments all round the Pacific basin.

Moreover, it was followed in exactly a month by another sudden and unilateral act of American policy which suggested that the President's diplomatic right hand and his economic left hand were not acting in concert. After the most serious down-turn in the American balance of payments since the early 1930s, President Nixon on 15 August announced a ten per cent surcharge on imports of manufactured goods and a decoupling of the dollar from the price of gold. For the industrial countries of Europe this was a significant sign of the times, especially coming at a moment of recession and high unemployment there. It reinforced those who had been arguing for some years that the dollar-based international monetary system, negotiated at Bretton Woods in 1944, would need radical overhaul if the expansion of world trade and therefore of employment were to be sustained in an economic order which the United States no longer dominated. But for Japan, thirty per cent of whose foreign trade is with the United States, the surcharge was a direct blow and, coming as it did immediately after a major turn-about in Sino–American relations, it raised widespread and serious doubts as to where in the emerging international system the real interests of Japan lay. True, the surcharge was lifted at the end of 1971, the dollar was devalued and the yen revalued, but Japan had been cast adrift from her moorings in a way which no pragmatic or detailed readjustments of American policy could now wholly rectify.

Unravelling Europe's Gordian knot

It is best to discuss developments in Europe separately because the story contains several different though interrelated threads, including the normalization of the Federal Republic's relation with her Eastern neighbours, the development of the European Community and its relationship with the super-powers and the movement towards East–West negotiation. All these were indirectly affected by developments in Soviet–American–Chinese relations, but the change in the structure of great-power relationships did not have the same direct impact there as in East and Southern Asia.

By the beginning of 1969 discussion between the Federal Republic of Germany and the Soviet government about the basis for a new relationship had been in train for nearly three years and were only interrupted for a short time by the Czechoslovak crisis, despite the fact that Soviet propaganda had tried to incriminate Germany in the responsibility for the events in Prague of 1968. In a sense the Soviet intervention there had made easier the task of Herr Brandt, the Foreign Minister, by disposing of a number of illusions, among both young and old, about the feasibility of a more radical reorganization of European relationships than the definite acceptance of the post-war status quo in Europe that he had in mind; it also illustrated the infeasibility of trying to encircle the DDR by West German rapprochement with all her neighbours and made it necessary to confront directly the necessity for a new relationship between the two Germanys.

The first move in the process was German agreement on the eastern frontier of the DDR – the Oder–Neisse line – and, when Gomulka proposed Polish–German negotiation on the subject in May 1969, Herr Kiesinger, the highly conservative Chancellor of the broad coalition of which Herr Brandt's SPD was the junior member, reciprocated in a matter of weeks. In the autumn the SPD itself became the governing party (in coalition with the Liberals) and Brandt as Chancellor was in a position to concentrate on the *Ostpolitik*. This involved a number of related moves: the negotiation of a treaty with Poland to settle the question not only of the frontier but of the German minorities there; formal diplomatic signalling to Moscow that the *Ostpolitik* was not aimed, as earlier versions might have been thought to be, at undermining the Soviet position in Eastern Europe; reassurance of West German public opinion that the freedom of West Berlin would not suffer from a consolidation of the Federal Republic's relations with Eastern Europe (which involved pressure by the United States, Britain and France on the Soviet Union for a new Berlin agreement); and finally direct negotiation with the DDR.

By August 1970 a non-aggression treaty had been signed between the Federal Republic and the Soviet Union which accepted the existing frontiers of Europe including those between the two Germanys. In December Chancellor Brandt visited Warsaw for the signature of the West German–Polish Treaty. But although there were two direct discussions between the Chancellor and the Prime Minister of the DDR in that year, negotiations between the two Germanys did not at first prosper: this was partly because the DDR insisted that there could be no 'special relationship' between them and that they could normalize relations only on the basis of recognizing each other's state sovereignty; in part it was because the DDR exerted continuous interference in the negotiation of a new Berlin agreement.

However, by the autumn of 1971, after, that is, the opening of American communication with China, it was apparent that the Soviet Union was now anxious to move on to a new phase of multilateral diplomacy in Europe and in September a new four-power agreement on Berlin – the first since 1947 – was negotiated.

On his way back from Paris the following month, Brezhnev exerted pressure on the government of the DDR to work out the details of an agreement on access and traffic with the Federal Republic. The Berlin agreement was finally signed in June 1972 by the Soviet Union after the Bundestag had, after stormy debates, finally ratified the Moscow and Warsaw treaties. But throughout 1971 and 1972 the parliamentary majority of the SPD–Liberal coalition in Bonn had been gradually eroding; Brandt, however, had based his diplomatic calculations on the belief that his *Ostpolitik* commanded a popular majority in the country, and he pursued negotiation on a Basic Treaty with the DDR on assumptions that his victory in the general election of November 1972, which gave him a parliamentary majority of forty-six seats, in fact confirmed. On 21 December 1972 the Basic Treaty, by which each German state recognized the independence and autonomy of the other but held open the option of eventual reunification, was signed in East Berlin. Though neither the Berlin agreements nor the Basic Treaty are formal peace treaties, they substantially conclude the unfinished business of the Potsdam Conference of 1945, and Brezhnev's visit to Bonn in May 1973 suggested that the Soviet Union was now ready to endorse the spirit as well as the letter of these agreements.

But there have been other forces at work which have contributed to a rapid pace of developments in Europe, so rapid as to make this new period of détente certainly a complex and, in some ways, an uneasy one; the desire of the Soviet Union to explore and if possible exploit a new relationship with the countries of Western Europe; the desire of the Eastern European countries to find ways of increasing their autonomy without the risks to which Czechoslovakia exposed herself; the expansion of the European Economic Community and new problems in its relations with the United States, as well as growing Western anxiety about the military foundations of détente in Europe.

The Soviet proposal for a conference on European security goes back to 1954, the year before the Geneva summit meeting when phrases like 'roll back' were still current in the West. Its purpose has been to gain acceptance of the territorial status quo and the political division of Europe; it rose again to the top of Soviet priorities in the mid-1960s after the failure of de Gaulle to undo the supranational aspects of the European Economic Community implied that Western Europe as a Community would exert an increasing economic and political magnetism on the countries of Eastern Europe. At a meeting of the Warsaw Pact in Bucharest in 1966 a call was issued to the NATO countries to engage in a negotiation on the dissolution of the two blocs in Europe. The Western reply was merely the qualified negative that the European NATO powers had no intention of entering a multilateral negotiation with the Soviet Union unless their North American partners, the United States and Canada, also participated.

By the beginning of 1969 there had been a number of developments. The Czechoslovak crisis and the evolution of the Brezhnev doctrine had made it necessary to strengthen rather than contemplate the dissolution of the Warsaw Pact. Both the Soviet Union and the East European countries were anxious to find means of acquiring Western technology and attracting certain forms of Western investment. On the Western side, fear that American public and congressional *ennui* with overseas military commitments might not be confined to Asia, made governments, some more than others, anxious to explore mutual force reduction in

Europe. They were also influenced by the argument that if the United States was going to be engaged in a bilateral negotiation with the Soviet Union on strategic weapons, while Germany was embarked on the normalization of its relations with Eastern Europe, decisions might be taken by either the United States or Germany that could affect the security interests of Western Europe as a whole if there was no general multilateral negotiation between East and West. Finally, they were responsive to East European diplomatic urgings about the desirability of such a conference as a means of narrowing the Soviet definition of the Brezhnev doctrine. Consequently, when in March 1969 the Warsaw Pact conference in Budapest issued a fresh invitation for a European security conference, without mentioning a dissolution of blocs, it elicited by the end of the year a cautious acceptance from the NATO Council.

In the succeeding two years the Soviet Union kept the pressure on and accepted the presence of the United States and Canada at a European Security Conference. But, in the leisurely battle of half-yearly communiqués between the two alliances and in private diplomatic soundings, it became clear that the Soviet Union wished to discuss European 'security' only in the political sense of recognition of frontiers and so on, while many NATO powers desired discussion on arms control in Europe. By 1971 the American Administration, which like Britain and France had been sceptical about the prospects of a successful negotiation on force reductions, had become sufficiently alarmed at the prospect of being forced by Congress into unilateral reductions to be disposed towards such a negotiation. On the Soviet side, Brezhnev at the 24th Party Congress in March and again at Tiflis in May – just before the Mansfield Resolution calling for a fifty per cent reduction in American forces in Europe was about to come to a vote in the Senate – indicated Soviet willingness to negotiate on the subject. Largely as a consequence, the Mansfield resolution was defeated. During 1972 it was bilaterally agreed by the superpowers that in fact two conferences would be convened in 1973, one a European Conference on Security and Cooperation with a broad agenda including – at Western insistence – freedom of personal movement, and involving every European state (except Albania who refused to participate) plus the United States and Canada; and another between members of the Warsaw Pact and NATO on mutual and balanced force reductions (MBFR).

Preparatory talks on the Conference on European Security and Cooperation (CSCE) started in Helsinki in November 1972 and MBFR in Vienna at the end of January 1973.

It was against this background of diplomatic movement between East and West in Europe and of uncertainty about the emerging pattern of relationships among the very largest states, that the enlargement of the European Community took place. It was evident before President de Gaulle left office that his own view about the need for the Western European countries to act in concert in world politics was changing: he had for instance spoken privately to the British Ambassador, Sir Christopher Soames, about the desirability of Franco–British discussions on the development of a wider political grouping in Europe. When M Pompidou succeeded him as President in April 1969, this sense that the Western European countries must draw closer together was made more specific, and at the Hague conference in December 1969 the heads of government of the Six had little difficulty in finding consensus on the need to expand the Community to include Britain, Norway, Denmark and Eire. It is worth noting, as an indication of the necessity that was perceived in Bonn to keep *Westpolitik* in balance with *Ostpolitik* that this was the first international engagement of the newly elected Chancellor Brandt and that in fact he played a leading role in the whole discussion of expanding the Community. By May 1971 Mr Heath and President Pompidou had agreed, after a meeting in Paris, that differing French and British perspectives on the future organization of the Community were now relatively unimportant; by June Britain had secured terms of entry into the EEC which met her principal problems (particularly the safeguarding of New Zealand's market for dairy produce and that of the Commonwealth Caribbean countries for sugar); and on 28 October the House of Commons voted by a large majority (including nearly half the Labour opposition) in favour of entry. Of the other three candidate members, all of whom required a popular referendum for a constitutional step of this magnitude, only Norway fell by the wayside in 1972 (a decision that may well be reversed in the next few years). On 1 January 1973 the Community was formally enlarged to include a total of nine powers.

In theory this was the consummation of a long-standing American desire to have a comprehensive European Community as a partner. But the circumstances of enlargement were not entirely propitious for the future of European–American relations. For one thing, the Community now had preferential trading agreements of one kind or another with some forty countries, in Europe, the Middle East, Africa and elsewhere in the developing world. This was a fact at which the United States could not fail, now that her balance of trade was adverse, to look askance. Second, the early 1970s have been characterized by growing European nervousness about its future security relationship with the United States. The regular statements of President Nixon that there would be no unilateral reduction of American troops in Europe, that Western Europe was as important to American security as Alaska, could not allay the fear in Western European capitals, including Paris, that NATO could not travel far into its second quarter-century without a drastic reorganization of the European–American military or strategic relationship.

The end of the Third World

The Philippines, India, Pakistan, and Ceylon became sovereign states in the 1940s. In the succeeding twenty years some seventy other former colonial areas in Asia, Africa and the Caribbean acquired sovereignty, so that by the beginning of the 1970s only a small group of dependencies remained under the control of the former colonial powers, either for reasons of size (St Helena, or Bermuda), strategic significance (Puerto Rico, Djibouti or Micronesia), the political difficulties of offering them statehood or their own reluctance to assume it (Hong Kong, Gibraltar or Tristan de Cunha) or their political backwardness (New Guinea). Only Portugal continues to believe in her mission as a colonial power.

Thus a process of political change as significant for world order as the emergence of strategic and economic super-powers proceeded in parallel throughout the years of the bipolar world and its erosion. The early objectives of the new states, as formulated for instance by Jawarhal Nehru, were primarily those of non-alignment in the East–West conflict, of peaceful co-existence with the members of both power blocs and with their neighbours, freedom from interference and respect for their sovereignty, acceleration of the process of decolonization elsewhere and the fostering of an international climate that permitted them to get on with their own development. These objectives, political rather than economic, were the formal cement of the Afro-Asian bloc that emerged in the United Nations during the 1950s. But with the economic regeneration of Western Europe and Japan, the economic differences between the countries of Africa and Asia and those of the developed world assumed increasing significance, as did those between North and South America. During the 1950s both a policy and a practice of economic and technical assistance, multilateral and bilateral, was evolved among the industrial countries, deriving partly from a sense of conscience, partly from fear of the influence the Communist powers might come to exert in weak, poor and angry states, partly from traditional concern for the safeguarding of sources of raw materials.

By reason of the fact that there was by the middle of the 1960s a majority of members of the United Nations who seemed to exhibit a number of characteristics in common – poverty, high population growth, illiteracy, dependence on the export of primary products and above all political non-alignment – characteristics which they did not for the most part share with the countries of either Western or Eastern Europe, North America, Japan, or Australasia, it became part of the jargon of international political analysis to describe them as the Third World.*

But by the beginning of the 1970s it was clear that no such sweeping – and condescending – categorization of the non-industrialized states any longer fitted the facts and that it was a hindrance to any accurate perception of the real world of international politics. In the first place, though the conception of 'non-aligned' is still largely valid in ideological terms – only Cuba has become aligned in this sense in the past fifteen years, though to a curious kind of Marxism – it is no longer true in the political sense. Of the developing countries that became allied to the United States or other Western powers in the 1950s, all but Iraq remain within the ambit of SEATO or CENTO and are reluctant to see these organizations dismantled (Pakistan has left SEATO but places increased emphasis on her relations with Turkey and Iran in CENTO). Iraq, briefly the capital of CENTO's predecessor, the Baghdad Pact, became a formal ally of the Soviet Union in 1972; and, more significant, the countries that provided Nehru and

* As the Pearson Commission noted there is no satisfactory generic term to distinguish rich or poor, advanced or backward states without implying value judgements and I have followed its example in using the distinction of 'developed' and 'developing'.

Nasser, the two great leaders of the Afro-Asian bloc in its heyday, the two great exponents of non-alignment, in 1971 entered into formal treaties of cooperation with the Soviet Union. In terms of dependence on a great power for military assistance, Israel, which only a decade ago saw itself maintaining close relations with Europe as well as the United States, has been almost totally dependent on the United States since then and Iran has become partly so. Pakistan has become increasingly dependent on China for arms and Syria on the Soviet Union. In terms of older forms of association France remains the primary political, economic and military partner of the countries of the French Community. And, though Britain is no longer the sole support, in terms of military or economic aid, of most of the new Commonwealth countries, and has seen her relations erode with many small as well as with some large members of it, Malta as well as India for instance, the multi-lateral relationships of the Commonwealth retain a certain political value. Britain's old treaty relationships with the Persian Gulf States came to an end in 1971, but a five-power defence agreement with Australia, New Zealand, Malaysia and Singapore was re-negotiated in the same year and looks as if it may last for a few years. The Rio Treaty, the Inter-American Treaty of Reciprocal Assistance, signed in 1947, a year before the Atlantic Alliance, still provides the political framework of relations between the United States and all the significant countries of Latin America (except Cuba who withdrew in 1960).

These relationships, formal or informal, vary greatly in their significance and it would take a separate book to describe or compare them. All I wish to suggest is that their diversity is almost as great as the political diversity of the regimes of the non-industrial states. Mexico, for instance, has had forty years of political stability and the basic framework of democratic institutions has been maintained for over twenty-five in the much larger and more diverse polity of India. Elsewhere it is largely a landscape of one kind or another of authoritarian rule or of endemic instability, whether by reason of the preference of some middle-class elements for dictatorship rather than populism, as in some Latin American states, of the impatience of the military with disorderliness and the corruption of the democratic process which the metropolitan powers attempted to bequeath in much of Africa, or of ethnic and tribal rivalries. It is true that on certain issues – the General Assembly vote on China's admission to the UN in October 1971 or in condemnation of Portugal or South Africa, for instance – the countries of the so-called Third World can be expected to act in unison. There are certain new preoccupations of the industrial powers, concern with environmental problems, for instance, which the poorer developing countries can hardly be expected to share, as the Stockholm Conference of 1971 on the subject illustrated, and they tend to resent being addressed on the subject by well-meaning environmentalists. The unity of their ranks is still maintained on issues of development and investment, even though the Third UNCTAD conference at Santiago in 1972 did lead to some serious arguments between its Asian and African members. The increasing scarcity of certain raw materials gives rise to new forms of functional cooperation among developing countries, as in the case of the oil states. But on less specific issues of international politics the major powers do not move in a uniform climate of interests, opinion or objectives among the developing countries. Local balances of power are emerging, between Nigeria and her neighbours for instance, between Singapore and Malaysia as well as in Southern Asia, and also local ententes such as that between Kenya and Ethiopia. The Arab–Israel dispute has secondary ramifications in the relations of many other states. Consequently in discussing the relations of the great with the less great it is important to talk of areas, countries, leaders rather than in terms of generalities.

This does not mean that the distinction between the new or the developing states and the industrial ones is disappearing. During the 1960s, the industrial states added $700 billion to their annual real incomes, a sum far greater than the total annual incomes of Asia, Africa and Latin America.[6] Put another way, income per head in the developed countries rose by $300 during the 1960s, whereas in the developing countries it rose by $10. This is an indication of the size of the 'development gap', even though the average rate of increase in the GNP of the developing countries attained 4.8 per cent by 1965 (which is double the growth rate of Britain, the United States or Japan during their period of industrialization). But comparisons of GNP conceal desperate deficiencies in education, literacy, medicine and nutrition. Above all they take no account of the population problem, which was not foreseen twenty years ago. Population grew at an average rate of 2.5 per cent through the 1960s in the developing countries, more than twice the rate of growth in the developed. The governments of many developing countries, China and India among them, are now fully aware of the way in which rapid population growth can end in negating increases in production. But in other parts of the world population growth remains enormous, either by reason of the baleful policy of the Vatican on contraception which has created a population growth rate of 3 per cent in most of the Catholic countries of Latin America (excluding, that is, countries like Jamaica) or because population is seen as a form of power, as in Kenya, Libya or Israel, or for both reasons as in Zaire which had a growth of 4·2 per cent from 1969 to 1971.[7] The consequence is that production per capita has at best increased only at the rate of 3·3 per cent in the developing world as a whole, and unless population increase is got under better control is not likely to increase significantly whatever happens to the level of aid and investment. In addition the developing countries have a very large amount of external debt to service (nearly $50 billion in 1968) and have had a declining share of world trade.

But global figures conceal marked differences between regions. The region with the highest growth-rate both in production and product per capita (allowing, that is, for population increases) has been Southern Europe: Spain, Greece, Turkey, Yugoslavia, Cyprus and Malta, countries which it will soon be difficult to regard as part of the developing world.[8] The other area of fairly rapid growth is the Middle East, not surprisingly in view of the demand for oil and the industry of Israel, which has been developing faster than any other area, not only in terms of Gross Domestic Product (7·2 per cent), but of agricultural, steel or energy production. (Real living standards would have risen faster in the Middle East if there had not been a general rise in defence budgets in the 1960s.) Somewhat behind came the countries of the Pacific littoral, sustained principally by the remarkable performance of both South Korea and Taiwan. Latin America stands a little ahead of Southern Asia and Africa largely because of the 'economic miracle' that has occurred in Brazil since 1968, though Brazil is under an authoritarian regime which seems to have little concern to spread the benefits of growth either socially or regionally. To illustrate the spread of domestic capabilities, it is worth quoting three figures for energy consumption per capita in 1965 (in kilograms of coal): the United States, 9201; Argentina 1341; Nepal 8.[9]

This differentiation between the well-being or power of different parts of the developing world is likely to increase for reasons that

I shall attempt to examine later. But by the beginning of the 1970s it was clear that a small number of countries had emerged from the developing world as middle powers. India, of course, has been one for a quarter-century and is more powerful on her own sub-continent after the events of 1971–2, even if Mrs Gandhi's influence on world politics in general is markedly less than that of her father. To India must now be added Indonesia, which is the most significant state in South East Asia by reason of its population (130 million), its size and its control of the passage between the Indian and the Pacific Oceans; Indonesia has in the past been courted by all the great powers, and her significance affected, though it did not determine, the increasing American involvement in Vietnam in the decade after 1954. But it is only now after Indonesia has started to achieve political stability and a respect-able rate of real growth that she is beginning to acquire some independence of her own. In Latin America, Brazil, with a popula-tion of 100 million people and a GNP of $40 billion in 1971, is becoming increasingly an autonomous actor in world politics; so also is Mexico. In their own region Iran and Saudi Arabia are emerging as the leading powers, both having an income per capita considerably above the average for the developing world (though the league table is actually lead by little Kuwait which is second only to the United States in this respect). Both powers are strategically situated and with the prospect of rapidly increasing external revenues from oil (and in the case of Iran, copper).

The diversification of the fortunes of the developing countries has had its reflection in the policies of the developed. On the one hand détente among the developed powers (coupled with increasing domestic demands on public resources) has had the unfortunate effect for the developing countries of robbing development aid of its political appeal to the legislatures of the developed. The Pearson Commission was asked in 1968 to survey the whole field of development on behalf of the World Bank, and to investigate all the problems of maintaining the best possible rate of economic and social development that could be considered in terms of political realism. It emerged with a firm conclusion that the level of development assistance should be increased, that more of it should take the form of grants and that more national funds should be directed through the multilateral agencies. As a con-sequence of its findings a target for the 1970s of a total annual contribution of 1·0 per cent of national income for the aid-giving countries was set by UNCTAD, of which 0·7 per cent should be in the form of governmental development aid (a modest target by comparison with that for the developing countries themselves, who were asked to increase to 7 per cent the proportion of their national income devoted to investment).

But one salient characteristic of the late 1960s was the relative decline in the flow of American and other Western resources to the developing world, compounded partly by the disenchantment of both political and expert opinion with the social achievements of fifteen years of development aid, partly of diminished fear of Soviet or Chinese encroachment in the developing countries, partly of the redirection of private investment towards Europe. The level, both in 1970 and 1971 of American official aid amounted to only just over 0·3 per cent of GNP, half the Pearson target, and the total flow of her resources to the developing world (public and private) to 0·65 per cent (two-thirds of the Pearson target). The total flow of French resources fell from 1·24 per cent in 1970 to 1·00 per cent of GNP in 1971 (the lowest proportion of her wealth devoted to aid since consistent development programmes began). The flow of British resources in 1971 was 0·40 in terms of official aid but with a substantial increase in private investment that brought the total figure up to 1·15 per cent of GNP. The combined figure for Germany had risen to 0·88 per cent and for Japan to 0·96 per cent.[10] Projections made by the World Bank of the period 1970–5 show that official aid for the developing countries will hover around the 0·35 per cent mark during these six years with only the smaller countries where popular idealism affects foreign policy, the Netherlands, Norway, Sweden, providing sums approaching the target of the Pearson Commission and with the United States trailing the pack at 0·24 per cent of GNP or less.[11] In most developed countries, aid now has only two not very powerful lobbies behind it, the churches and the young.

The prospect for many developing countries of keeping pace with the growth of the developed countries or of markedly accelerating their own social and economic strength is consequently not a very encouraging one. In part it is the reverse side of a subtle change that has been occurring in the perceptions of the great powers about their relations with each other. One aspect is a change in the American attitude to spheres of influence. In theory the United States has always been in favour of an open world in which all states had access to each other, but in practice this has historically been limited by the application of the Monroe Doctrine to Latin America, and more recently by the attempt to exclude external Communist influence from South and South East Asia, as well as, for a while, from Africa. In recent years, however, the American acceptance of the late Allende regime in Chile, which was not linked to the Soviet Union by the same dependence as Cuba but which was nominally Marxist, represented a significant modification of traditional attitudes. The foundation of a formal treaty relationship between India and the Soviet Union in 1971 produced little reaction in the United States, though it would earlier have been regarded as of prime importance to keep India within 'the free world', as well as to mitigate her appalling problems by maintaining a high level of development assistance to her. Conversely, in Eastern Europe the visit of President Nixon to Rumania in 1969 and of other senior American public figures to other East European countries represent an attempt to water down the exclusivity of the Soviet sphere of influence there. And in a field that affects the American pocket book much more directly, the beginnings of the 1970s were marked by an increasingly hostile reaction to what was seen as an attempt on the part of the countries of the EEC to create their own sphere of economic and political influence by the development of preferential arrangements with the countries of the Mediterranean littoral and sub-Saharan Africa.

At the same time the logical counterpart of the Nixon doctrine, the acceleration of the internal progress and stability of the major developing countries by increased aid, technical assistance and private investment has foundered, in fact, upon the disillusionment of Congress, and the President's lack of concern for the problems of the developing world as a whole except where they affect the direct interests of the United States. Since about half or more of the resources flowing to them have been from the United States this crucially affects the prospects for the future, as well as placing enhanced emphasis on the stimulation of their earnings through the elimination of various forms of trade barriers in the developed lands.

4
The Emerging Pattern

The road to Peking

The process of change which I have attempted to describe became temporarily consolidated in the twelve or so months after February 1972. They witnessed President Nixon's visit both to Peking and Moscow and his overwhelming re-election to a second term; the normalization of Japan's relation first with China then to a considerable extent with the Soviet Union, as well as changes of policy on the part of other Pacific states; the preliminary definition of the enlarged European Community's objectives for the ensuing decade; the approach to multilateral negotiations with Eastern Europe and the Soviet Union; and a more accurate definition, if no solution, of the problems of Western trade and monetary relationships. The impending alteration in the nature of the developed world's relationship with the Middle East also became visible.

On his return from seven days in Peking on 28 February, the President spoke of 'a week that had changed the world'. If that was an overstatement, given the intractability of the international system, the visit was both a remarkable initiative and a remarkable accomplishment on both sides. But the only point of real substance that eventuated, from discussions that were longer and more candid than had been expected, was a deliberate act of American appeasement* when in the communiqué it was stated that 'the United States acknowledges that all Chinese on either

---

* The word 'appeasement' has acquired a pejorative meaning as the result of Chamberlain's policy towards Hitler. Properly it means to assuage, pacify or to bring peace. Its pejorative connotation derives from Chamberlain's misjudgement of the possibility of assuaging Hitler except at the expense of other powers and of the balance of power.

side of the Taiwan Strait maintain there is but one China and that Taiwan is part of China'. (It was also an acknowledgement of the truth since this has always been the position of the Chiang Kai-shek regime.) But, more significant, in the agreed section of the communiqué the United States declared that it 'would progressively withdraw its forces and military installations in Taiwan as tension in the area diminished, with complete withdrawal as an ultimate objective'. It also spoke of a new programme of Sino-American scientific, technological and cultural exchanges and declared, without mentioning formal diplomatic recognition, that the two countries would maintain contact by various means. Within the year this had led to an exchange of quasi-diplomatic missions.

But though there were signs, ranging from the President's deferential references to Chairman Mao to the fashion for Mao jackets among the smart East Siders of New York, that a traditional American Sinophilia might be re-emerging, the discussions of February 1972 did not produce a complete diplomatic *volte-face*. In the communiqué, for instance, the Chinese stressed their desire for the reunification of Korea and Vietnam, and their opposition to Japanese militarism. The United States declared its interest in self-determination 'for each country of Indochina', its support for South Korea, and its friendship for Japan. On the latter point the President was clearly able to convey assurances that the Nixon Doctrine did not involve encouraging the massive rearmament of Japan, which had significant consequences later in the year.

Hardly had Mr Nixon returned to Washington than pressure began to build up on the left and in the centre of the Japanese political spectrum for a similar revision of Japan's relation with China; in part it was motivated by resentment at what was regarded as yet another instance of American unilateralism, especially as Japan has a keen interest in the future of Taiwan. The government of Mr Sato came under increasing criticism for not having defined Japan's interests more clearly and for not having asserted them more cogently. In June he resigned and was succeeded by Mr Kakeui Tanaka, who gained majority support within the ruling Liberal Party because he seemed a more independent figure, from a different social background, than the characteristically cautious, American-oriented, type of Japanese post-war politician.

In late September he visited Peking – less than a year after

Japan's vote against China's entry into the UN – from which emerged a nine-point agreement by which Japan recognized the People's Republic as the sole legitimate government of China and recognized that Taiwan was an inalienable part of China. (This had been declared in principle by Mr Sato immediately after the Nixon visit to Peking.) China renounced her claim to indemnities for damage in Japan's fourteen years (1931–45) of undeclared war with her, and the two countries agreed to resume normal diplomatic relations. In October a new trade agreement was signed. In March 1973 the embassy of Taiwan in Tokyo was handed over to the Peking government. European visitors to Peking in the winter of 1972–3 found that the Chinese no longer raised the spectre of Japanese militarism though they continuously inveighed against the 'dual hegemony' of the super-powers.

The prospect of the opening of relations between Tokyo and Peking had led to a mellowing in the Soviet attitude to Japan even before it actually happened. In January 1972 Mr Gromyko, the Soviet foreign minister, visited Japan and reached an agreement to open talks on a peace treaty (which the Soviet Union had not signed in 1951, though the two countries resumed diplomatic relations in 1956) and on joint economic development. Japan had for some time been interested in the development of oil and timber and coal resources in Siberia, and felt that the return of the four Kurile Islands (which had been wrested from her at the end of the war by the Soviet Union, partly as consequence of Roosevelt's hints to Stalin at Yalta that, if she would take an active part in the final defeat of Japan, the United States would not stand in the way of such adjustments) was essential to a peace settlement. Negotiations got under way in Moscow in November 1972 but the Soviet Union, whose interest had cooled somewhat after the Tanaka visit to Peking, seemed at first ready to consider only the return of Shikotan and the Habomais, among the Kurile group of islands. By March 1973 the Japanese had decided to separate the question of investment in Siberia from that of a peace treaty, and to make proposals on the joint exploitation of the Tyumen oil fields in Western Siberia and a 4,000 mile pipeline to the Pacific coast. There was a slight softening of the Soviet attitude on the return of the Kuriles. As we shall discuss in chapter 9 Japan does not feel that she possesses much leverage in dealing with her mainland neighbours. The Chinese protest at any mention of the Tyumen pipeline, which would come near its border, raises the question of whether Japan can have close relations with both mainland powers, if they remain in a state of enmity.

But there were other consequences among the smaller Asian powers of the emergence of a quadripartite relationship between the United States, the Soviet Union, China, and Japan. One was in the relation of the two halves of Korea, to which I will return in chapter 10.

In Thailand the change was muted, despite the Thai government's emission of pacific signals to Peking, by the increased American dependence on bases there during the final phase of the Vietnam war. In the Philippines it was similarly muted by increasing domestic unrest and the imposition of martial law. Perhaps the most striking changes were in the two countries of Australasia, whose Labour governments were returned at the end of the year. The newly elected Prime Minister of New Zealand announced his government's intention to withdraw from SEATO (though this does not seem imminent), and both countries established diplomatic relations with China in December. More than that, Mr Gough Whitlam, the new Australian Prime Minister, sought to reverse the perspective of his countrymen on their position in the Southern hemisphere, which during a quarter century of Liberal-Country Party rule had often been conceived in terms that Israelis would recognize, as an outpost of Western civilization among traditionalist societies, an advanced society surrounded by hostile neighbours, which must keep the United States (and Britain) intimately involved in her security to maintain order in the region. Instead he emphasized the inherent strengths, geographic and economic, of Australia, and her ability to let the balance of power in Asia sort itself out without Australia playing a continuous diplomatic and military role in the process of change.

The consolidation of change in the politics of Asia was further ratified by the achievement of a cease-fire in Vietnam on 27 January 1973. To have attained a negotiated armistice of any kind was a considerable diplomatic feat, given the animosity of North Vietnam to the United States, and South Vietnam's nervousness at the prospect of American withdrawal. Its achievement was partly an index of the changing interests of the Soviet Union and China who, though they both continued to support Hanoi materially throughout 1972, made clear, each in its own way, that a prolongation of the conflict did not suit their interests, and therefore left North Vietnam hanging in something of a diplomatic void. It

was also an index of the changing nature of great-power relationships that President Nixon could exert cruder and cruder forms
of pressure upon a nominal ally of the Soviet Union, mining
Haiphong Harbour, for instance, in May just before his visit to
Moscow, or bombing the Hanoi area in late December, without
creating a crisis in Washington's relations with either Moscow or
Peking. But the actual attainment of a ceasefire was a considerable
tribute to the political skill and diplomatic tenacity of Henry
Kissinger, who commuted almost weekly to Paris throughout the
summer and autumn of 1972 until he had created a relationship
of confidence with his North Vietnamese opposite number, Le
Duc Tho.

In the course of these negotiations each party made one central
concession from its earlier position in the Paris Peace talks; North
Vietnam agreed to accept a cease-fire before a political settlement
of the future of the country had been decided, and the United
States agreed to withdraw all its forces without insisting on the
withdrawal of North Vietnamese forces from the South. But the
cease-fire agreement could by no means be regarded as the basis
of an enduring peace. For one thing it did not cover the whole of
Indochina and left the future of Laos and Cambodia, to be settled
by internal conflict. For another it left unclear whether the signatory powers, the United States, North Vietnam, and the Provi-
sional Revolutionary Government of South Vietnam (the NLF)
had in mind a unified or a divided Vietnam, in either the short or
the long term. Thirdly, it created machinery for enforcement and
inspection which presupposed not only an identity of interest on
the part of the signatory powers but of a number of other countries,
the four powers of the Independent Control Commission (Canada,*
Indonesia, Hungary and Poland), and the states which the United
States sought to associate with the settlement, the Soviet Union,
China, Britain and France, whose views on its implementation
were by no means identical. The rights of Washington to continue
to replace the existing armaments of South Vietnam, and of
Moscow or Peking to replace those of North Vietnam (though in
neither case to increase or reinforce them) are, moreover, specifically safeguarded in the agreement. Though the conflict in Vietnam
may no longer have the aspect of formal war, one must, therefore,
assume that there will be an indefinite period of political confusion,

* Canada withdrew from the Commission in the summer of 1973 and was
replaced by Iran.

including fighting, and of oscillating tension between the parties to the cease-fire, before anything that can properly be called peace in Vietnam can be achieved. Nothing in the negotiations or subsequent developments suggests that North Vietnam has abandoned its objective of taking over the South or exercising a dominant influence in Laos and Cambodia. In that sense she has won the war and the United States has lost it.

By the beginning of 1973 the mould that had been constructed by Acheson at the beginning of 1950, of a 'free Asia' stretching from Hokkaido to the Himalayas supported by the United States and the European powers around the perimeter of a communist Eurasia, had been entirely broken, only partly as a consequence of victory and defeat, and more by a change in the domestic perspectives of every country concerned, local and external.

The adversary partnership

If the President's visit to Peking was primarily a diplomatic *beau geste*, there was, by the time he reached Moscow in May 1972, a long agenda of substantive Soviet-American business to be concluded. It may have been made more urgent but was not occasioned by the opening of Sino-American relations; SALT had been under way for two and a half years, and two minor bilateral arms-control measures – to diminish the risks of war as a consequence of the accidental or unauthorized use of a nuclear weapon, and to improve the 'Hot Line', which had first been established in 1963 – had been concluded in September 1971. In addition the Soviet Union was running into endemic problems of food production, for the rise in the yield of her cereal production was less than half that of the rise in demand caused by population growth: this was accentuated by a severe winter in 1971–2 which led in fact to the purchase of 32 million tons of American and Canadian grain. At the same time the United States was becoming increasingly interested in the potential export surplus of the Soviet Union in oil and natural gas, while on the Soviet side the American trade deficit with her western partners offered the prospect of tempting the United States into liberalizing the definition of 'strategic' goods, acting as a market for medium and high technology products, and thus expanding the relatively narrow base of her own high technology industries. Despite denials it was also clear that the United States saw trade and technology as a certain form of leverage.

What eventuated was a statement of twelve Basic Principles which appeared to be largely of Soviet drafting and which emphasized the importance of the responsibilities of the superpowers towards each other and to the international community without making any ideological concessions to each other; an agreement on environmental protection through the establishment of a joint committee; one on public health of no particular significance; and an accord on space which envisaged cooperation in manned space flight including experiments in docking each other's space craft in 1975, and which is important in signifying the end of space exploration as the form of deutero-war, the rival search for prestige, that it had been in the 1960s. Next came an agreement on scientific and technological cooperation whose significance really depends on what the United States chooses to make of it: this was followed by an accord on the control of 'incidents at sea' which really represented instructions to the Soviet Navy to lay off the dangerous tactics of buzzing and jostling NATO ships. In the field of trade the two governments could do no more than create a US–USSR commercial Commission, because the United States Congress was unwilling to extend most-favoured-nation treatment to the Soviet Union until the Soviet Union made some gesture on the repayment of lend-lease funds which it had received nearly thirty years earlier. These negotiations were completed in October; a new three-year trade agreement was signed which envisaged a level of about $500 million a year in trade, a target which was doubled in 1973. The Senate, however, remains hostile to the grant of most-favoured-nation treatment, partly because of the Soviet government's treatment of its Jewish minority, partly from a feeling that commercial concessions simply help finance the Soviet defence budget.

Finally, two agreements emerged out of SALT. One was a treaty of unlimited duration restricting each power to two complexes of 100 ABMs and associated radars, one covering the national capital, one covering a complex of ICBM launch silos: a restriction of ABMs had been a prime Soviet demand almost from the beginning of the negotiations, as American ABM technology was more advanced than Soviet. An important feature of the agreement was that it forbade the transfer of ABM technology to other powers or the undertaking of international obligations inconsistent with the agreement, which put an end to any talk of, say, an ABM system for NATO Europe, or Japan. The United

States had made it equally clear by 1971 that she would not sign an ABM limitation agreement unless it was linked with an agreement on the limitation of offensive systems; the Soviet Union was extremely reluctant to see this applied to submarine-launched missiles. What emerged was an interim agreement to last for five years to halt construction of land-based ICBMs after 1 July 1972, and – by a compromise reached only at the last moment – to place ceilings on both ICBMs and submarine-launched missiles (SLBMs). The latter made provision for the fact that both powers were modernizing their submarine fleet and might wish to shift part of their deterrent forces from land to submarine bases as particular categories of ICBM (those deployed before 1964) become obsolete.

The two agreements are different in character. The ABM agreement 'implies a permanent situation of quantitative and functional symmetry between the two sides'.[1] It involved the cancellation of the American *Safeguard* programme designed to protect *Minuteman* silos, and it is not clear that either super-power will now necessarily feel disposed to deploy ABMs up to the ceilings prescribed in the Treaty. The agreement on offensive weapons is much more complex and is less clear-cut. Essentially it is designed to prevent the Soviet Union acquiring such a commanding lead in numbers of deployed missiles as to force the United States to abandon the doctrine of 'sufficiency'. But it embodies a numerical superiority in Soviet missiles which, if she retains her diesel-powered as well as nuclear missile firing submarines in service, could produce a total of 2,424 Soviet launchers of which 950 would be SLBMs, contrasted with an American total of 1760 including a ceiling of 710 SLBMs. The reasons that President Nixon could put his signature to an agreement embodying a disparity of this magnitude were, first, that it was cast in terms of launchers only and made no reference to MIRVs, in which the United States had a clear lead over the Soviet Union; second, that at current Soviet rates of construction of both submarine and land-based missiles the disparity would have been even greater if it had not been signed; and third, that the United States possesses a considerable superiority in long-range and medium bombers which are not covered by the agreement.

The negotiation of these agreements was a considerable achievement, since it involved a process of mutual comprehension not only of each other's broad fears and problems but of the particular technologies which each had developed in an attempt to offset them.[6] But they were in no sense a measure of disarmament as there were a number of gaps in the agreements, regarded even as a measure of stabilization. Though the interim agreement did impose a standstill on the construction of 'heavy' missiles – notably the Soviet SS9 with its very large warhead which the United States has seen as a disarming weapon which could destroy her 1,000 land-based ICBMs in a first strike, it did not cover either strategic bombers or what are called FBS (Forward Based Systems), that is medium bombers or missiles based within striking distance of the Soviet Union on the territory of allies of the United States, nor the number of warheads per missile, nor missiles on aircraft, nor the relative size of missiles, let alone the question of continuing research and development by the super-powers in this field.

The partial nature of the agreements of May 1972 was evidenced by the fact that both powers agreed that the second round of negotiations must get under way again as soon as possible, and the first meeting of the negotiations on SALT Two began in Geneva less than six months later. In an earlier period of Soviet-American relations, a President might well have hesitated to put his signature, in an election year, to a treaty which institutionalized an American numerical inferiority in missiles. There was domestic opposition to it, and when the interim Agreement came up for ratification in the Senate in September an amendment, moved by Senator Henry Jackson, calling on the President to secure quantitative levels in American strategic forces 'not inferior' to those set for the Soviet Union, was passed by fifty-six votes to thirty-five. But the President's triumph over Senator McGovern in November was, in part, a popular ratification of his own belief that he had set world politics upon a new course.

The undermining of Western unity

If a certain degree of symmetry in the political interests of the United States and China and in the security interests of the United States and the Soviet Union has become both evident and accepted, this was not true of the parties to the two multilateral European negotiations that got under way in the winter of 1972–3, except in the most basic sense of a common interest in peace and prosperity.

The Soviet Union in the previous three years had pursued an ambitious foreign policy – with the Indian and Egyptian treaties and yet another treaty with Iraq in 1972, Brezhnev's state visit to France in October 1971 and the extension of her naval power. But in 1972 she suffered various reverses: the ejection of 17,000 Soviet military advisers from Egypt, China's diplomatic successes and growing influence, minority unrest in the Ukraine, the Baltic states and elsewhere and the emergence of what could be a permanent deficit in food grains. Though Soviet foreign policy is permanently that of a universal power, her immediate objectives appear to be concentrated on three fields in particular, those of strengthening her bilateral relationship with the United States, of entrenching her position in Eastern Europe, and of extending it in Western Europe. The second of these was helped by the legitimation of East Germany, and toward the end of the year Mr Brezhnev, who has in recent years accepted the reality of the EEC (as an economic, not as a defence or political association) suggested that it should negotiate bilaterally with the Council for Mutual Economic Assistance (COMECON); this would have the effect of strengthening Soviet control over the economics of the Eastern European countries. This is the last thing that Poland (where industrial unrest forced a change of regime at the end of 1970), Hungary (which is an industrial economy to a certain extent in competition with the Soviet Union) or Rumania (which has successfully asserted its economic and political autonomy over the past decade) now desire. Consequently, the appearance of détente in Europe may conceal a growing cleavage of interest between the East European states and the Soviet Union which is focussed primarily on their economic, and secondarily on their political, autonomy, although since 1968 they have had only modest hopes of asserting the latter. In so far as it is possible to generalize about a diverse group of states whose similarity lies only in their political and ideological structure, their ambition is to use the concern of the West with readjustments in the security relationship between the two halves of Europe to create a more plural or diverse network of interstate relationships in Europe as a whole, which will give them greater protection from intervention by the nominal guardian of their security, namely the Soviet Union.

The debate within Western Europe and between Europe and the United States is more complex and has been more articulate than its Eastern counterpart. Two of its mainsprings are, first, the fact that the United States, while continuing to be the custodian of the strategic security of the Western alliance, has become only *primus inter pares* at the level of trade and monetary relationships; second, that the growing dependence of all the Western industrial powers on imported raw materials, most particularly oil, implies either a major work of political construction in order to coordinate and reconcile their requirements or a competitive struggle between the United States, Japan and Europe for supplies, which would weaken the solidarity of their alliance at other levels, as well as creating new lines of stress in the developing world itself.

By 1972 it was impossible to ignore the re-emergence of strong protectionist sentiments in the United States, most notably in the attitude of the major trade unions. But this was not simply the result of an increasingly adverse trade balance of $2 billion in 1971 and $6·4 billion in 1972 (primarily with Japan). It was partly a consequence of the extensive operations of American multi-national corporations, whose overseas investments – nearly a third of which are now in Europe – are now conservatively estimated at $80 billion (nearly triple the figure for 1960).[3] Quite apart from the effect in diminishing the economic autonomy of other countries, these operations have created triple political problems in the United States itself: labour's charge that American job opportunities are being transferred abroad; the fears of both labour and management, which find their reflection in Congress, that the overseas products of the multinational company – for instance, cars made by General Motors in Germany or Japan – are undercutting their domestic equivalents in the American market; and the fear of labour, management, and government that they are undercutting domestic American products in third markets. The fact that investment returns from such overseas operations are large and increasing, and help to redress the adverse balance of trade, tend to be overlooked by those who are hurt directly by them.

If one adds to this relatively new problem the exclusion of some American agricultural products from Europe as a consequence of the Community's Common Agricultural Policy (though the United States has never seriously lowered its own barriers to agricultural imports) – a long-standing problem which is accentuated by the addition of Europe's largest food importer, Britain, to the EEC – and the fact that the Community has preferential arrangements with some forty other countries in Europe itself, the Mediterranean, and Africa, the basis of a sour European–American divergence on trade matters has become only too evident. This also helps foster a belief, both in Europe and the United States, that increased trade with the Soviet Union or Eastern Europe may alleviate the transatlantic stresses in trade and this could lead to a process of competitive European and American investment east of the Elbe which could in turn have political implications. By 1972 it was clear that, to put it at its lowest, there was an urgent need for a new round of trade negotiations if the overall framework of the post-war General Agreement on Trade and Tariffs (GATT) was to be preserved, but with the additional complication that, unlike the Kennedy Round, it would also have to tackle many problems of non-tariff barriers to trade such as price supports and import quotas which have a direct impact on domestic politics, if it was to be successful. By the spring of 1973 President Nixon had also made it clear, by submitting a bill to Congress which would give the Administration negotiating power of a kind that would permit increases as well as decreases in the level of American tariffs, that, in response to domestic pressure, he intended this to be a round of tough bargaining.

Inevitably these stresses in transatlantic and transpacific trade relations have had their reflection upon the Western monetary system. The difference is that on this plane the United States is not one actor among several but still the central one: the Bretton Woods agreement of 1944 was, by American choice, based on a dollar-gold standard which gradually became a pure dollar standard as the supply of gold proved inadequate to the enormous expansion of world trade, and the position of sterling as an alternative reserve currency largely disappeared throughout the 1960s. Western Europe would never have recovered from the Second World War without a massive injection of American dollars, partly under the Marshall Plan, partly in the form of long-term loans and military aid which involved a total transfer of \$33·5 billions to Western Europe in the ten years after the war. But in the 1960s, the outflow continued as a consequence of increasing overseas investment and governmental expenditure abroad so that the United States had an endemic balance of payments deficit, both on current accounts and in terms of long-term capital flows.

This was not one of the crucial problems of the Eisenhower–Kennedy years: it was accepted as being the function of the largest power to stimulate international liquidity and trade, as Britain had done in her half-century of economic hegemony. But after 1964 the outflow of dollars began to accelerate, partly as a consequence of direct expenditure on Vietnam; partly because President Johnson's unwillingness to finance the cost of the Vietnam war by increased taxation created domestic inflation which put American prices out of line with that of her major trading partners: partly by reason of the investment opportunities the great American corporations found outside the United States. Throughout the 1960s American reserves, the famous gold in Fort Knox, dropped dramatically; they stood at $26 billion in 1949, $14·9 billion in 1966 and $12·1 billion at the end of 1971. By the end of the decade not only was the American balance of payments in fundamental imbalance but there were now very large dollar balances in the hands of other countries. Various expedients were attempted; in 1967 the pound, whose support had been one major source of strain on the United States, was devalued; increasing fluctuation in the gold market was temporarily subdued by a gold pool among central banks, though this fell apart when in 1968 the United States had to separate the market price of gold from its official selling price; in 1969 the Deutschmark was revalued. Yet because the world was on a dollar standard it was thought impossible to devalue the dollar. But as the external American position continued to be weak in 1970 and 1971, more drastic measures were thought necessary,* so that in August 1971 the convertibility of dollars into gold was stopped, and by the Smithsonian Agreement of December 1971 the dollar was in effect devalued by 10 per cent through an agreed revaluation of the other major currencies.

It seemed that this might be all that was required to adjust the Bretton Woods system to a changed balance of economic power, but in fact throughout 1972 it became clear that, despite the fact that European rates of inflation were now higher again than American, the United States was running a heavier trade deficit than in 1971. In February 1973 the desire of the multinational companies, the Arab oil states, and other large holders of dollars outside the United States to maximize their interest rates, led to vast quantities of dollars moving into the mark and the yen and to a second American devaluation in March. It was now a more open question whether a universal dollar standard could be maintained

* It is an index of the scale of monetary movements to recall that in the sterling crisis of 1947 which led to the devaluation of the pound, $100 million was withdrawn from Britain on its worst day, whereas in the crisis of 1971 $2,500 million entered Germany in twenty-four hours.

without leading to such uncertainties as to arrest the growth of world trade, or to resurrect the spectre of the 1930s, competitive devaluations of major national currencies, based upon short term mercantilist calculations of protecting reserves, employment, or trading positions in individual countries.

The politics of economics

It was in this atmosphere that the Heads of Government of the enlarged Community, a group of states that in combination deploy two-thirds the economic strength of the US, met in October 1972 to consider the immediate priorities of the enlarged EEC. In other circumstances, say of sharp political tension in central Europe or the Mediterranean or of unmistakable and irreversible sign of American withdrawal from all its security commitments, they would probably have set as their prime objective the creation of some form of political and defence union (though the latter would have involved extending the Treaty of Rome). If the problems of energy and raw materials had seemed as serious then as they may only a year later, they might well have made their first objective the evolution of new relationships with the developing countries. But it was presumably because monetary relations was the aspect of international politics in the greatest disarray that they chose as their prime objective the creation of a European Monetary Union by the end of 1980, beginning with a European Monetary Cooperative Fund under the control of the nine central banks in 1973.

European monetary union is a very ambitious objective for it assumes a commitment within seven years to an irreversible stability of par values among the currencies of the Nine, which means that the constituent countries would by then have relinquished their principal form of leverage vis-à-vis each other, and would have successfully created not only the central institutions to govern the internal and external monetary relations of the Community but the democratic institutions, an effective European parliament, for instance, to monitor their actions. But 1973, the first year of the enlarged Community's existence, had, as I write, witnessed not only the Community's failure successfully to take the first step towards monetary union, but also no significant progress on subsidiary but still politically important issues such as regional or industrial policy, let alone any serious prospect of reforming its agricultural policy. Thus whatever its long-term promise, the Community at this stage offers no great inspiration to its new members; at the same time, its decisions and policies have brought to the surface a new American ambivalence about the Community. If on the one hand, the Community achieves political and monetary coherence only very gradually, it will be regarded in Washington through much of the 1970s as a flabby organization which can either be ignored or whose individual governments can be handled bilaterally. If, on the other, it finds its coherence and evolves its own collective policies, not only on trade questions but on monetary and other issues in reaction to American pressures, then it enters into what is partially an adversary relationship with the United States. Thus the events of the early 1970s have raised the spectre of a shifting balance between the United States, the European Community and Japan, each with its own sphere of political and economic interest in a developing world whose interests also are increasingly fragmented. This could be a break with the past almost as significant as the Sino-Soviet rift. In such circumstances the continuation of the security alliances that have hitherto been accorded a higher priority than economic relationships, NATO and the American-Japanese alliance, would be open to question.

Such thoughts would be mere speculation at this time, had not the impending problems of energy resources impressed themselves by 1973 so forcibly upon governments. I will deal with this problem in greater detail in the next chapter. But the fact is that the United States is now joining Europe and Japan in being a major importer of petroleum products. She consumes today nearly one third of the world's energy. By 1980 at least one-third and by 1985 two-thirds of her requirements may have to be imported. Moreover to achieve the level of production that is envisaged in 1985 will require enormous capital investment. This means that unless ways can be found of restricting demand, or increasing domestic production, the United States will have to find very large additional resources – a figure of $30 billion a year by 1980 has been suggested, though it is impossible to make an exact calculation at this stage – of foreign exchange to meet her energy requirements, unless she can either make some special arrangement with key producer countries or unless some wholly new arrangement both among the major states and between them and the producer states can be negotiated. The complexities of the latter open the temptation to consider the former.

New balance or new anarchy?

I have deliberately cast most of the last three chapters in the form of historical narrative, for I think it is a useful basis for an analysis of the structural, quantitative and qualitative changes that are occurring in world politics. It saves one from the mistake of becoming preoccupied with what is novel and forgetful of what Marxists call 'the permanently operating factors'.

The era of high bipolarity, the period when world politics was not only dominated by the confrontation of two ideologically hostile coalitions which embraced both hemispheres and stretched the whole way round the northern half of the world, but when few governments felt disposed to make major policy decisions without reference to Washington or to Moscow, began to dissolve a decade ago. But power has become diffused by a different route from that which then seemed the most probable to many people including myself, namely the acquisition of nuclear weapons by a growing number of states, so that alliances would tend to break down and be replaced by a strategic balance of power that had a number of independent partners or participants.[4]

True, Britain and France are still nuclear powers and China, having first detonated a nuclear device in 1964, was reported in the autumn of 1973 to have tested its first batch of 3,500-mile missiles. But Britain is now more wedded to the Atlantic Alliance than ever. France has doubts about the future of her own nuclear force, while the emergence of China as an important independent actor on the world stage is only partly related to her nuclear capability. True, the Non-Proliferation Treaty is only a normative instrument which provides no formal sanctions against its infringement – and two significant potential nuclear powers, India and Israel, have not signed it. But nuclear proliferation is no longer perceived as the principle threat to world order or the principle agent of change.

Change has come by different routes, on the one hand through the apparent decline of ideology as a principle motive force of political decisions, on the other by the fragmentation of state power into different objectives in different fields, so that the bipolarity or multipolarity of the international system is different on the strategic, the political and the economic planes of interaction.

Nothing is more rash than to make categorical assertions about the role of ideology in world politics. The heralds of its demise in the late 1950s and early 1960s, largely Western, largely basing their judgements on the progress of de-Stalinization in the Soviet Union and moves towards détente and arms control, were proved wrong by the entrenchment of the American commitment in Vietnam which was largely ideological in motivation, by the Cultural Revolution, by the rise of the New Left in Western politics, and by a Soviet intervention in Czechoslovakia that was partly ideological in its motivation. There is still an ideological gulf that separates the industrial democracies from the Communist powers and that, to an extent, divides them both from many countries of the developing world. The theory of a convergence, which held that ideological differences between the major powers would gradually disappear as their material interests and their internal problems were seen to converge, has not proved true so far;[5] and just as there are serious ideological differences between Yugoslavia and the Soviet Union, or the Soviet Union and China, so there are between France and the United States and the Soviet Union, or between Britain and South Africa. These could re-surface rapidly, as a consequence of personalities, of domestic conflicts or as a rationale of the need to foster allied or domestic unity by creating an external adversary. It is true that a world in which China proclaims the virtues of peaceful coexistence which she vehemently denounced when the Soviet Union first proclaimed them under Khrushchev, has a different language of intercourse from that of a decade ago. But it is also true that even in the days when national objectives were cast in their most idealistic form in the most ideologically motivated of the powers, the United States, China, and the Soviet Union in particular, their actions continued to be largely governed by more earthy considerations of the national interest. All that has happened is that these mundane calculations are for the time being more influential in the counsels of the major governments.

It is important to make this reservation, lest in the discussion that has been going on, ever since the first sign of Sino-American rapprochement, about the return to a pentagonal balance of power similar to that which kept the peace in Europe for long periods of the eighteenth and nineteenth centuries, an analogy be mistaken for reality.[6] For one thing ideological contention and other forms of suspicion still rule out one form of the balance of power, namely a concert of the great powers, the system of Metternich. It is true that the political influence of the Soviet Union and the United States has contracted markedly, while that of China has grown. There are now five nuclear powers, and economic strength has tended to aggregate unevenly around the United States, the Soviet Union, Japan and the countries of the enlarged Community. But to assume that there is any fundamental similarity between this situation and that in which the classical European balance of power operated successfully overlooks at least three factors. The first is that the five power centres exercise quite different forms of power in quite different proportions. Only the Soviet Union and the United States are both great military and great industrial powers; China can exert influence on both of them and in certain other areas as well, but in economic terms is still a developing country; Japan is the world's third most powerful economic state but has only the military capacity to defend her home islands from conventional attack; Europe, though both economically powerful and heavily armed, has yet to acquire the institutions to take political, strategic or even major economic decisions centrally.

Moreover, any talk of a return to a traditional balance-of-power system not only overlooks factors of geography and wide differences of interest, but also the fact that war is no longer acceptable to any of the five, except as a desperate last resort, in order to adjust imbalances between the major power centres or to settle conflicting interests in third areas. Finally, the fact that ideological differences are not dead means that another characteristic and normal mechanism of adjustment in a historical multiple balance – changes in alliances and alignments – is difficult, if not absolutely impossible, to conceive.*

It is only by examining the different planes of power that one achieves any comprehension of the different kinds of balances that are emerging. In the first place, on the strategic plane, there are only two fully competent powers, the two super-powers, and their relationship is still a bilateral one as it has been through most of the post-war era. Some simple orders of magnitude illustrate this fact: the Soviet Union and the United States possess over 90 per cent of strategic delivery vehicles, missiles and aircraft: despite the recent growth of military expenditure in parts of the developing world, notably the Middle East and Asia, the two super-powers still account for nearly two-thirds of global military

---

* I have attempted a somewhat more extended examination of the difference between classical balances of power and the contemporary situation in *Power and Equilibrium in the '70s* (New York: Praeger. London: Chatto & Windus, 1973).

expenditure; most significant of all, they account for 85 per cent of the world's expenditure on military research and development (about $15 billion a year as contrasted with $4 billion spent annually on medical research) while between them Britain, France, Germany and China account for only 10 per cent, and all the rest of the world for the other 5 per cent. And unless there is a serious débacle in political relationships, especially within the American alliance system, these relative orders of magnitude are unlikely to change markedly in the foreseeable future, even though China's share in the total of strategic weapons will gradually increase, and the strategic relationship may eventually become tripolar.

So for the time being there can be no argument that if a situation were to arise that implied, however obliquely, the use of strategic power or the threat of deployment of it to deter action by either super-power or some third country, it would again be Washington and Moscow that would be the decisive centres of decision in operating what Professor T.C. Schelling called 'a balance of prudence'. And because there is a qualitative difference between, on the one hand, riches and poverty and, on the other, life and death, the strategic plane inevitably has a certain primacy and governs the judgements of the other powers about their relationships to the super-powers at other levels.

But there is a second plane of relationships in between the strategic and the economic which can loosely be called the political, though it embraces not only diplomatic activity and influence but also the potential use of non-strategic military force as well as economic and military aid. Here there has been a considerable change. In the first place, the United States no longer has the self-image as the central pillar of world order, which, to be fair, was only a temporary abberation of the 1960s in a longer tradition of encouraging and supporting a plural international system. With this change in its perception of its function has come a diminished readiness to contemplate such things as military intervention of the kind that occurred in the Lebanon in 1958 and in the Dominican Republic in 1965, or over a much longer period in South East Asia. We must examine later whether the pursuit of strictly national interests may not make the United States again an interventionist power, but for the time being she is not. At the same time, the Nixon Administration has been tolerant, if not exactly encouraging, of policies of greater independence on the part of her major allies, the German *Ostpolitik* or Japanese relations with

China and the Soviet Union, for instance, in considerable contrast to the impatience of the Johnson and Kennedy administrations with President de Gaulle's attempt to assert the political independence of France within the framework of the Atlantic Alliance (though it was as much de Gaulle's style as the substance of his policies which accounted for the difference).

No such tolerance of the independence of her allies in Eastern Europe has been observable on the part of the Soviet Union, but the reverse in her relations with Egypt and her failure, despite a prolonged programme of massive military aid, to help North Vietnam to achieve a clear-cut victory in Indochina, have illustrated the limits of her ability to pursue interventionist policies. More important, she has had to accept the emergence of China as a fully independent actor on the international scene, even though China's most active diplomacy is for the time being primarily concentrated on the maintenance of some political influence in Southern and Eastern Europe (encouragement of Rumania's autonomy within the Warsaw Pact, continuing support for Albania, a £17 million loan to Malta in 1972) and also in East Africa and parts of the Middle East. The Soviet Union has to a certain extent become reactive to Chinese policies. The principal effect has been a determined attempt to forestall the new Sino-American relationship from disrupting her own special relationship with the United States. She also attempted in a rather half-hearted fashion to pre-empt Sino-Japanese rapprochement in 1972. It is generally accepted, though the evidence is obscure, that her willingness to normalize her relationship with the West European countries, by signing a new Berlin agreement and accepting the other measures of normalization of relations between West Germany and herself, Poland and the DDR, was related to her increasing preoccupation with her confrontation of China.

There has emerged, then, a trilateral relationship between the Soviet Union, China, and the United States. It can hardly be called a balance of power since China possesses so little strategic or economic power by comparison with the other two. It is probably better described as a balance of influence. There are only three partners to it, since neither Western Europe nor Japan nor other large powers in Asia such as India or Indonesia can effectively alter the policies of the three towards each other. It does have an effect on the policies of all three powers outside Asia even though its focus may be there.

Many students of international politics have pointed out the ambiguity of a triangular relationship of this kind, especially if more than one of the partners in the triangle think they are the apex of it. *'Nous tenons la balance de l'Europe'*, wrote Napoleon to the Directory in 1797. *'Nous ferons pencher comme nous voudrons.'* Thus at the moment China appears to believe that she can advance her interests, particularly in her adversary relationship with the Soviet Union, by manipulating her relations with the United States and its allies. Similarly it can be argued that the United States, while correctly disclaiming any responsibility for the Sino-Soviet conflict or any desire to exacerbate it, clearly feels that she is *tertius gaudens* to it and that she advances her interests both with China and the Soviet Union by manipulating her relationship with both of them. The only partner that can be under no illusion that she is the apex is the Soviet Union, and this itself creates its own instability for it must seem in her interest to destroy the Sino-American side of the triangle. There is also a danger that a relationship of three power centres will either become two against one, the great contemporary Soviet fear, or if it remains a relationship of mutual distrust will lead to a ruthless attitude towards third areas. The disposition of Taiwan with no reference to the wishes of its inhabitants, or the rivalry of the three powers in the Indian subcontinent could be the contemporary equivalent of the partition of Poland in the 1790s to maintain the peace between Russia, Prussia and Austria. A triangular balance of power or influence has in the past often become a balance of compensation in other areas.

Japan has so far exerted little influence on the plane of political relationships, partly because she is acutely conscious of her strategic vulnerability, largely because she is unsure of her objectives. The countries of the European Community have for the present neither the ambition to make it a major force in world politics nor the internal cohesion and the central institutions to achieve such an ambition. But on the plane of economic relationships a different triangular constellation has emerged between the Community, the United States and Japan. On the one hand stand the current orders of magnitude of contemporary economic power: the fact that the gross national products of the countries of the enlarged Community totalled about $700 billion in 1972, nearly two-thirds that of the United States, while that of Japan stood at nearly $255 billion (nearly five times greater than that of ten years earlier).

The nine Community countries accounted for nearly 37 per cent of world exports in 1970 and Japan for 6·2 per cent, while the American share had dropped in over a decade from 16 per cent to 13·7 per cent, a reduction especially in primary products and consumer goods: the productivity of Japanese labour has nearly doubled in the previous five years while that of the United States had gone up by only 13 per cent. On the other hand, it is clear that the Western monetary system cannot be reorganized simply by the return to the dollar standard which has prevailed through much of the past quarter century. Though the American economy is still the world's largest, the dollar can no longer be regarded as the immutable basis for the calculation of the value of other currencies. Its devaluation twice in fifteen months, with further adjustments probably still to come, has demonstrated that the United States, in order to protect its own interests, can no more behave as the universal or core power in the monetary than it can in the political arena. And the fact that the weakening of the dollar has been the result of a massive and rapid outflow of American investment funds to Europe and elsewhere, does not smother domestic resentment at what are regarded as discriminatory practices in trade on the part of Europe, Canada and Japan.

I once shocked a university audience at the beginning of the 1960s by suggesting that by now we might look back with nostalgia to the simple character of international politics in the years of the Cold War, despite its dangers; but possibly I was right. For despite the current absence of serious armed conflict, despite the high level of prosperity in the developed world and its heightening in the semi-developed countries, despite the diminution of ideological pressures, and the disappearance of such dangerous fictions of the post-war era as the non-existence of mainland China, we have entered a period of such complexity that it makes the clear distinctions of the previous quarter century – distortions and myths though they may often have been – seem like the boyhood world of Rousseau's noble savage.

For what eludes us is a clear understanding of the link between these different planes and kinds of interaction. Clearly the two strategic super-powers, though they remain differentiated from all others in their possession of this form of power, no longer exert the broad authority of a decade ago: yet the cost of maintaining strategic power is rising while its political influence may be diminishing. Faced with considerable and costly domestic problems as well, will they decide to control and reduce their strategic force levels by an interlocking series of agreements, especially if they see other states making greater economic and social progress than they? If so, do they run the risk of losing what control they still possess over the incidence of conflict between lesser states? Do they run the risk that China, far weaker strategically and economically but also less muscle-bound than they, may be able to gain influence at their expense?

If the climate of American opinion becomes increasingly hostile to the continued assumption of military burdens which she feels her Japanese and European partners are unwilling to shoulder to the same degree, will the United States withdraw a strategic umbrella that covers a wide group of powers around the world to the confines of her own continent? Yet can she shed her strategic and political obligations without risk to her own safety? Conversely, if Western Europe and Japan begin to see an irreconcilable conflict of economic interest with the United States, if the coherent trade and monetary system of the post-war era seems to be but a bright interlude of interdependence in a long history of mercantilism and national autarchy, will they feel constrained either to acquire an effective autonomy on the strategic plane or else make political accommodations with their ideological adversaries? But could European–American relations degenerate without endangering the cohesion of the Community itself? If access to raw materials becomes an overriding preoccupation of the industrial powers, may we see in a different form a late twentieth-century equivalent of the late nineteenth-century scramble for colonies and concessions?

Henry Kissinger wrote before entering office in 1969, 'In the years ahead, the most profound challenge to American policy will be philosophical: to develop some concept of order in a world which is bipolar militarily but multipolar politically.'[7] How much headway have he and his President made in the confrontation of this challenge? Can the task of construction, of aligning perspectives, negotiating the agreements, and devising the institutions to avert these dangers be accomplished in an era when states are for the most part led by men of very ordinary substance?

These are some of the questions which the developments of recent years have raised in the minds of both optimists and pessimists. In what follows I have attempted to gather the raw material on which intelligent hypotheses about their answers might be founded.

PART TWO

5
The Context of Continuing Change

We turn now from an examination of the immediate past, of a consideration of the alterations that have occurred in the nature of the international system, to the present and to the foreseeable future. It is a system which is still primarily upheld or changed by the policies and activities of governments, despite the significance of various forms of transnational activity and the importance of many forms of international institutions. But although the extent to which the foreign policies of governments are simply a reflection of domestic interests and pressures varies widely, there has never been any argument that all conceptions of the national interest are significantly influenced by them. Governments may feel a broader duty than simply to advance the interests, political or economic, of the influential pressure groups within the borders of their state, and that their task is to make the best resolution that is possible at any particular time of the particular national interest with those of the international community as a whole; yet the way in which they attempt this resolution is intimately affected by the play of domestic forces and debate.

But what distinguishes the period of international politics through which we have been passing from earlier historical periods, a distinction that is likely to become even more obvious in the later twentieth century, is that the growth of communications, on the one hand, and, on the other, the similarity of domestic concerns in the industrialized countries, have tended to create an increasing uniformity in the preoccupations of the major states, even though they may not be identical. It is thus both possible and necessary to attempt some general examinations of the climate of domestic debate and attitudes to the external world in which governments, especially those of the major states, will make their choices and take their decisions in the years immediately ahead.

To do this in a really scholarly or comprehensive fashion would involve a study in its own right in which many disciplines or forms of expertise would have to be enlisted. All I have attempted in this chapter is to point to certain disparate subjects where attitudes and preoccupations are clearly changing and are likely to continue to change still further: social and political expectations; the dichotomy between growing economic interdependence and the survival of political nationalism; attitudes towards the use or maintenance of military power; the new problem created by the increasing dependence of the industrial powers on imported oil and raw materials; and the parameters within which a new system of trade and payments will have to be negotiated. All these subjects now form part of the context of international politics. I have not attempted to deal with the much broader question of whether the demands of an increasing world population may necessitate a fundamental revision of attitudes to economic growth and distribution of wealth.

Society versus the state

It is extremely difficult to make generalizations about the nature of social change, even if one were possessed of the insight of a de Tocqueville, Marx or Weber, still more to base firm assumptions upon them. Many phenomena that strike the public imagination – the student unrest of the later 1960s for instance – may not necessarily be constants. Profound alterations in personal or national values and priorities may occur so gradually that their incidence is hard to measure or detect. Nevertheless, if one looks back over the past two decades one can observe a number of significant changes in the values of at least European and American society, using the word 'value' to imply more than just norms or patterns of expectation, to mean objectives for which individuals or more likely groups are prepared to make sacrifices and incur costs (not necessarily economic costs).

A group that discussed this question at one of the Ditchley conferences concluded that it was possible to identify four such areas of change: diminishing readiness to accept the judgement or leadership of established authority in the conduct of both internal and external policy simply because it is established authority; a

declining belief in the intrinsic value of work, and a more questioning attitude towards science and technology; increasing tolerance
of deviation in personal conduct parallel with a decline in the
coherence of the family or a shift in loyalties from the family to
the group; rising expectations, in some instances still primarily in
economic terms, in many others in social terms as well. Many
other European and American sociologists have reached substantially the same conclusions and all these changes affect, some
more directly than others, the climate of international politics,
even though their onset can be traced to the interwar years or even
earlier.

All of them are probably linked in one way or another to the
rising level of education and to the development of mass media of
communications, notably the emergence of television in the past
fifteen or twenty years as the primary source of public information;
to the more powerful hold over the attention which audio-visual has
than purely audio or written communication; and the inevitable
tendency of broadcasting to simplify what are for the decision-
makers complex issues, while at the same time immensely diversi-
fying the recipient's sources of information, about his political
leaders, about other countries or other cultural groups within his
own country. But there has been at least one other powerful factor
at work, namely that as countries become more extensively
governed, as the power and size of companies, corporations, or
urban administrations have grown so there has been a measurable
growth in unionization, in such things as tenants' associations, consumer associations, or associations to protect the rights (or a
particular right) of the citizen, minority groups especially. And
with the increasing self-consciousness of the citizen there has
diminished the traditional deference to authority (perhaps more
associated with European or Latin countries than with countries
like the United States or Australia) which has made democracies
easier to govern in the past than in the present.

The implications of these various forms of changes, whose force
is far from spent, for the domestic structure of societies is so
considerable that there is a natural tendency to introversion in all
major states. If there could be any choice I am sure that both
governments and the publics whom they serve would wish to take
a holiday from all forms of international relationships for the next
generation – while, for instance, the constitutional processes of
the United States were radically overhauled, while the environ-

mental problems and the implications of the decline of the nuclear family in Japan are sorted out, or while the countries of the European Community decided which subjects should be elevated to the control of Brussels to ensure coordination, which diffused to the control of Yorkshire, Brittany or Schleswig-Holstein to promote participation and which left with existing national governments. But no such holiday is possible for the reason that the very forces that are creating rapid domestic change are among those that are also creating an increasingly interdependent international system.

Consequently, one must consider the implications of these kinds of change for the continuing conduct of external policy, particularly as this process of interdependence continuously blurs the never clear dividing line between domestic and foreign policy. This is a phenomenon especially noticeable in the countries of the Community where agricultural, industrial and social ministers now have to engage in the kind of bargaining with each other before arriving at common positions in relation to the United States or the Soviet Union which Europeans had hitherto tended to associate contemptuously with the 'wheeling and dealing' of the US Senate. But it is also noticeable in broader international negotiations as well, such as the preparatory discussion on the trade talks or on the conference on the Law of the Sea.

One fact is clear: the bitter controversies of the past twenty years, over Suez in Britain, over Algeria in France, over Vietnam in the United States, the fact that major governments have also made major errors of judgement, has, when combined with the rise of the media, stripped the making of foreign policy of the remnants of its arcane quality, of any popular sense of its greater propinquity than domestic policy to the sacred core of royal or presidential prerogative. It is true that more of the conduct of foreign and defence policy is conducted behind closed doors in Britain, France or Japan than is the case in the United States or in Germany, but this is no longer necessarily an advantage. The sluggishness of British public opinion about participation in the Community, the mindless Gallocentrism of many Frenchmen, appears to be related to the candour with which they insist on being treated by governments. The greater openness of the German debate on the various phases of the *Ostpolitik*, though it produced great controversy, ended also by producing a broad consensus of support for it. Since public opinion in Western countries is not prepared any longer to be governed by a mandarin class, is less ready to accept the social concept of a foreign policy establishment, governments are faced with the alternatives of either letting the news media set the agenda of debate on foreign as well as domestic issues, as has happened in the United States over much of the past decade, or themselves taking more initiative to explain the complex decisions with which they are faced. That greater public participation in the foreign policy debate complicates diplomacy no one would deny, but equally a government that is unsure of the support of its own opinion negotiates from weakness.

The other changes in social values may have a somewhat less direct impact upon foreign policy than does the decline of confidence in government, but they all contribute to the presumption of more restless and possibly more aggressive societies. The diminishing belief in the ethic of work induces frustration, anger replaces the older fatalism, the satisfaction of material wants coupled with an observable decline in 'the quality of life' creates increasing tensions even in the most prosperous societies (though it may not diminish their prosperity). This means that violence is unlikely to be the province only of those societies that feel themselves materially deprived, and 'post-industrial' societies may well become chauvinistic and adventurist, even though this may not be the case at present.

At the same time the decline in respect for science and technology, and the growing contempt, at any rate among the educated younger generation, for economic growth as a major social objective of states, changes the arena of international competition and removes a traditional yardstick for measuring power and prestige. Much of Soviet-American conflict, the competition for influence and prestige, was conducted harmlessly if expensively in outer space in the decade or so after *Sputnik*. Will the next arena be as harmless? If economic growth is really no longer an agreed objective in the advanced countries on what basis are such things as trade negotiations to be conducted, or policies of development aid to be based and supported? If, as seems more probable, concern with the implications of technology rather than its achievements, with the safeguarding of the environment rather than the expansion of the economy, is symptomatic only of the more prosperous areas of developed countries, then it still has the effect of creating tensions between them and the poorer regions in the same countries, as well as between the developed and the developing world.

At the same time the increasing acceptance of social deviation, while usefully undermining many of the stuffy class shibboleths of post-Victorian society, appears to have three significant implications. First, it also undermines the old foundations of social discipline without laying the basis for new ones, at a time when increasing population pressures and the increasing scarcity of resources such as land and raw materials make it likely that both non-industrial and industrial societies will have to achieve a high measure of such internal discipline and restraint if the very improvement in their environment which they desire is not to be frustrated. Second, it diminishes the appeal of those disciplined callings and professions, most notably military service, on which the security of states still to a significant extent depends. Third, by increasing the self-consciousness of minority or ethnic groups, even in old states, it calls in question, especially when coupled with rising social expectations in the sense of desire to participate in decisions affecting their own governance, the continuing viability of existing constitutional and political structures. It is not merely Nagas, Kurds or Ibos who have challenged the validity of the present state systems but also Ulster Catholics, Flemings, Basques, Catalans, and Quebecois, to say nothing of American blacks. The processes by which the forces of internal integration have tended to slacken while those of differentiation have accelerated does not yet seem exhausted, so that one must assume that states will be much more preoccupied with the processes of domestic adjustment and will also present less of a united or 'national' appearance to the world in the coming years.

Before examining other aspects of change anyone concerned with their impact on international politics must ask whether these changing social values may not be creating a disparity in the strength and influence of the industrial democracies and the Communist powers. Superficially the difference is striking. In the Soviet Union, in China, in Eastern Europe it is the government and the party, not the media, that fully control the agenda of public debate and a very simple picture of the external world is presented to the citizen. The Russians who have always been deferential towards authority appear still to be so, while the Chinese who have a long tradition of incompetent central government seem to have acquired in the past generation not only the political but the industrial and social discipline necessary to pull their country up by its boot straps. The angry and the dissident are harried and repressed in the Soviet Union and in most of the Eastern European countries. In all the Communist countries science and technology remain enthroned and economic growth as a social objective far overrides any concern with the quality of life. With draconian systems of conscription military manpower remains no serious problem.

But before accepting any simple contrast between a still disciplined group of powers and a series of 'soft' and divided Western states, there are other considerations to be put into the balance. For one thing, some of the social phenomena that are observable in the West – the alienation of intellectuals from the objectives of government, the frustration of workers with the discipline of the assembly line – can also be detected in the East, as evidenced by the Polish strikes of 1970, even though the speed with which they mature may be slower. More important, the self-consciousness of minority groups appears to be increasing as fast in the Slavonic states as in Western ones, with the difference that there are many more of them. Both China and the Soviet Union, being states that developed out of empires, are in fact honeycombs of different ethnic groups, though in China they are kept under firm control at present. (The problem of the Soviet minorities will be examined more closely in the next chapter.)

Consequently, although the *dirigiste* states of the developing world may appear to be more stable than their democratic counterparts, many of the same forces of social change are at work within them. The difference, apart from the slower tempo of change there, is that when it occurs it is likely to take a more violent form and to create greater external repercussions than the domestic explosions within Western societies. For resistance will be motivated by greater idealism, by greater readiness to die upon the barricades, as the youth of Prague would have done in 1968 if Dubcek had been Wenceslaus, by a more romantic conception of progress, than in the more confused debates of Western post-industrial societies.

Nationalism versus transnationalism

What we have been principally discussing so far is what Isaiah Berlin has recently described as 'a world reaction against the central doctrine of nineteenth-century liberal rationalism itself, a confused effort to return to an older morality. It is the revolt against the planner in all his expert roles and it springs', he adds,

'from the feeling that human rights, rooted in the sense of human beings as specifically human, that is, as individuated, as possessing wills, sentiments, beliefs, ideals, ways of living of their own, have been lost sight of in the "global" calculations and vast extrapolations which guide the plans of policy planners and executives in the gigantic operations in which governments, corporations and interlocking elites of various kinds are engaged. Quantitative computation cannot but ignore the specific wishes and hopes and fears and goals of individual human beings. This must always be so, whenever policies for large numbers must be devised, but it has today gone very far indeed.'[1]

And one focus for those 'individuals or groups whose members do not wish to be dragged along by the chariot wheels of scientific progress' is identification if possible with some ethnic minority, Red Indians, Aborigines, Welshmen, Herzogovinians, Bohemians, the list is indefinite; this is one form of national assertion. But contemporary nationalism also assumes a more conventional form, the assertion of the authority and individuality of the nation state against the apparently increasing forces of transnationalism, the multinational corporation, the overseas military base on one's soil, the Catholic Church, guerrilla movements, the Ford and Rockefeller Foundations, the Pugwash movement, the World Bank, all those organizations, governmental, intergovernmental or non-governmental which, for whatever purpose, operate across national frontiers.[2]

The phenomenon of transnationalism, of the movement of ideas, materials, services, people, power across state frontiers without the necessary cognizance of governments is as old as the nation state itself, and nineteenth-century writers as different as Comte and Marx assumed that the common interests of men of business or of the industrial working class in different countries would eventually override the political relationships of governments. Men, money and ideas moved freely across borders until 1914, but the First World War and the autarchic political and economic policies of governments during the inter-war years appeared to reassert the predominance of interstate relations over transnational movements. The major fount of transnational activity appeared then to be the Comintern with its objective not just of by-passing governments but of eventually destroying them.

But the greater contemporary impetus towards transnationa-lism has been only partly ideological in character, and has been accelerated by technological developments and needs, by com-munications, by the need for raw materials, by the necessity to organize the sale of many products over a much wider market than that provided by any nation state, by the control of aid pro-grammes, the need for overseas military bases (now diminishing), by new types of international organization, by the growth of inter-national fraternities of scientists and other experts, which is much more of American inspiration than that of any other country. The significance of this form of change is that it has coincided histori-cally with a near tripling of the numbers of nation states, most of which have a natural anxiety to assert the comprehensive authority of their government, a concern which, particularly as regards economic transnationalism, they share with much older states such as those of Latin America, and indeed many in Europe as well.

Writers like George Ball may assert that the transnational corporation 'is a modern concept evolved to meet the requirements of the modern age' while the nation state 'is still rooted in archaic concepts unsympathetic to the needs of our complex world'.[3] But nationalism remains a potent factor, especially in poorer countries, and it is very easy for politicians, particularly those with a weak domestic base, to assert that they have exchanged one form of colonialism for another, that the European empires are being suc-ceeded by the American or Japanese empires. As issues like over-seas air and naval bases diminish in importance (at any rate for the time being), so the activities of the multinational corporation, which it is calculated now account for some fifteen per cent of world production, have become an increasing source of friction. Moreover, when one looks at figures on the size of General Motors, Ford, IBM, Unilever or the great oil companies, most of them with revenues greater than the national income of Belgium, and ten times that of most of the African countries, employing nationals of many countries but still taking their essential decisions in their original country of registration, one can see why the multi-national company has become such an easy target of attack. And this quite independent of the revelations of foolishly run multi-nationals such as IT&T or memories of such high-handed operators as the United Fruit Company.

One can argue that the multinational corporation is only one aspect of the growing transnationalism of society (the growing mobility of capital being another) that it is more vulnerable to local political decisions than is commonly supposed, and that it has had the effect of accelerating the spread of techniques, products and training more rapidly than older patterns of international trade. One can suggest that the multinational company plays, in the words of the Rey Report of OECD, 'an important positive role in the transfer of financial resources, technology and even general skills between developed countries and from these to developing countries. In the host countries they create new jobs, increase the occupational skills of the labour force, improve industrial structures, often contribute to regional development and generally stimulate economic growth.'[4] One can point to the fact that they have played a major role in trebling the direct investment flows of the OECD countries during the past decade. One can emphasize the vulnerability of the multinational corporation to the laws and the political climate both of its country of origin and of the host countries in which its subsidiaries operate, as exemplified by the positions in which the oil companies now find themselves.

One can also contend that the dynamism of the multinational company even when combined with the dominance that some have acquired in certain countries or in certain sectors of the economies of others and the centralization of their decision-making processes, is only one form of transnationalism. It coincides with a steady increase in radio propaganda on the part of the major states towards each other and third countries.* The increasing speed with which ideas now travel is generally identified with the spread of bad ideas such as techniques of terrorism, or the actual operations of terrorists groups, rather than of good ideas or men. International fraternities of experts may produce conclusions hostile to the views of governments whose citizens participate in them. Even large flows of tourists may undermine traditional or local cultural patterns. Lumped together in this fashion as they tend to be, the increasing facets and degree of

* In 1950 the Soviet Union was broadcasting in other languages programmes totalling 553 hours per week, China 66 hours, and Egypt not at all. In 1972 the Soviet Union was broadcasting 1,900 hours a week, China about 1,300 and Egypt 600. Between them these three countries now broadcast in 44 languages, affecting 500 million people which the Voice of America, whose overseas programmes have gone up from 500 to 929 hours a week and the BBC, which has registered a much smaller increase, do not attempt to reach.

transnationalism accentuate a sense of powerlessness over their environment which affects not only governments in new, poor or vulnerable states, but also interest groups in the richer ones who think, for instance, that American jobs are being transferred to other countries with lower wage levels, or that the core of French culture is being deliberately undermined by a host of transatlantic influences. At this moment, perhaps the institution with the greatest sense of powerlessness is the British Treasury.

Transnationalism in its economic aspect is primarily a source of tension between the industrial democracies or between them and the countries of the developing world. It is not a problem that the Communist powers are desirous to exploit because most of them are anxious to enter into partnership arrangements with many of the major Western multinational companies. (The extent to which they are prepared to accept the logic of their position by permitting greater freedom of personal movement and information across frontiers will be partly tested in the forthcoming Conference on European Security and Cooperation.)

The less developed countries have in certain instances, notably as far as the oil and mining companies are concerned, the alternative of nationalizing the foreign installation, as the Chilean government has recently done with Kennecott Copper and as a number of countries have done with oil. If they do, experience suggests that the Marxixt analysis is false in asserting that the government of the country where the offending company originates will take political action against them. All that may happen is that the country pays a certain price in terms of technological and economic benefits (notably investment capital) for the assertion of its political persona. It may also be the case that, as problems of the supply of oil and other raw materials become increasingly crucial for the security and economic prosperity of industrial countries, their governments will become increasingly involved in negotiations that hitherto have been conducted between governments of developing countries and Western companies, converting a transnational relationship into an international one. Equally, Samuel Huntington may be right in suggesting that there will be an important distinction between different kinds of government:

'Weak governments resort to nationalization as a way of mobilizing popular nationalist sentiment behind the government. Strong governments, on the other hand, even though they may be committed to a radical nationalist ideology, do not need to appeal to popular chauvinism and are able to deal as equals with foreign business. Post-revolutionary governments in Mexico, Algeria, Yugoslavia, as well as in the countries of the Soviet bloc in Eastern Europe, have made mutually beneficial arrangements with private corporations that would be beyond the capacity of less stable Third-World polities. In a broader sense, also, the more stable and highly developed political systems in Western Europe and Canada have been able to tolerate levels of transnational activity far beyond those which would be possible in countries with more fragile regimes.'[5]

If a conflict between nationalism and transnationalism is inherent, or is thought to be, one of the challenges of the coming decade is to discover the extent to which internationalism – cooperation between governments – can be revived as a mediating force between the two poles. For the alternative to it may be an attempt to put greater emphasis on the aspiration of national autarchy, to try and build artificial barriers against the revolutions in communications, demands and expectations.

The particular problems which the activities of the multinational corporation present in political relationships within the West or in North–South relations appear to be amenable to control. An international convention to monitor multinational business enterprises seems politically both essential and attainable. To avoid the danger that this would be simply an agreement among the rich countries which would leave the poor embittered, it has been suggested that the UN, in which the developing countries predominate, should take the lead in this process of monitoring, mediating and establishing norms for transnational economic activity.[6]

Moreover, the past decade has witnessed three international conventions designed to control a particularly odious transnational activity, namely aerial piracy, even though the loopholes in them still illustrate the difficulty of controlling activities that do not occur under the jurisdiction of one particular state. Nations are beginning to cooperate more effectively in the control of another, namely the drug trade. And as I will mention shortly the future exploitation of the oceans for minerals or fishing, and the future control over narrow waters, occurs in a situation where the power of the nation state has been more intensively and successfully asserted than ever before; only an agreement between governments can avert the virtual demise of the historic notion of the open sea.

Energy, raw materials and interdependence

New patterns of dependence are emerging between the industrial and the developing countries in the supply of raw materials. But, in view of the amount of professional Cassandras in this field of activity, it needs emphasis at the beginning that there is no crisis. Most of the resources of the world are finite: man's ingenuity is infinite – even though the supply of certain raw materials will have to be carefully guarded, by price or other mechanisms, if they are not to be wasted or exhausted before it is necessary.

Since energy fuels are the basis of so much human, industrial and political activity, it is on their supply that attention has become primarily focussed. But again the point needs reiterating that there need be no energy crisis. Even assuming the world's consumption of energy in the year 2000 to be five times what it is today, there will remain available 200 years' worth of fossil fuels which can be exploited, at a price, by new technologies, 600 years' worth of nuclear energy with the use of breeder reactors, 5,000 years' worth of exploitable solar energy, and, when the deuterium in the ocean can be converted into energy by nuclear fusion, enough to satisfy demand from the beginning of the third millennium after Christ for another million and a half years, in addition to local sources of energy, geothermal, tidal or hydro power.[7]

What is developing is a short-term crisis in the supply of the most convenient and cheapest forms of energy, namely oil and natural gas, which will be at its most acute throughout the next ten to twenty years, and in the solution of which the price of energy in whatever form, petrol, natural gas, electricity, coal, will rise markedly with significant social and economic, strategic and political consequences. In fact, it is already clear that the half-century from 1920 to 1970 has been a quite aberrant period of human history in which cheap energy has been more abundant throughout the world then it has ever been before or will, in all probability, ever be again.

Since this is not a work of distant futurology but rather an attempt to grapple with contemporary circumstances and the immediate problems they throw up, I propose to concentrate primarily on the basis for the present sense of anxiety about oil, on how much foundation it has, and on the different ways open to governments for its alleviation. This means concentrating principally on four topics: the likely increase in demand up to 1985; the availability of oil and its distribution; changes in its price; and the political and economic implications of these three changes.

But first of all, why has the situation caught us, as it were, unawares, especially as energy is a quantifiable product, the industries that supply it are studded with research organizations, and governments are continuously interested in the subject? First, projections made in the 1950s of the point at which nuclear energy would become competitive with fossil fuels proved quite wrong. Second, and partly as a consequence, the demand in the coming decade for oil was being underestimated as late as 1970, and the potential of oil and natural gas supplies under the domestic control of the industrial powers (in the United States, Canada, Alaska and the North Sea) was overestimated by industry. The demand for oil doubled between 1962 and 1970 and is now expected to double again by 1985. Contributory factors in this have been the growing concern with environmental considerations which have forced governments to be careful about the siting of such nuclear power stations as will come into operation in the ensuing decade, about the use of oil or coal with a high sulphur content plus the increasing unpopularity of coalmining as a vocation. Third, it was not until 1970 that OPEC (Organization of Petroleum Exporting Countries)*

TABLE I. World Oil Consumption†

(Thousands of barrels per day)

	1971	1980
North America	13,180	23,750
Western Europe	16,390	24,300
Japan	4,440	9,180
Others	7,350	17,200
Non-Communist Powers	41,360	74,430
Communist Powers	7,350	15,300
Total World	48,770	89,730

† The 1971 figure is from the BP *Statistical Review*. The 1980 figure is an EEC projection; some experts put the figure of world oil consumption in 1980 at 90–100 billion barrels per day. But it should be emphasized that these projections antedate the events of late 1973, with the economies or substitutions to which dramatic price increases may give rise.

* This includes four non-Arab states, Iran, Indonesia, Nigeria, Venezuela; the five oil states of the Persian Gulf, Kuwait, Saudi Arabia, Iraq, Abu Dhabi and Qatar plus Libya and Algeria.

which had been founded in the later 1950s became an effective cartel for the control of prices and levels of supply. The balance of strength then swung sharply from the consuming states with whom it had long rested to the producing ones.

Consequently in the past three years several things have happened. First, estimates of oil consumption have been slightly revised upwards giving the projection shown in Table I:

These are in strong contrast with projections of production and potential production.

TABLE II. Estimates of Liquid Hydrocarbon Capacity*

(Thousands of barrels per day)

	1975	1980	Potential Deficit 1980
North America	12,100	15,400	8,350+
Western Europe	1,500	3,000	21,300
Japan	—	—	9,180
South East Asia	3,000	4,000	
Africa	9,000	11,000	
Latin America	5,800	7,000	
Middle East	30,000+	40,500	

* Source: US National Petroleum Council. Liquid hydrocarbons would include oil from coal, shale and the beginnings of oil from the Canadian tar sands, so the North American figure may, therefore be rather optimistic. Many experts put the figure of US imports at 11 billion barrels a day in 1980, assuming the OPEC production restrictions are lifted.

What this suggests is that the dependence on imported oil will by 1980 be of the order of 50–60 per cent for the United States and Canada, 85 per cent for Western Europe and, as it has been in the past, 100 per cent for Japan. As most people in the Atlantic world will by now be aware, half and probably more of the industrial world's oil supply must come from the Persian Gulf, while developments like the Alaskan North Slope or the North Sea can only modify this dependence, not reverse it (even though the latter may fortify some Scots in advocating secession and making Scotland a member of OPEC).

This raises a number of questions. The first concerns the future of oil itself as a source of energy. Between the beginning of 1972 and 1980 the non-Communist world will have consumed about 200 billion barrels of oil, out of total present and proved reserves of 550 billion barrels of which over 60 per cent or more is in the Middle East, only 9 per cent in North America and 12 per cent in Rumania and the Soviet Union. Suppose no more oil were found, which is virtually impossible, there would at 1980 consumption rates be only a few years' supply of oil left in the world. May most readers of this page see the end of such amenities as oil-fired central heating, let alone air conditioning, and a marked drop in industrial production before they are very much older? Briefly, it is most improbable, even though the rising cost of oil may make them more careful with its use. Though intensive exploration by the great oil companies outside the Middle East, wherever there are sedimentary basins, has so far not produced dramatic results, there are a great many ways of increasing proved reserves. For one thing probably one half of Middle Eastern oil has not yet been found. For another, at present only thirty per cent of a normal oil field can be exploited economically and 'an improvement of only one per cent from all known commercial fields would add to proven reserves something like one and a half year's production at current rates';[9] already the productivity of the heavy oils in old fields in Venezuela and the United States has been improved by the injection of steam to make them more viscous. Leaving aside natural gas, there are large deposits of oil in shale (200 billion barrels worth, though very costly to extract), and in the Canadian and Latin American tar sands (1,350 billion barrels or more than double existing proven oil reserves, for which the techniques of extraction have now been mastered). Moreover, there is the equivalent in the world of almost 25,000 billion barrels of oil in coal, over half of it in the United States, and some countries are working on processes of liquefaction underground rather than mining; the cost both of conventional mining and other methods is, however, likely to keep it uncompetitive with oil over the next decade, so it is regarded at present more in the nature of a last ditch reserve should strategic factors make oil imports impossible or prohibitively expensive. But oil in the Northern hemisphere, indigenous or imported, will be costing between $8 and $12 per barrel, and liquefied coal as well as nuclear energy is likely to be competitive with such a price

It is time, therefore, to turn to the strategic aspects. (I will deal with natural gas a little later.) Although Japan and Western Europe have got used to living with a high level of imported oil, the United States has not; and with a global conception of her responsibilities she had fought shy of dependence on Middle Eastern oil where her support of Israel has complicated her diplomatic position, to put it mildly, and which in any case has a long transit journey to the United States. Moreover, the Arab states have imposed oil boycotts four times in the past twenty-five years, in 1948, against Britain and France in 1956, and against the United States and others in 1967 and 1973. Earlier there was an oil surplus in the world, but today the withholding of oil production by any one of the seven larger OPEC producers, Saudi Arabia, Iran, Iraq, the Arab Emirates, Kuwait, Libya or Venezuela produces a significant, and of any two a critical, shortage in the consuming countries.[10] American dependence on Middle East oil is now of the order of 10 per cent of consumption and will grow, some say, to a fifth, some to a third of total consumption. Consequently, the OPEC countries stand in a quite new relationship to the Western industrialized countries, which will continue until other sources of energy production begin to make a more significant contribution to demand some time in the 1980s. The industrial countries of the western alliance system cannot for the next fifteen years or so pursue a policy in a crisis of more than a few weeks' duration which would involve the active hostility of the OPEC states without a drastic reduction in domestic consumption. This has been proved by the events of October–November 1973. This among other things must force a modification of American official support for Israel in the protracted political crisis that has ensued since 1967. Before 1973 it had already had the effect of altering American policy on arms supplies to the extent of encouraging Israel to be a manufacturer rather than a purchaser of all but major weapons systems, and of permitting the sale of American arms to Saudi Arabia as well as Jordan. In addition, the lack of oil reserves in Western Europe should give impetus to a reconsideration of the feasibility of fighting a protracted nonnuclear war in Europe as an aspect of a NATO strategy of 'flexible response' (a problem to which I will return in chapter eight).

The second and natural consequence of the solidarity of OPEC has been a rise in the cost of oil which is by no means ended. The interesting process whereby OPEC gradually acquired coherence during the 1960s – the first producer organization in the developing world to do so – has been described elsewhere.* It was a mixture of political solidarity plus a skilful capitalization of Europe's lack of reserves by President Ghadafi of Libya plus the desire of the big oil companies to remain in a contractual relationship with the Gulf States in the face of competition from the national companies of both the producing and consuming states. The upshot was the Teheran agreement of 1971, which added 45 cents a barrel to the price of Gulf oil and 80 cents a barrel to Libyan oil, with a schedule for further increases over the years to 1975. In consequence an OPEC government was getting exactly twice as much revenue per barrel as in 1960 ($1·66 as against $0·83) before the vast increases of late 1973 which sent the selling price of Gulf oil up to over $10 a barrel.

The third consequence, of which the end is not yet in sight, is a change in the whole structure of relationship between the consumer and producer states. There have been emerging an increasing number of national oil companies both in the producer countries and in countries such as France and Italy which have been jealous of the Anglo-American multinationals and readier to enter into partnership agreements than the seven great international companies; and in consequence 'participation' has come to be as important an objective for the producer states as a rise in the price paid for their oil. A year after the Teheran agreement, some OPEC countries under the leadership of Saudi Arabia reached the Riyadh agreement of 1972 whereby the host countries would acquire a 25 per cent share of operations on their territory and by 1982, 51 per cent, that is to say, control.† This represents an aspiration on the part of the Middle Eastern countries to become more than mere reservoirs, to use their oil and financial reserves to turn themselves into industrial states, or important international actors, and the master in general in their own house. If participation is steadily increased, as the agreement envisages, the international companies will gradually slip downstream, that is, become primarily concerned with processing, distribution and

* See especially 'The Oil Crisis' by James E. Akins: *Foreign Affairs*, April 1973. For a challenge to the orthodox view, which suggests that the bargaining power and solidarity of OPEC and its success was largely a product of the alarmism of the State Department and the desire of the multinational companies for a quiet life, see 'Is the Oil Shortage Real?' by Professor M. A. Adelman, *Foreign Policy*, Winter 1972–3.

† Iran and Libya have already moved faster than this, and so most probably will the others.

exploration, purchasing their oil at the tap rather than being con-cessionaries.[11]

But the new situation is also revealing different priorities and policies among consumers and producers. Saudi Arabia, far the largest producer, whose reserves constitute probably a third, per-haps half, of all those in the Middle East, appeared before October 1973 to be primarily concerned with assured markets and may well become so again, despite taking the lead in production cut-backs during the crisis of November 1973. Kuwait, all of whose proven reserves are already explored, is anxious to conserve its oil and turn it into assured income. Iran, the only country with a big population, also wishes assured markets and has sought to make special arrangements with Germany and Japan. Iraq, a radical state, which nationalized the British IPC in 1972, has had an immediate task of finding outlets for its crude and has been making arrangements with a variety of countries, particularly France. Libya, which has demanded immediate 50 per cent parti-cipation in the operation of foreign companies, and which has nationalized parts of British and American companies operating on its territory, has been making arrangements with European national companies, notably Italy (which must if possible obtain its oil from within the Mediterranean).

The new situation raises a number of questions of political significance for the future. The first is whether what has been primarily a commercial arrangement between the producer states and the international oil companies will now inevitably become a government-to-government one with the risk of further politicizing the confrontation of interests that this may create. There is no doubt that the pre-1972 situation, in which the oil companies acted as a buffer or intermediary between the two kinds of government, did forestall a good deal of diplomatic stress. But, equally, there seems little doubt that the situation has fundamentally altered, for two reasons in particular. The first is that the governments of the consumer states are becoming increasingly concerned with the future of their energy supplies in all its aspects, and therefore concerned to make the relationship with the producer states the stuff of diplomacy rather than pure commerce. The second is that the maintenance of the production increases that will be necessary to satisfy consumer demand over the next decade or so will require such high capital investment, not so much in the Middle East as elsewhere, as to be beyond the scope of normal private finance; it has been estimated, for instance, that it will require capital investment over the ensuing decade of the order of $400–$500 billion or more, particularly to bring high-cost fields such as Alaska or the North Sea into full production, whereas the seven major international companies spent only about $8 billion in 1971, and this only by considerably increasing their debt commitments. Moreover, if the oil producing states are going to become as rich as the figures in Table III suggest, is there not a case for shifting part of the capital burden on to them?

But if the oil nexus is to become largely a government-to-government one, what form should it assume? At the moment a network of different consumer–producer relationships is developing which is likely to bid up the price of crude oil beyond the levels negotiated between OPEC and the companies, and also to force the more moderate producer states to emulate the lead of the more radical ones in forcing the pace of 'participation', i.e. nationalization. It also undermines confidence between the consumer states, particularly as the Japanese, who feel themselves in the most desperate position of all, seek to make bilateral bargains throughout the Middle East, and as the national oil companies of the European countries that are not the home of the traditional multinational oil companies, notably Germany and Italy, seek to do the same. (The French national oil company CFP is in process of making a bilateral deal with Iraq.) Behind this stands the threat, sometimes advocated quite openly, that the United States might make a bilateral deal with the largest single exporter, Saudi Arabia, although the balance of official opinion seems at present against it.[12] Alternatively, there have been fears in Europe that because so much European oil is shipped under the auspices of American companies, a worsening of American political relations with the Arab states, over Israel or some other cause, could affect Europe's supplies of Middle Eastern oil as happened in 1973.

It was this which led to discussion and advocacy of a co-ordinated Japanese–Atlantic energy policy, before the American suggestion of an Energy Action Group.[13] Britain, who as a consequence of North Sea oil and the fact that it is the headquarters of two of the seven multinational companies, has a brighter national future in this respect than other Community countries, nevertheless laid emphasis, with Dutch support, at the Paris Summit meeting of October 1972, on the development of a Community energy policy, and the Commission at the time of writing was labouring to produce one. President Nixon, in his message to Congress on Energy of 19 April 1973, suggested that the United States should work with the Community in this respect; the Administration in general has considered the problem in a wider context than Japan or the Six. But before deciding whether the oil nexus can, over the next decade, take the form of a straight-forward relationship between a consumer and a producer associa-tion, one must examine three other considerations.

One concerns the position of the Soviet Union. I have not hitherto discussed natural gas, which is particularly valuable to the industrial countries as it raises virtually no environmental problems. At the present it accounts for some 18 per cent of world energy consumption but in the United States for 32 per cent, and because the price has been set too low there, the consumption of American reserves has been unexpectedly rapid, and domestic production will probably decline after 1975. But the OPEC countries are not in the same dominant position in the possession of natural gas as in oil, and the largest single area of proven reserves is in the Soviet Union, which has 32 per cent of the world's known store of gas as compared with 12 per cent of its known oil reserves (though these are still considerable).[14] Though Europe has some indigenous supplies, its consumption of gas has gone up nearly six times in the last six years and will rise much further, while Japan is an eager customer, though having some close at hand in Sarawak. Consequently, if the international trade in energy is being considered in any comprehensive fashion, and if the objective of policy is to create stable world prices and depend-able agreements on supply over the foreseeable future, it is difficult to consider excluding the Soviet Union from such an arrangement, particularly as Japan is negotiating the extraction of oil from the Tyumen fields, and the American gas companies are now anxious to explore the possibilities of a natural gas pipeline from Siberia to Murmansk (despite the formidable cost of building such a pipeline over thousands of miles of permafrost and constructing a fleet of pressurized ships to take it in liquefied form to the east coast of the United States). The Nixon–Brezhnev communiqué of 25 June 1973 spoke of Presidential encouragement to 'American firms to work out concrete proposals on these projects'. The Soviet Union, moreover, though it is self-sufficient in oil at present may become a significant importer of Middle Eastern oil by the 1980s if it is to maintain oil and gas exports to Japan, Europe and the

United States as a means of acquiring hard currency. But if the Soviet Union is included in a producer–consumer agreement, does it not simply invite trouble, especially for Japan, to exclude China whose energy requirements are also increasing?

A second consideration that must make one hesitate about a simple OPEC-OECD arrangement is the implications of the vast wealth that will henceforth flow into the Middle East.

TABLE III. *Estimated Middle East Production and Revenue**

	Production: Thousand Barrels per Day		Revenue: Billion Dollars a Year	
	1975	1980	1975	1980
Iran	7,300	10,000	4·7	12·8
Saudi Arabia	8,500	20,000	5·4	25·6
Kuwait	3,500	4,000	2·2	5·0
Iraq	1,900	5,000	1·2	6·4
Abu Dhabi	2,300	4,000	1·5	5·0
Other Persian Gulf	1,800	2,000	1·0	3·2
Total Persian Gulf	25,300	45,000	16·0	58·0
Libya	2,200	2,000	2·0	3·1
Algeria	1,200	1,500	1·1	2·3
Total Mid-East	28,700	48,500	19·1	63·4

It is possible to make too much of these figures. It is true that between 1973 and 1980 the Arab oil producers will have a cumulative income of well over $200 billion; it is also true that none of them except Algeria are at present spending all their current income and that all the Gulf states, except Iran, have small populations on which to spend it. But it is also true that there are many poor parts of the Islamic world, Pakistan, Bangla Desh, Egypt, Indonesia, the Islamic countries of Africa, which could use much more by way of grant aid than they are likely to get from traditional

* These were the estimates of Mr James Akins, Director of the State Department's Office of Fuels and Energy. They assumed (1) that the price of oil remained during the 1970s at a figure which did not produce a significant switch from oil to other sources, (2) that the level of production conformed to demand, not to what the oil states say will be their production level. But these estimates were made before the large increase in the price of OPEC oil and the 25 per cent cutback in the production of Gulf oil in November 1973, and the working figure of Middle East oil revenues is now closer to $100,000 million a year, not in 1980 but in 1975.

sources. So that the case, that has been mooted, for an inter-Arab Development Bank is a strong one. The prospect of enormous unused reserves, of $100 billion or more, floating around the world's money markets and destabilizing them can be overdrawn.

But there will be a considerable surplus and, at the same time, it must remain an Arab interest to see that the reserves of the Gulf and North Africa are drawn down as slowly as possible and not, at it were, sucked out of the ground by consumer demand over the next twenty or thirty years. Even if they made very high profits in this period, these could be converted only into (a) domestic economic growth and military power for which there is a limited requirement, (b) Western securities and industries which puts their value at the mercy of the economic stability of the industrial world, and makes them fallible to a depression, or (c) into gold whose future is uncertain despite the current boom in its value. The use of oil in petro-chemicals is steadily increasing and oil will always be the preferred form of energy in industrial states, if it is available and its price is competitive, because it is easier to handle and raises fewer environmental problems than other sources, except gas. The Arab states have, therefore, a direct interest in financing both exploration, especially in the Middle East itself, and techniques for improving the amount of oil extracted, indeed; an argument can be made that they have a direct interest in the development of other sources of energy to conserve their reserves. There does seem, therefore, a reasonable case for suggesting that, if the right institutional framework can be constructed, they should bear a share of the capital costs of exploiting the world's energy resources while at the same time playing an influential role in the framing of international policy.

The third, and in many ways the most important, reason why a simple OPEC-OECD relationship may not meet the case is the problem which the increase in the price of oil poses for the rest of the developing world. OPEC refused in the early 1970s to consider the feasibility of a differential price for the developing countries, on the grounds that this would lead to circumvention and re-sale to the developed. But this has had the effect of forcing India to cut back on oil imports and has upset many calculations about growth in the poorer countries which had been counting on declining energy costs in real terms to sustain it. As the history of the industrial revolutions in Britain, Germany and the United States illustrates, the prospects of 'take off' crucially depend on this. Though some World Bank and other loan finance may be available, it will be difficult to persuade legislatures in the industrial states to provide the development finance to exploit indigenous sources of energy, such as hydro-electricity in parts of Africa and Latin America, or solar energy in India, which have a high initial cost, particularly when there are so many other demands on development resources. An embittered relationship between the OPEC countries and the non-OPEC developing countries, between, say, Venezuela and the rest of Latin America, between Algeria and Libya and their sub-Saharan neighbours, or between Iran and Turkey, can hardly be in their political interest. Consequently, there seems a strong case for reconsidering the need for a differential oil price for the other developing countries with adequate safeguards to ensure against its diversion to Japan or Europe – always provided that the rich countries bear part of the cost of financing such a differential.

These considerations make me believe that what confronts us is the need for a new international agency or standing conference or commission with membership open to all interested states and which is responsible for monitoring all forms of international negotiation in this field, for encouraging the exploration of the remaining reserves of oil, and for the research – which is already largely international – on alternative sources. Its central instrument would be a new kind of international commodity agreement similar to the wheat agreements of the post-war years of scarcity, in which producers and consumers periodically determine among themselves the volume of supply and prices. One must contemplate the creation of a new UN agency with some reservations, knowing the cumbrous bureaucracies of some of them; but it is difficult to see how the international community can intelligently tackle a problem that is truly universal in its proportions on any other basis. If the OPEC states choose to maintain their solidarity within such a framework, if the OECD countries succeed in speaking with the same voice in it, this does not invalidate the need for a wider framework of discussion, bargaining and research than is simply provided by a dialogue of two cartels.

I have attempted to deal later in this chapter with the implications for the international monetary system, and the American balance of payments in particular, of very large expenditures in imported oil. But one question must be raised at this stage: namely, are the calculations of the future demand for oil correct, and is there a possibility that the impending 'crisis' may be simply a nightmare of the planners, just as earlier assumptions about an oil surplus in the 1970s have been found quite wrong? The United States and Canada consumed in 1971 three times as much energy per head as Western Europe, seven times as much as the Communist states, nearly twelve times as much as the countries of the Middle East and Latin America, and forty times as much as the average for Africa. Might not quite modest economies in the use of oil and energy in the United States, an hour's less central heating a day, a month's less air conditioning a year, increases in gasoline taxes that persuade Detroit to build cars of European size rather than those that do only seven miles to the gallon, modify the demand curve that is now being projected, and hence change the politics of the situation?

So far there seems little will to contemplate any serious measure of energy conservation. President Nixon's Energy Message of April 1972, published before the Watergate scandal undermined his authority, issued no clarion call to his countrymen although he later recommended a massive programme of research on domestic American resources. Moreover, the high cost of labour in industrial countries, especially the United States, makes it essential to mechanize every possible industrial and commercial operation, and machines use energy. It is also true that increasing concern with environmental problems is leading to greater not less consumption of oil; the imposition of higher standards for automobile exhausts has led in some cases to a 30 per cent increase in the gasoline consumption of American cars. Concern with the disposal of radioactive waste, and the possibility of leakages in nuclear power plants, creates local opposition to the expansion of their numbers. The highest estimate of the contribution nuclear power will make to American energy consumption by 1985 is 17 per cent.

But the dilemma cannot now be obscured. Either the industrial powers, the United States in particular, take fiscal measures such as increasing taxation on gasoline and fuel oil to reduce the personal and commercial consumption of oil (which together with the production of electricity accounts for about 45 per cent of total American oil consumption)[15] or their relations with both the oil producing states and with each other may be in an endemic state of crisis and tension over the next twelve years or so until other energy sources can make a greater contribution, and probably far beyond that. Thus oil now presents both an international and a domestic political problem which is of a high priority.

Oil, moreover, is not the only raw material which will create a growing problem of reserves on the one hand and demand on the other. According to calculations made by the Meadows Report, *The Limits of Growth*,[16] we shall see the end of the existing supply of the following minerals within the next thirty-five years, assuming that consumption is allowed to grow at the rate that it has averaged in the recent past and that no more deposits are discovered: gold (9 years), mercury (13), silver (13), tin (15), zinc (18), copper (21), lead (21), tungsten (28), aluminium from bauxite (31), molybdenum (34). By these calculations only a decade beyond stands the threat of the extinction of supplies of platinum and manganese. These figures are open to criticism because they are based on known reserves and take insufficient account of the much wider resources of these metals that would be worth exploiting if their value rose. But it stands to reason that even if the consumption of oil cannot be much abated over the next decade or so, governments of all kinds will have to exercise much greater care over the use of many other raw materials than they have been inclined to do in the past. And as a recent report of the American Academy of Sciences has noted, such concern cannot fail to have political consequences:

'As industrial nations use up the cheap supplies in their own countries, they inevitably become more and more dependent on recycled or "scrap" metal and on foreign sources for raw materials. At present all industrial nations except possibly the Soviet Union are net importers of most of the minerals and ores used by them. The dependence of the United States on foreign sources will almost certainly increase greatly during the next generation. Increasing dependence on foreign sources brings increased vulnerability to military, political, or economic action. This is emphasized by the fact that some of the metals most vital to the economic well-being of free-enterprise industrial nations are in areas of political instability or in Communist countries. Most of the known reserves of tungsten and antimony lie in such areas, as well as a large part of the world's manganese, nickel, chromium, and platinum. The present and near-future sources of manganese for North America are mostly in South America, Australia, and Africa, the sources of tin in Southeast Asia, the sources of aluminium ore in various underdeveloped tropical countries.'[17]

Just as British industrial power and political influence in the nineteenth century was largely based on the exploitation of her own natural resources, coal, iron, lead and so on, so the rise of the United States to world power and her dominant position over the past quarter century has rested partly on occupying half a continent rich in the raw materials of industrial and strategic power. Though this may still be the case for the Soviet Union, one factor of change is that the end of American self-sufficiency is in sight and this must inevitably find its reflection in American diplomacy, for I can detect no signs that post-industrial, high-consumption economies will need fewer raw materials than those in the first flush of industrialization.

The politics of trade

Someone who is not an economist and who has not been continuously involved in discussions about the future of the international trade and payments system can make no independent contribution to the controversies which the subject now evokes. But equally no student of world politics can now ignore this aspect of the intercourse of nations, for partly by coincidence, partly because other considerations such as security relationships have lost some of their urgency, it has risen to the top of the agenda. In the mid-1960s the Kennedy Round of negotiations on the reduction of tariff and other barriers was a conference of experts in GATT which had little or no bearing on initiatives like the Multilateral Force, American decisions about Vietnam, or East–West relations. Today no statesman meets another, whether it be Brezhnev and Nixon, Heath and Brandt or Pompidou, Tanaka and Chou En-lai without questions of trade figuring high in the communiqué. And this enhanced concern about international economic relations is matched by increasing political and popular pre-occupation with the subject.

In many ways this is a healthy development. Material concerns about wealth and welfare, employment or innovation are the basic stuff of politics, whatever political philosophers may say, and the fact that they now have equal precedence in the minds of governments with more dire considerations of security or more meta-

physical calculations of ideology or prestige can be taken as a sign
that international society is returning to its more usual preoccupations, if not to anything as chimerical as 'normalcy'. But the
fact is that, in a situation when ideological conflict has only been
tamed and not abolished, and in which different societies possess
the means to inflict marked damage as well as to confer real
benefits upon each other, the connection between economic,
political and security relationships is necessarily a close one. If
Japan, the United States and the European Community retreat
into autarchic policies, or into a search for new economic partners,
their political relationship and the whole framework of world
politics cannot fail to be affected. 'Linkage' between the different
levels of power and activity is inherent.

This is nothing new; the attempt to confront the recession of
the 1930s largely by national economic policies was a major factor
in the steady decline in international confidence as the decade proceeded; the redefinition of Britain's security and political interests
in the early 1960s was largely a consequence of its weakened
position in the international system of trade and payments. What
is new, in this generation, is the manifestation of a similar kind of
economic weakness on the part of the core power of the western
political system. In part, the quiescence of economic issues in the
1950s and 1960s, the general acceptance of the view that trade
concessions should be negotiated for their own sake, was a tribute
to the post-war negotiations, notably the Bretton Woods Agreement on the outlines of an international monetary system based on
fixed parities in relation to the dollar, and the General Agreement
on Trade and Tariffs, which laid down specific rules about trade
relations, established a general commitment to the lowering of
trade barriers and provided an orderly procedure for the resolution
of tensions arising from economic relations. In part it was a consequence of a deliberate decision on the part of the United States
itself in the 1950s to bend the rules of these agreements, even to its
own economic detriment, in order to accelerate the economic
recovery of Japan and the economic cohesion of Europe. Recently
she has felt the material consequences of this political choice, in
the form of adverse balances of both trade and payments as well
as the dominance of certain of her consumer markets by imported
goods, without having any sure sense that she has reaped a political
advantage in terms of having acquired firm and lasting friends on
whom she can also devolve a measure of her political responsibilities.

And further to complicate the issue, this situation of American disillusionment has coincided with a period in which not only are new patterns of dependence on imported energy and other raw materials certain to raise the magnitude of international trade and diffuse its control still further, but in which changes in domestic social values have made the process of adjustment harder. As a distinguished, international group of economists, who attempted to survey the problem after the first American devaluation in 1971, pointed out,

'political and social trends within the industrial nations inevitably influence international economic relations. Increased stress on social equity leads to special economic policies for particular groups or regions; resistance to the disruptive consequences of economic change is growing; and the wholly desirable concern for protecting the environment has grown up. In pursuing these objectives, governments may choose to forfeit some of the gains from international specialization and thereby create problems for other countries and the international system.'[18]

To put it another way, in the industrial world, international issues have more important domestic overtones, and decisions on domestic issues larger international implications, than ever before.

Perhaps the greatest difficulty of all is one that has affected other processes of change in the international system, but is more apparent in economic relations than in others. The evident need to overhaul the structure of inter-government agreements on monetary and trade relations has not arisen as after a great war when there is a general consensus, as there was in 1815, 1919 and 1945, that international society must make a fresh start. It is the result of the accumulation of a large number of factors whose significance is seen in different perspectives in different countries; there are no victors and no vanquished; no towering figure like Keynes; and the men who must design and operate the successor systems to those which kept economic tensions out of high politics in the generation after 1945 are largely those who grew up in, and have operated, the existing ones.

It is easier, I think, to grasp the issues that are involved in monetary reform if one tackles first those involved in the trade negotiations which the members of GATT agreed should start in the autumn of 1973, and which it was hoped, rather optimistically perhaps, to conclude within two years. (The Kennedy Round which, it is true, was not animated by the same sense of urgency, took the better part of four years.)

Obviously one issue in a general negotiation of this kind is the level of tariffs, on which an initial assault was made by the Kennedy Round, resulting in a reduction of about one-third of customs duties on industrial products and affecting transactions valued at some $40 billion, leaving a general average across the whole spectrum of trade of 6 per cent for the EEC (Britain's entry into it involving a reduction in her own average level of tariffs), 7·1 per cent for the United States, 6·4 per cent for Canada and 9·7 per cent for Japan.* On this aspect of trade, the Community thus feels itself in a strong position, especially as the American average conceals some tariffs of 25 per cent. There appears to be a growing consensus that the time has now come for a commitment to the abolition in the foreseeable future of all industrial and raw material tariffs, no matter whether it is accomplished across the board or sector by sector; it is argued that tariffs are an obsolete technique of nation or community building which create fears of rival trading blocs without really protecting the security or promoting the welfare of states. Such an objective would have to be approached with care, for there are a number of industrializing states such as Iran, Mexico, Brazil, Singapore and others which are not yet in a position to withstand the full force of Japanese or European competition. But in general, industrial exports from the developing to the developed countries are increasing, and with the static level of development aid, there is every reason to encourage this by tariff reductions. Yet it is difficult to feel optimistic about the abolition of tariffs in the foreseeable future. President Nixon's Trade Bill, which will provide the legal basis for American authority to negotiate, contains provisions for the raising as well as for the lowering of tariffs, and Watergate cannot fail to augment the power of Congress, with its greater susceptibility to the pressure of interest groups, at the expense of the Executive.† It is still entrenched orthodoxy in Brussels that it is the combination of internal free trade with a common external tariff that provides the cement of the Community, and most industrial countries have

---

* Different methods of weighting lead to somewhat different allocation of percentages. These are the European Community's figures.

† By November 1973 it was no longer clear that the President would get a trade bill through Congress at all in the foreseeable future – in other words that the launching of the trade negotiations themselves might be in jeopardy.

backward regions whose interests are often cheaper to protect by external duties than to promote by internal pump priming.

But industrial tariffs may not be the main bone of contention in the Tokyo Round, especially as the American multinational company has largely succeeded in negating European and Canadian tariff barriers. A more difficult problem is that of agricultural protection, where the Americans and the Europeans argue both with acrimony and from a weak legal position. American agricultural exports to Europe have risen by over 40 per cent since the Community's Common Agricultural Policy was first instituted in 1965 but in American eyes the CAP with its system of variable levies on imports over a large sector of agricultural trade – cereals, sugar, livestock, tobacco, to name only the more important – is now seen as a violation of the whole spirit of international cooperation. Yet the United States never formally objected when the CAP was mooted and several years earlier, in 1955, insisted in GATT on a blanket waiver for its own domestic agricultural price support programmes.[19] The basic economic principle of the division of labour seems to have got lost as far as temperate agricultural products are concerned, owing to the disproportionate political influence of agricultural lobbies and both sides of the Atlantic have become committed to costly support programmes that are socially irrelevant to the protection of the poorer farmer. The essential difference, as Richard Cooper has pointed out,[20] is that if both sides could tame their agricultural pressure groups in the interests of the consumer, as general inflation may force them to do, it would be apparent that the United States would be a major exporter and Europe a natural importer of many agricultural products, so that Europe's policy hurts both her consumers and her partners. In a later chapter I have suggested reasons why the CAP must be modified, but this is going to be a ferocious aspect of the negotiations because it is not so much two sets of governments arguing but two groups of societies. Yet if the major governments do not get control of the argument they run real risks not only in their relations with each other but with parts of the developing world. For the GATT negotiations are among eighty countries, not simply among the rich, and many poor countries have little to export but agricultural produce. American bilateral deals with the Soviet Union may take some heat out of the purely European–American argument. But it happens, for instance, that the American legislation on sugar, the Commonwealth Sugar Agreement and an international sugar agreement covering part of the free market, all come up for revision in 1974, and sugar is the only export of some Caribbean and other poor countries.[21] The recollection of what happened to Cuba should make individual governments wary of letting their own arguments, of pitting the sugarbeet growers of New Jersey against those of Picardy, take precedence over wider considerations.

Then comes the contentious question of preferences, again largely a European–American argument, with the Community contending that the United States is creating a storm in a teacup in the pursuit of an abstract principle, and the Americans that Europe is threatening to plunge the world into 'a trade jungle in which special deals become the practice rather than the exception', to quote a recent American Secretary of Agriculture.[22] The fact is that the preferential agreements that the Community has negotiated with Spain, Greece, Turkey, the EFTA countries, Israel, or in the association agreements with the states of the former French Community in Africa and the East African Commonwealth countries do no great harm to American economic interests (with the exception of those with EFTA). They are the consequences of traditional ties and a certain case can be made for many of them. (See chapter 8.)

But equally Europeans, and especially the French policy-makers, fail to appreciate the extent to which the American emergence from political isolationism a generation ago was conditional on the creation of rules of universal applicability in the relationship of states, even though for special reasons they might be waived for limited periods. If the rules are flouted, an Administration's ability to resist the domestic forces of protectionism becomes weakened. The Community's apparent creation of a swathe of preferential arrangements, especially in the Mediterranean and Africa smells in American nostrils like the traditional French arguments for a special European responsibility for Eurafrica, which now not only cuts across American lines of communication on oil but carries the implication of a European sphere of economic influence; yet, even if it were economically desirable, Europe as an entity is no longer ready to assume political and strategic responsibility for such a sphere. The European case has also been weakened by the negotiation of 'reverse preferences' with many of these countries, preferential access, that is, for European industrial products, which in the eyes of the developing countries themselves carries overtones of neo-colonialism. If no broad commitment to the elimination of all tariffs emerges from the Tokyo Round, the very least that must be attempted is a generalization of such preferences to bring them back into line with the basic principle of most-favoured-nation treatment on which GATT rests; otherwise GATT itself is in danger. And as I have implied, the will to draft a completely new code of conduct is not demonstrable.

Another heading of the trade negotiations concerns the removal or mitigation of import quotas, on which all the industrial powers are sinners but of which the chief is Japan, as well as those European countries that maintain quotas on certain Japanese goods, even though the latter are legal since they were entered as reservations at the time Japan adhered to GATT. They infuriate the United States, which now regards it as the Community's moral responsibility to help absorb a greater share of the flood of Japanese consumer exports. The fact that by the end of the decade the level of wages in Japan will probably be within 20 per cent of the American level and is already nearly on a par with Europe's should make this problem easier to confront.

Side by side with this goes the question of 'voluntary restraints' which the United States has forced some countries, notably Japan, to adopt on products such as steel and textiles and which in the words of a distinguished American economist are 'a clear and flagrant contravention of the purposes and spirit of GATT'.[23] Finally, there is the thorniest question of them all, the reduction or elimination of the 800 non-tariff barriers which most major industrial powers maintain in some form: regulations on packaging, licensing, health or safety standards, customs valuation (the American selling price, for instance), governmental procurement (the Buy American Act, for instance). They can only be tackled on a case-by-case basis: they are in theory an aspect of domestic, not foreign policy, and to assume their rapid elimination also assumes that the same spirit of 'community' animates the governments of both sides of the Atlantic and both sides of the Pacific, a hypothesis that is harder to prove now than a decade ago. Yet if tariffs are simply replaced by some form of non-tariff barrier, one party or another to the agreement will feel defrauded.

Will the Communist powers play any role in this process of readjustment? Formally, some of them will, since Poland, Rumania and Czechoslovakia are members of GATT and Hungary is becoming one. But the level of trade between the OECD countries and the Communist powers, including China, is so small (it was one-thirtieth of the former's total trade in 1970, though it is rather higher now), that it cannot materially affect the infighting that must take place between the Community, the United States, Japan and Canada or between them and the developing countries. Nevertheless, if the Tokyo Round goes badly, there will be a temptation on the part of all of them to try and offset what they consider to be their losses by increased barter trade with the Communist powers, a situation which would find the United States in the strongest position since she has both foodstuffs and technological products to offer and may need Soviet gas if not oil as well. So wider political implications hang upon the Tokyo negotiations than simply diminished confidence and rising frustrations among the consumers and producers of the countries of the Western Alliance system, politically significant though this would be.

Who leads? This was not a question in previous trade negotiations, since the United States' economy was ten times and more larger than that of any other and she was more *concessionaire* than *demandeur*. Now the Community disposes of over one third of world trade and it is the United States whose balance of payments difficulties have provided the impetus to the negotiations. But it is the latter who still has the broadest responsibilities and the strategic power to support them, even if her political influence is now much less than a decade ago. On the other hand, the Community can negotiate more flexibly than the United States because the legal basis of its positions rests not on one act of Congress but on decisions of the Council of Ministers in more or less continuous session. Although it is with Japan and Canada that the United States now runs an adverse balance of trade, the key to many American frustrations lies in Europe. Consequently in many ways it is a confrontation of two equals and a great deal depends on the personal style of the European and American negotiators if what is inevitably a game of patience is not to degenerate into beggar-my-neighbour. This particular negotiation is no place for hard-faced men, for those with a quick reputation to make or for narrow specialists who do not see the wider implications of trade. The tone of the negotiations under Article XXIV (6) of GATT, whereby the United States claims compensation for the altered tariff levels of the new members of the Community and for her devaluations, that were in progress in the summer of 1973, did not augur well for the broader negotiation.

Towards monetary reform

The politics of monetary relations are different from those of trade relations in that they are *ab initio* the business of governments and involve not only considerations of national well-being, through their eventual effect on trade, but also considerations of prestige, influence and even security. But in the 1970s we seem to be the victims of a paradox, namely that as a consequence of the dramatic increase in economic interdependence, monetary relations are no longer wholly within the control of governments.

The Bretton Woods system, based on a norm of fixed parities, administered partly by an international agency, the IMF, and partly by the central bankers of the major countries, founded on a gold standard that soon became a dollar standard, was a remarkable product of human ingenuity. Because the strongest economic power since Babylon stood behind it, it permitted a phenomenal increase in foreign trade, held currencies reasonably steady through crises of rearmament or decolonization, and permitted the resurgence of two wartime enemies, Japan and Germany, who had had no hand in its design. But it faltered, possibly beyond repair, on 5 August 1971.

There is a professional debate as to exactly why this happened, but the central weakness of the Bretton Woods system was that it did not envisage capital movements on anything like the scale or speed that has occurred over the past decade, primarily from the United States outwards; it made insufficient provision for changes in the market value of currencies that might arise from this and other causes; and it made inadequate provision – since the men of 1945 could not have envisaged the vast expansion of world trade that has occurred – for providing the liquidity and the reserves to keep pace with such expansion. The system has been in trouble since 1964 when American overseas investment, which had been $1,674 million in 1960, rose to a figure of over $3 billion a year, channelled primarily toward Western Europe, so that by 1970 the book value of American overseas investments stood at $78 billion, as compared to only $13,200 million of foreign investment in the United States. Thus over the last seven or eight years it has been increasingly difficult to rest content with any such generalization as that the strongest power in any free system of trade and payments inevitably runs a deficit, as Britain did throughout much of the nineteenth century. By 1971, the overall American balance of payments deficit had reached the staggering figure of $29·7 billion and in 1972 it had only dropped to $10·2 billion (a figure still higher than 1970) despite devaluation. Yet only $2·6 billion of this derived from an adverse American balance of trade in 1971, though the figure rose to $6·8 billion in 1972; still less, $2·8 billion in 1971 and $3·5 billion in 1972, was attributable to gross overseas military expenditure (that is, before taking account of European offset arrangements). It is true that in the American balance of trade was in surplus by the third quarter of 1973, but much larger payments for oil and raw materials means that this may not be maintained.

The last two or three years have, consequently, brought a marked change of perspective. Throughout much of the 1960s the citizen of middle America and his representatives in Congress had assumed that the deteriorating position of the dollar was largely a consequence of American military commitments (to which for some three years the external costs of the Vietnam war lent some colour) and of the protectionism of America's allies. To many Europeans and Canadians the activities of the American multi-national company seemed a new form of American imperialism designed to subvert their political independence. Since President Nixon's dramatic suspension of the convertibility of the dollar in August, 1971, its formal devaluation in December of that year, and a second devaluation in the spring of 1973, the monetary situation is now seen less in terms of confrontation between the United States and her principal economic partners – as issues of trade barriers are still largely so conceived – and more as a common problem to which no ready answer is apparent.

Europeans may grumble that this situation need never have arisen if the United States had imposed effective controls over external investment, as France still does, an idea which finds an echo in proposals put forward by the more conservative elements in Congress. But not only is the European view about *le défi Amercain* changing, as I shall mention later, not only is it seen as providing a new form of American involvement in the independence and safety of Europe, but any objective scholar must recognize the difficulty for a nation so committed to the ideology of free enterprise in considering, and successfully imposing, such a form of *dirigisme*. American labour may grumble about the export of jobs which American overseas investment is thought to imply; but a large part of it is concerned with exploiting new sources of oil or raw materials which do not exist in the United States, and, more-over the overseas manufacturing subsidiaries of the American multinationals are among their parent company's best clients. The magnitude of the energy problem alone shows that there is no such simple solution to the problem as turning off the tap of American overseas investment, or even redressing the balance over time by encouraging greater foreign investment in American industry. For one thing, there is now a large accumulation of dollars and gold in the hands of foreign central banks, $51 billion in 1971 and still rising, which though no longer threatening the United States with bankruptcy since the dollar was made inconvertible in 1971, makes the monetary system no longer Americocentric as the Bretton Woods system assumed. The world's strongest economy no longer provides the world's strongest currency.* The con-vertibility of other major currencies, combined with the unwilling-ness or inability of the United States to restrict the flow of fresh dollars for investment, means that there can be rapid shifts of capital reserves from one country to another to take account of differential interest rates which diminishes the control of govern-ments over their domestic economic policy. Germany's attempt in the spring of 1973 to curb domestic inflation by raising interest rates led to a massive inflow of dollars and to a revaluation of the mark at the end of June.

Yet it is difficult to be confident that a permanent remedy can be negotiated in the near future, despite the attempts of a special Committee of Twenty, drawn from the developing as well as the industrial world, to do so. But before chronicling the difficulties, it is worth noting the areas of agreement. The first is that there can be no question of returning to the system that obtained until the Great Depression – the gold standard – whereby governments gave precedence to their balance-of-payments relationships over domestic economic policy, even if it involved deflation or unem-ployment. The second is that the economies of all countries except the Communist states are now so interdependent, so sensitive to each others' policies, that the system of the 1930s, which gave virtually overriding precedence to internal economic policy, is not to be considered either. No political leader could survive the advocacy of either course. The third is that the supply of gold, even if it is still the most widely trusted medium of exchange and

* This judgement may need revision now that the rise in oil prices is seen to have a more drastic effect on the economies of Europe and Japan than of the United States.

even if its monetary price were raised, is inadequate to provide the basis of the liquidity necessary to finance a continuing expansion of world trade, except at the cost of giving its two principal suppliers, the Soviet Union and South Africa, considerable leverage over the free economies. And even if we assume a deceleration of economic growth in and trade between the major industrial powers, expansion of both investment and trade flows are vital to the developing countries. Even France, which for many years was the principal protagonist of a shift from a dollar standard to a managed gold standard, appears to have modified her views in this respect. Finally, there is no argument that there must be an international currency of some kind to play the role that once gold, then sterling, then sterling and the dollar, and latterly the dollar alone have played.

There appear to be two interrelated problems that confront the experts and their political masters. The first is to evolve a basis for international liquidity that is not primarily dependent on the dollar. A start was made on this in 1969 with the creation of Special Drawing Rights under the aegis of the IMF, artificial money available to central banks and recognized by others to supplement the inadequate resources of national currencies made available to the Fund under its original charter; at the end of 1972 SDR's stood at the figure of $9·3 billion. This is still only about 8 per cent of the world's reserves, and one school of thought argues that the level of SDR's or a similar agreed reserve unit should be steadily and rapidly increased to ensure the adequate growth of reserves without total dependence on gold or dollars.[24] In 1971 the idea was mooted that the 'dollar overhang', excess dollars held by other central banks, should be funded.[25] One political difficulty of adopting this course is that Japan and the major European countries who now have large reserves feel for the time being no shortage of liquidity, and do not appear to have the economic and political incentive to engage in the complex problems of re-drafting the rules and strengthening the powers of the IMF to the same extent that the United States does.

The other problem is to create a better mechanism of adjustment when national currencies become overvalued or undervalued in relation to those of their main trading partners. The post-war system which assumed that virtually fixed parities (that is, fluctuating within only a very narrow margin) would be the norm and changes in exchange rates the exception, rested on the assumption that such a rule was essential to the maintenance of international confidence and the forward planning which capital investment across national borders and within them requires. This economic judgement was reinforced by considerations of national pride; a British reader has only to recall the intense reluctance with which the Wilson government confronted the necessity to devalue the pound in the years between 1964 and 1967, being prepared to make political sacrifices such as a marked reduction in Britain's military presence and political influence in South and South East Asia, before facing the inevitable.

But today it is more difficult to find consensus on a successor system to that of Bretton Woods. On one thing all governments are agreed, namely that despite their anxiety not to pursue policies of beggar-my-neighbour, they insist on maintaining their sovereignty to the extent of protecting themselves against the import of inflation from other countries by the greater use of flexible exchange rates: European governments especially feel that the rapid eastward flow of dollars has been a significant factor in their increase of costs and of living and in the general rise of commodity prices. In the wake of the first American devaluation in December, 1971, it looked as if it might be possible to obtain agreement on a re-drafting of the rules of the IMF to permit small but frequent changes in parities on agreed rules. In September, 1972, the United States put forward a formula whereby a country in persistent deficit would lose its access to SDR's and have its drawing rights restricted, while a country with disproportionate reserves 'could', in the words of Mr George Schultz, the Secretary of the US Treasury, 'lose its right to demand conversion, unless it undertook at least limited devaluation or other acceptable measure of adjustment'. It was assumed in the discussion that took place in the year or so after the 'Nixon shock' that the European Community would form an exception internally, since its nations were committed to monetary union through economic harmonization, and that European par values would move as one. What was then envisaged was a system in which the European Community currencies, the dollar, the yen and the currencies of the other industrial countries would be adjusted in a regular, fairly frequent and orderly fashion under the aegis of a strengthened IMF rather than through large, sporadic changes as in the 1960s.

But the currency crisis of the winter of 1972-3 undermined such an assumption. For one thing it proved what large sums of money, larger than the central banks could equalize, could now cross the exchanges as a consequence of decisions of non-governmental actors, such as the multinational corporations or the great international banks, or of minor countries such as the Arab oil states. It also showed how difficult it will be to institutionalize control of the huge Eurodollar market. For another, it showed that the level of a particular exchange rate no longer seemed to have the political importance it had had earlier. The pound and the lira were floated, left to find their own value in the world's money markets, incidentally putting in doubt the prospect of economic union by 1980 as the necessary step to political union. Other currencies, the Canadian dollar, the Swiss franc, were also floated. Fourth, it also showed that countries with an undervalued currency such as Japan were prepared to revalue only under extreme pressure.

In consequence, the prospects of reaching agreement on a revision of the rules of the international monetary system in the immediate future are not exactly promising. For one thing, it is difficult to see how any firm progress can be made on the reconstruction of the system as a whole until the debate about monetary relations within the European Community, to which I will return in chapter 8, has been resolved. For another, although it is accepted by governments, bankers and experts that an orderly code of conduct must be re-established if the expansion of international trade and investment is not to be arrested, the end of the dollar's overvaluation and the floating of other currencies has taken some of the stress out of international monetary relations, and to a certain extent reduced the incentive for reforming them or strengthening the authority of the IMF as the United States desires.

It is recognized that monetary and trade relations are interdependent but the atmosphere in which they are negotiated may be different. Because trade relations have such a direct bearing on the bread-and-butter issues of domestic politics, negotiations on them have an embattled quality of confrontation which is absent from the arguments of central bankers whose mutual concern is with order and stability, however sharply they may differ on the means by which this may be achieved. It may well be that we shall not see a successor system to that of Bretton Woods emerge until, first, national positions on the various trade issues have been clarified or reconciled, and, second, until agreement has been reached on a code of conduct for the great transnational investors and manufacturers, and the capital movements they generate.

But, though some problems in international politics and economics seem more formidable in prospect than they prove to be in reality, there is one reason in particular for suggesting that international monetary relations will need as explicit and thorough a reorganization by governments as trade relations, namely the large movements across the exchanges that the energy problem of the next ten to fifteen years will necessitate. Even if controls could be successfully imposed in both short and long term movements of American capital to finance manufacturing investments in Europe or elsewhere, the United States will be the country with the greatest interest in exploring and expanding proven reserves of oil, and therefore in generating a large share, say half, of the $400–$500 billion needed for the purpose over the next decade. Though some of this will be spent within her own borders much of it will not, and a figure of the order of $15 billion a year in capital outflow for energy purposes alone seems a conservative guess for the United States. In addition, if by 1980 she is importing 30–40 per cent of her oil from OPEC countries, her annual royalty payments will be of the order of 25–35 billion dollars a year. The European Community countries will be faced with similar or larger orders of magnitude; the difference is that, by reason of Europe's greater dependence on oil imports, the strain on their balance of payments will be felt sooner.

I do not know how the problem is to be solved. All I know is that it will stare governments in the face throughout the period of the trade negotiations, since major changes in parities can negate trade concessions overnight, and must affect the atmosphere of all negotiations on economic cooperation. It carries the danger that if it is not confronted, the United States may apply quite ruthless means to maintain a trade surplus in order to meet the current costs of imported energy, or that the dollar will become steadily devalued so that it cannot serve even as a secondary reserve currency to SDR's, the international character of the monetary system will erode and the United States will feel impelled to revise its political and strategic commitments and to enter still further into bilateral relations with the Soviet Union or the Gulf states. Clearly whatever solution does emerge will involve making the major developing countries, especially the OPEC countries, partners in the management of the international monetary system (only two of the developing countries in the Group of Twenty are oil states), for they will increasingly hold the power to wreck any agreement of which they are not founder members and active supporters.

Power, influence and force

In the acceleration of existing processes of change, towards a re-definition of the domestic priorities of states, towards a world in which transnational activities are unlikely to decrease, towards an increasingly interdependent world economy in which industrial states become more dependent on each other and on some develop-ing ones as well, and when pressures on resources seem likely to create new forms of tension, is the function, the necessity or the utility of military power changing also?

The next decade or so will be as much characterized by gross disparities in military power as its predecessors. The United States and the Soviet Union will still have the obvious characteris-tics of super-powers in this domain, whether expressed in terms of strategic forces, aircraft, cruisers, intervention capabilities or the power to support and reinforce allies. The more even distribution of power which has occurred on the economic plane, and which ten years ago seemed likely to apply to the strategic plane as well, has not occurred. Nuclear weapons have not yet spread beyond the three other powers, Britain, France, and China, that possessed or were developing them then; and, though the past decade has been characterized by a marked increase in the expenditure of the developing world on military hardware, China at present possesses the means to exert military influence at only a short distance beyond her border, the proportion of the Japanese GNP spent on defence is only a quarter that of the West European powers while the military capabilities of the latter, even those with the remnants of global interests like Britain and France, are largely concentrated on the maintenance of the European balance. At the same time the nature of social change in Western societies, when combined with increasing demands for other forms of public expenditure, means that if military power cannot be shown to serve a central national interest, the pressures to reduce both forces and expenditure will be considerable.

It is impossible to discuss this subject, still less to make any assumptions about the future, without first considering the changes that are occurring in men's conception of the utility of war as an instrument of policy. In the first place, we are unlikely to see in the perspective of the next decade or so radical steps towards the reduction, still less the elimination, of nuclear weapons despite the pious words in the Nixon–Brezhnev communiqué of June 1973, about their commitment to the ultimate objective of general and complete disarmament. The next round of the SALT negotiations seems likely to be focussed on preventing certain technological innovations, such as multiple warheads, from undermining what stability as has been achieved in the super-power balance (though this may well involve secondary agreements on the overseas deployments of American strike forces or Soviet missiles targeted on Europe). Any resort to conflict, therefore, not just as between the nuclear powers but as between their friends or allies, will take place against a continuing sense of alarm about the dangers of escalation or super-power involvement of the kind that has characterized attitudes to Arab–Israel or Indo–Pakistan conflicts. The irenic language of the Soviet–American agreement of June, 1973, on the prevention of nuclear war cannot dispel this.

Second, to the current sense of the illegitimacy of war as an instrument for the pursuit of interests or to redress an imbalance of power, which Klaus Knorr suggests has been growing throughout this century,[26] has been added the depressing experience of the United States in the use of military power in South East Asia. 'The rudimentary development of a universal human conscience', he points out, using a phrase of Raymond Aron's, has a longer and broader history than the Vietnam war, as the damage done to the political standing of Britain and France by the Suez incident, to France by the Algerian war, or to the Soviet Union by its interventions in Hungary and Czechoslovakia, suggest. Hedley Bull has pointed out that of the traditional objectives for which states have made war, to increase their economic power or prosperity, to achieve ideological objectives, and to protect their own security, only the third is now generally considered as legitimate*[27] (though Arab radicalism and Soviet support of certain revolutionary conflicts as well as Vietnam showed that the ideological motivation still persisted into the 1960s).

The distinction between legitimate and illegitimate use of force

---

* I support this judgement even though there was no general or serious condemnation of the attacks on Israel by Syria and Egypt on 6 October 1973, and war may have strengthened their negotiating position.

is, of course, very difficult to define, as the UN's failure over twenty-five years to get agreement on a definition of aggression exemplifies. What looks like a war of aggression to one group of powers can be identified as liberation by another. All one can say is that, at this point in time, the restraints on the use of military power even by small powers seem to be stronger than at any previous moment in the century. It is true that the Soviet Union had to make only modest adjustments in its general foreign policies to compensate for the damage done to confidence in its intentions by its intervention in Czechoslovakia. Yet Vietnam has had a profound effect not only on the external policy of the United States but on domestic attitudes to the use of force, to a point, for instance, which has severely constrained President Nixon's ability to use force to support the existing regime in Cambodia; even military aid to those developing countries thought to be significant to American interests is under severe attack in the United States, and the amount of American forces deployed outside the borders of the United States has already been halved in the past four years.* The ability of Malta to defy Britain and the other NATO powers over the price of a base, the determination of riparian countries to impose fifty mile or wider fishing limits, of Egypt to dismiss Soviet advisers, exemplified a characteristic of the present state system which differentiates it sharply from that of the late nineteenth or early twentieth centuries, namely the ability of the small to defy the great.

In part this springs from the recognition that, as Henry Kissinger wrote just before entering the White House, '... power no longer translates automatically into influence. This does not mean that impotence increases influence, only that power does not automatically confer it.'[28] And with this recognition has come, in the world's most powerful state, a more political definition of security and deterrence, the notion that American security depends more on preventing combinations of power hostile to the United States or promoting friendly constellations of powers than on the maintenance of particular levels of military force, or the defence of particular geographical areas. In other words, military strength is seen more as an instrument of bargaining and negotiating than for the physical defence of what W.W.Rostow

* One sign of changing American attitudes was the failure of President Nixon to make any real headway in advancing his credibility on the Watergate issue by invoking considerations of national security.

has called the Cold War truce lines. As Samuel Huntington has expressed it:

'In an era of confrontation, there is not much that military force can be used for except to confront, that is to deter. In an era of negotiation, paradoxically, the potential uses of military force multiply: military buildups, weapons decisions, deployments, and even actions, all become ways not simply of deterring military aggression by the other power, but also ways of putting pressure on him to make concessions at the negotiating table. So long as there were no negotiations, there was no opportunity for military power to perform this function.'[29]

The one area where this conception raises and has raised immediate problems is central Europe, where stability continues to depend both on a higher level of deployed force than in any other part of the world to maintain a political balance of power, and on a high level of American and Soviet control of potential crises, which inevitably involves their military participation in the two alliance systems. President Nixon has continuously reiterated that there are strong arguments why the general redefinition of American strategy cannot be applied to Europe as it has been in Asia. Nevertheless, as the MBFR negotiations illustrate, even in Europe American military power has a bargaining as well as a security function.

But it also seems to raise a second question. Does the Soviet's move towards equilibrium with the United States not only at the strategic level but in naval and other forces which would be used for intervention, either in outlying areas of the American alliance system or against non-aligned countries, mean that at the point in time when the restraints on possible American interventions are becoming increasingly evident, the Soviet Union is acquiring not only the means but the will to move into the vacuum created by the retreating Western powers? There is a great deal of special pleading on both sides of the Atlantic in support of this view, but personally I am sceptical. The Soviet presence in the Mediterranean, the Indian Ocean or off the coast of West Africa is still a modest one, and the keels to maintain it appear to have been laid down in the immediate aftermath of the Cuban missile crisis when the Soviet Union felt profoundly humiliated by her inability to meet the American challenge to her power at the level at which it was presented. It was continued and accelerated during a period when American interventionism was more spectacular than at any time since the early twentieth century. In my view the Soviet navy has as much the characteristics of a counter-intervention force, the extension of deterrence to an arena not hitherto covered by the spectrum of Soviet power, as the basis of a new Soviet strategy, while also serving the secondary function of demonstrating that the Soviet Union is now a power with global interests.

The military strength of the super powers or the great powers is likely to be exercised in the immediate future with greater selectivity, discretion or reluctance than in the past, to be latent rather than deployed, to be seen more as a diplomatic than as a peace-keeping or conflict-preventing instrument. But this does not mean that the number of conflicts in the world will necessarily decrease. There may be new civil wars or local wars, especially if the problem of greater self-consciousness of minorities, mentioned earlier, continues to grow, and there is no law of nature or of politics that suggests that the major powers may not get involved in them, even if this is now much less probable. They still run a certain risk as long as they continue to try and extend their influence or acquire foreign exchange by arms deals, which involve not only the sale of hardware but the training of thousands of technicians in their metropolitan establishments. All one can say is that for the time being Krushchev's declaration of support in January 1971 for wars of national liberation anywhere is in a pigeon-hole, together with Kennedy's go-anywhere, do-anything-to-support-free-peoples Inaugural Speech of a few weeks later. It might, as Huntington says, 'well be in the US interest to negotiate mutual abstention agreements with the Soviets on military action in the Third World areas.'[30] The need for such an agreement may become more evident as regional powers who have been hitherto the security clients of the major military powers, such as Japan, Iran, India, the Gulf States, Nigeria, and South Africa, acquire either the economic incentives or the military infra-structure, or both, to develop active foreign policies that may bring them into conflict with their neighbours.

There is one important *caveat*, however, to be entered in making any firm assumption that we are beginning a period when calculations of relative military power or the exercise of military force on the part of the major powers will play a less important part in world politics than in the years of the cold war and of rapid decolonization. It relates to the growing dependence of the western industrial powers on imported raw materials, notably but not exclusively oil. They have become used to a high level of material affluence, and in these societies, as I have tried to suggest, the older discipline of the industrial era is breaking down without yet becoming replaced by a new one governed by the need to make more careful use of all forms of resources.

If the efforts to evolve a common policy between Western Europe, Japan and the United States on the sharing of access to sources of oil and raw materials breaks down, if a situation of hostile confrontation should develop between them and the oil consuming countries, then there may be a temptation to resort to various forms of gunboat diplomacy. It is not difficult to imagine a situation in the late 1970s when the oil shortage may be at its height, when the price of gasoline at the pump has doubled, when central heating and other now familiar amenities have been drastically rationed and rising raw material costs are seen to con- tribute to inflation, in which some government in Washington or Tokyo, for instance, or in a European Community that is still finding it difficult to find other bases for united action, feels im- pelled by public pressure to threaten or exert force against a developing country to improve their bargaining position or avert some action that seems directly to threaten their material interests.

This contingency should be aired if only to ensure that govern- ments guard against the possibility of its arising. For it would be immensely damaging to the broader interests of the industrial powers, as well as internally divisive, given the extent to which the rudimentary universal conscience is on the side of David and against Goliath. It would also be risky, given the climate of nuclear parity in which it would occur and the counter-intervention capabilities of the Soviet Union. Anthony Eden attempted to justify the Suez operation of 1956 in terms of the importance of oil to Europe, the hand on the jugular of the industrial world. A second Suez twenty or twenty-five years later in Latin America, Africa or the Gulf would do infinitely more damage to the stand- ing and influence of the Western powers, to their relative influence in comparison with that of the Soviet Union and China, and therefore to the central balance of power, than did the first. Moreover, there would be no question of United Nations inter- vention to restore the peace as there was in 1956 (and in similar situations later). The application of techniques of UN peace- keeping were the product of special circumstances, a greater fear of super-power collision than exists today, the readiness of middle powers like Canada and Sweden to bear burdens with which they are now disillusioned, the personality of Hammarskjöld and other factors. The UN has an important role in the management of international crises, but the circumstances which gave it an active and almost independent one in the decade after 1956 have largely disappeared.*

Leaving such aberrations as the possibility of gunboat diplomacy aside, the question remains whether, in a period of rapid change, when so much has been accomplished in freeing the international system from the bonds of the Cold War years, the ensuing decade holds out real promise of reducing the colossal proportion of the world's wealth, some 7 per cent, that goes on arms and armaments, of finding new areas of agreement on arms control and entrenching techniques for averting conflict. I would like to be more sanguine than I am.

The area of agreement that would liberate most resources and most profoundly affect the climate of world politics would be a major modification of the central Soviet–American arms race. But one has to consider what this would involve. Despite the fact that the United States has accepted the reality of strategic parity without too much demur, the opinions that lay behind the Jackson amendment of 1972 to the Interim Agreement, mentioned on page 69, represents the present limits of American confidence in the trustworthiness of Soviet intentions (despite Mr Brezhnev's wooing of Congress during his visit to Washington in June 1973), unless the Soviet Union is prepared to agree to measures of international inspection and control of strategic and other force levels which for twenty years and more she has strenuously resisted. At the same time Russians, though not more or less aggressive by temperament than other races, have always had a crude attitude to power and would find it difficult to relinquish the position of potential dominance over countries other than the United States, with which two generations of low living and high capital accumulation have now endowed them. More than that, a real stabilization of the central arms race (and the two super-powers will have spent over $40 billion on the development and maintenance of strategic weapons between the signing of the SALT agreements

* These words were written before the Arab–Israel war of October 1973 but this seemed to support them. The UN was used then as the instrument of the two super-powers rather than asserting an independent role.

in May 1972 and the publication of this book) would involve other considerations as well. A far-reaching bilateral agreement that, say, involved the reduction of strategic force levels by ten per cent a year over eight years to one-fifth of what they are today, coupled with a treaty limiting military research and development or military budgets plus agreement on techniques of monitoring such limitations, would also involve a reordering of the relations between each super-power and its principal allies and friends if a super-power entente was not to create fresh dangers of nuclear proliferation or of new forms of tension between political systems that are still ideologically divided. It might well involve a normalization of Sino–Soviet relations with American encouragement and the full understanding and support of Japan. Such a thing is conceivable, but to embark on it successfully would require an assured period of strong political leadership, backed by domestic consensus, in each super-power if both the political and the technical problems involved were to be successfully overcome.

In the winter of 1972–3, just after President Nixon's re-election, it seemed possible that SALT Two might be cast in just such ambitious terms; both powers are in different ways feeling the economic pinch of maintaining deterrent positions at very high levels of force; both, though in different degrees, are aware of the danger that the rising generation may be alienated from strategies of deterrence by the maintenance of vast forces that both sides recognize should never be used. But by the summer of 1973 the prospects that SALT Two would take the form of a fundamental discussion of the requirements of world order had largely disappeared, partly because of the disarray of the US administration as a consequence of the Watergate scandal, but more by reason of the difficult negotiations involved in converting the Interim Agreement of 1972 into the form of a permanent treaty. Quite apart from the question of FBS, American aircraft that can be based around the perimeter of the Soviet Union to which the Soviet Union has no exact equivalent, or the American superiority in long range bombers, there is the fundamental disparity in the numbers of actual warheads each side deploys by reason of the American lead in the development of MIRV. The Soviet Union has some 2,400 strategic missiles, but, although the United States has a smaller number of missiles, as she deploys *Minutemen* III and replaces *Polaris* with *Poseidon* missiles in submarines, the number of warheads she can deploy will rise from about 4,000 in

1973 to about 7,500 by mid-1977, the point when the Interim Agreement expires.[31] Since all arms control agreements, to be politically acceptable, must be based on a broad symmetry of capabilities or restraints, the urgent problem has become to find a formula which will control MIRV. On 17 August 1973 Mr James Schlesinger, the US Secretary of Defense, announced that the Russians have mastered the basic technology of MIRV and by 1975 will have successfully deployed it on their new SS17 and 18 missiles; they may have only four and six warheads where *Minuteman* III has three and the new American SLBM *Poseidon* has ten to fourteen, but each warhead is one megaton where the American ones are considerably smaller. Since the Soviet Union has one-third as many missiles, by the Interim Agreement, as the United States, they have it in their power to negate the American superiority in 'throweight' (the aggregate of destructive power that could be projected against an adversary) and acquire what the US government would regard as a disarming capability in relation to the United States. One way to avert this would be to add a standstill on the deployment of American MIRVs to the existing Interim Agreement on launchers, or else to negotiate mutual self-denying ordinance on placing multiple warheads on land-based missiles, which because they are more accurate are seen more as disarming weapons, than their submarine-launched equivalents. Until this thorny question has been argued out in SALT Two, the prospects of converting the Interim Agreement into a broader measure of arms control are not high, and the fact that the attempt to set a deadline of the end of 1974 for the completion of SALT Two has failed suggests that it will probably be concentrated on this issue alone.

One must, therefore, accept the prospect that SALT Two will be largely a matter of hard, technical bargaining between the United States and the Soviet Union, and that it will not be until the second half of the 1970s, most probably after the next American presidential election, that they will have sufficient confidence that the one is not stealing a march on the other, to embark on more fundamental discussions. In the meantime, they will probably continue to transfer more of their retaliatory strength from land-based to submarine-launched missiles, which is not forbidden under the Interim Agreement. And it may be that, either by agreement or the pursuit of parallel policies, they will in ten years' time have shifted most of their retaliatory strength from the land to the oceans, even though in the process they may be relinquishing one of the geo-political advantages – areas of low population density – that made them super-powers in the first place. The only thing that may prevent this is the reluctance of the US Congress to face the enormous costs of building *Trident*, the successor to the *Polaris* submarine, which will cost $1,000 million per boat (even though its range, accuracy and number of missiles will be greater), unless the Triad concept of maintaining bombers as well as both land- and sea-based missiles, on which the US Joint Chiefs of Staff have hitherto insisted, is abandoned.

The fact that the central arms race is at best only likely to reach a plateau in the foreseeable future, and to show no serious signs of being on the downward curve, will have a secondary effect, namely on the prospects of nuclear proliferation. With the advances in the accuracy of missiles over the past ten years, no third power can hope to develop a secure retaliatory posture vis-a-vis either of the super-powers unless it too builds missile-firing submarines which are much more costly and require a broader range of technological skills than land-based systems. This is China's dilemma over the long term, though a force of hardened land-base missiles may be adequate to deter Soviet attack in the short term. But it must also affect the calculations of other countries who have the means to develop nuclear warheads or atom bombs such as India, Israel, Japan or South Africa, and eventually still others as civil nuclear energy spreads and plutonium stocks accumulate in a wide range of countries. There is still considerable semi-official discussion in India about 'going nuclear', for a variety of social and political reasons in which consideration of security plays only a part. And if India were to go nuclear it would hitherto have affected the debate in other countries; but the problems of developing a second strike force against a super-power or even China becomes for India year by year more formidable, while the deterrence of Pakistan has become relatively easier as the balance of power on the sub-continent has swung in India's favour.

Another possibility is that Israel, aware of declining American political support as the United States becomes increasingly dependent on Gulf oil, may feel constrained not to reach agreement with her Arab neighbours but to increase her deterrent power by converting the limited stock of fissionable material which she has been accumulating for the last five or six years into a small nuclear arsenal. The short distance between Israel and the capitals and bases of her neighbours would make her delivery systems adequate for such a purpose. It seems to me that the outcome of the fourth Arab–Israel war has enhanced this possibility. What may, and should, inhibit Israel from such a choice is the consideration that, though such a step might increase her territorial security, it would diminish her real security in the sense of being able to count on other influential countries, including the United States, to support her in a crisis.

But the fact that the restraints which have become evident in the use of military force by the great powers, and in both the vertical and horizontal proliferation of nuclear weapons, seem likely to remain, does not imply an international system free of conflict. The growth of communications, the rediscovery of old cultural and ethnic traditions, makes racial or communal conflict of the kind that we have seen in Ireland, in Cyprus or in Nigeria more not less likely, even if it assumes a primarily political form as in Belgium or Quebec. Ambitious and predatory men such as Sukharno may rise yet again to the leadership of significant states. It seems likely that there will be a period of near-anarchy in the Indochina states and in their relations with each other. The internal coup is an endemic risk in modernizing societies. And the Sino–Soviet conflict might even conceivably lead to forms of war by proxy in Southern Asia or elsewhere.

Moreover, the fact that a period in which the risk of significant armed conflict is lower is not synonymous with an orderly world is evident from the conflicting approaches to the regime of the Seas, on which a fresh attempt at codification will begin in June 1974.[32] Four kinds of technological development have in the past twenty years or so created a situation analogous to that which prevailed during the great period of maritime expansion in the sixteenth century, and have produced claims almost, though not quite, as extravagant as those then made by Spain or Portugal. Exploration has revealed important mineral deposits in the deeper ocean; continental shelves are becoming an increasingly significant place to search for and produce oil; the importance of fishing is increasing; and the maritime states, the great powers especially, feel an increasing strategic need to protect their access to the ocean bed, as well as to maintain access through straits and narrow waters.

It is coming to be accepted that the commercial exploitation of the deeper ocean should be internationally controlled; many developing countries would like to see control of its exploitation vested in a UN agency whose royalty earnings would be used for development; but some would like to extend national ownership to the deep ocean. But where does the deep ocean begin and end? The convention of 1958 is unclear. Countries like Iceland and Peru that are heavily dependent on fishing, and other developing countries that have coast lines, resent the way in which the developed countries, the Soviet Union, the United States, Japan, Norway, Poland and Britain especially, have industrialized their fishing operations with factory ships and are in effect taking *their* fish. Hence Iceland's claim of a fifty-mile limit and that of ten Latin American countries to two hundred miles. Thus the Law of the Sea conference will again be a confrontation of the rich and the poor countries like UNCTAD, with the difference that in this case the poor countries probably have greater leverage. It looks as if the nineteenth-century rule of absolute sovereignty for a country within a certain distance from its shores and only general rights beyond it will have to give way to a distinction between territorial rights and fishing rights.

But how wide are territorial rights to be? Most countries other than the super-powers do not want nuclear submarines prowling near their coasts, feel that the three-mile limit – the range of cannon shot – is out of date, and would settle for a twelve-mile limit. The United States is slowly backing away from her insistence on retaining the three-mile limit, on which she has stood shoulder to shoulder with the Soviet Union. But what bedevils the prospect of getting the super-powers to agree to a twelve-mile limit is the question of straits and archipelagos, which have emerged as one of the dominant political issues. The great straits like the Denmark Sound or Gibraltar have long been regarded as territorial for economic purposes but uncloseable to ocean traffic by virtue of the fact that they connect two oceans. But now, to the general desire of riparian states to get some advantage out of their position, has been added the fear of pollution from super-tankers in narrow waters; in 1971 this led Indonesia and Malaysia to introduce a regime governing passage of the Malacca Straits, which makes Japan nervous about her life-line, is considered by the great powers to interfere with their strategic interests, and might establish a precedent for similar behaviour elsewhere. A great deal hinges, therefore, on a redefinition of the concept of 'innocent passage'.

With ideas among the Caribbean states of converting that sea into a *mare clausum*, with the nationalization by some archipelago states of the waters between their islands, plus the increased national control of straits and the promotion of enormous territorial claims, there is a danger that new foci of conflict will emerge. The preparatory discussions in various parts of the world on the Law of the Sea conference have provided a revealing analogy of the state of international relations in general. The two superpowers for whom technological developments are making the sub-ocean strategically more important all the time have a wide range of common interests and positions which they have tended to assert rather dogmatically; but when they have been on the same side, the Chinese whisper that it is a consequence of collusion. There is, moreover, no agreed position between the United States and her European or Pacific allies. The new riparian states, most of whom have been provided by the great powers with arms and the means to block the passage of straits or to defend territorial claims, are determined to assert their local or national rights. The discussions have illustrated the diffusion of power that is occurring within the international system and, in this particular case, the risks of a possible retreat from a once well-defined order which it poses.

6
The Mainland Powers

The Nevsky Prospect

Brezhnev's achievements

The world which Leonid Ilyich Brezhnev surveys after some nine
years in power presents in many ways a pleasing prospect. At
home his colleagues, Podgorny and Kosygin, who together with
Kirilenko and Polyanski helped him engineer the downfall of
Krushchev in 1964, have been relegated to the thornier pastures
of domestic economic policy or Soviet relations with the developing world; he is the master of high policy. No palace revolutions
have shaken the stability, or undermined the external credibility, of
his regime. Despite many difficulties, including the increased flexibility of American diplomacy, Soviet external policy continues
to be dynamic and not simply reactive. Some of the problems
which it has confronted, the need for a more stable relationship with Western Europe or for technological and agricultural
imports, have to a certain extent been turned to good advantage.
Above all, the Soviet Union, heir to the broken, desolate Russia
of fifty years ago, now stands, by many formal indices of power
and influence shoulder to shoulder with a United States which
was even then the world's richest state and until very recently by
far the more powerful and influential of the two. Brezhnev's
Soviet Union, moreover, is regarded as a responsible actor on the
international stage in a sense that Krushchev's was not.

Fear, elemental fear of military attack, has stalked the corridors
of the Kremlin for the past century and more. So if the Soviet
Union is a more self-confident power, more considered and
sometimes more considerate in its statements and actions, the
adjustment of the strategic balance with the United States undoubtedly is a prime factor. One can argue that a good deal of this

fear was self-engendered, that the very structure of NATO made clear that it could only be a defensive alliance, that post-war Germany had neither the intention nor the capability to threaten the Soviet Union, that a nuclear first strike had ceased to be a rational option for the United States as soon as the Soviet Union acquired even a rudimentary capability to hit targets in North America, that is by the mid-1950s. But the fact remains that both the Soviet political and military leaders were slow to grasp the implications of a strategy of deterrence, and much of the astringent logic of McNamara's Pentagon with its emphasis on 'damage-limiting capabilities', a sufficient margin of American missile strength to cripple Soviet retaliatory power in a war situation, and justified by the existence of a much wider range of American than Soviet alliance commitments, induced real fears that the United States was preparing for just such a contingency. The attainment of parity with the United States in numbers of long-range missiles during the later 1960s, the American retreat to a strategy of 'assured destruction' and the refusal of the Nixon Administration with its rubric of 'sufficiency' to accede to right-wing pressures for an increase in those categories of weapons where the Soviet Union was achieving numerical superiority, eased certain gnawing anxieties, quite apart from such pleasure as it may have induced at becoming accepted as the strategic peer of the United States.

To this source of satisfaction has been added a second: namely that a man was elected President of the United States in 1968 and re-elected in 1972, who, together with his Adviser on Security Affairs (and now his Secretary of State), regards negotiations with adversaries as a higher priority, intellectually more intriguing and domestically more relevant, than consultation with allies and the consolidation of traditional relationships. Neither Nixon nor Brezhnev is in any doubt that the two political systems that they lead are ideologically hostile. (Nothing irritates Soviet commentators more easily than well-meaning Western speculation about the inevitable convergence of socialist and capitalist societies, or about 'the end of ideology'.) But the Soviet state has urgent reasons for wishing to engage the United States in a network of interlocking agreements on a host of specific subjects and has been lucky to find an Administration that has been intent on stabilizing great power relations and is prepared to go part of the way. Consequently, the agreements of May 1972 were followed by a trade agreement in October which normalized trade relations in the sense of removing most of the American restrictions imposed at the time of the Korean war; and this followed hard on the heels of a three-year grain agreement which made the Soviet Union the second largest American customer for cereals.

When Brezhnev visited Washington in June 1973, he had the double good fortune to find Nixon in the throes of a domestic crisis and anxious to take a positive step in any direction that suggested itself. One consequence, in addition to a number of specific cooperative agreements on civil aviation, agriculture and so on, and a doubling of the target for Soviet–American trade to $1 billion a year, was an agreement on the prevention of nuclear war, an objective estimable in itself but which contained the phrase '... if the relations between countries not party to this agreement appear to involve the risks of nuclear war between the USA and the USSR, or between either party and other countries, the United States and the Soviet Union ... shall immediately enter into consultations with each other and make every effort to avert this risk.' This could be read as no more than a recognition of the realities of crisis management as they have been accepted at least for the decade since the 'hot line' between Washington and Moscow was first instituted. It could be, and to a certain extent has been, viewed as a formalization of the priority which the two super-powers accord to their mutual security relationship (which was even more explicitly recognized in the accompanying statement on strategic arms limitation), over their support of an ally under pressure from the other.* Mr Brezhnev had to fly from Washington to Paris to assure President Pompidou that the super-powers were embarked on peace, not conspiracy against the interests of lesser powers, but with little success. Washington felt obliged to give the same sort of assurances to Peking. Ironically, each super-power assumed the burden of reassuring the most suspicious nominal ally of the other, which is the diplomatic essence of collusion. The two leaders also imposed – though without success – a deadline of the end of 1974 for the completion of the second round of SALT talks, thus emphasizing the urgency of strengthening their bilateral relationship, and President Nixon agreed to pay a second visit to Moscow even before then.

* In fairness to President Nixon, it should be made clear, however, that Brezhnev did not get what he had demanded, a ban on the use of nuclear weapons, which, with the Soviet conventional preponderance in Europe, would have seriously undermined the position of NATO

There is more satisfaction and less risk in this for the Soviet Union, which is committed to the continuance of a bipolar international system, than for the United States which seeks a more plural world order and which wishes to see confidence engendered between a number of power centres. Her own alliance, the Warsaw Pact, is in little danger of dissolution even if one of its members, Rumania, has attained a guarded measure of autonomy. In the name of European security she can oppose the political and military coherence of the European Community, knowing also that Europe is likely to be strategically dependent on the United States for a considerable period to come. In the name of non-proliferation she could oppose a decision on the part of Japan to develop her own nuclear weapons to replace an American guarantee in which Japan had lost confidence. At the same time she can draw both political and material profit from the frictions within the Western alliance to which trade and monetary arguments, compounded by European and Japanese irritation with American unilateralism in the sphere of security relations, are giving rise, even though she might not regard a rapid American withdrawal from Europe as being in her interests. In other words, the Soviet Union can, provided she is prepared to keep on reasonable terms with the United States by making concessions that keep their security relationship stable, maintain for some time a primarily bipolar structure of strategic power, which is her primary interest, while quietly capitalizing on frustrations within the West or in relations between the Western and the developing countries on other planes of interaction.

Moreover, whatever concessions the Soviet Union may have to make in the European Conference on Security and Co-operation – and she has already had to make some in the face of a united determination on the part of the West European countries that it should be a proper negotiating, rather than a largely formal, conference – it has been convoked at her urging partly to ratify a great Soviet diplomatic triumph. However warmly we may approve the realism that animated Brandt's decision to negotiate a new relationship with the Soviet Union, Poland and the GDR, however much one may admire the skill with which it was negotiated by the government in Bonn, the fact remains that, by a mixture of force and patience over a quarter century, the Soviet Union has achieved international recognition of the division of the most powerful nation in continental Europe. Decades of discussion about how the German problem might be solved, by 'roll back', by disengagement, by a new European security system, have washed up against the rock of Soviet determination and evaporated.

But Brezhnev has other reasons for satisfaction as well. He is the most powerful figure in a controlled society, bordered by other controlled societies. Few of the political and social troubles that affect Nixon worry him. Social, as contrasted with minority, protest is minimal despite the efforts of the *samizdat*. The Soviet approach to the CSCE has made clear that she is going to give little if any ground in permitting greater freedom of personal contacts – indeed, by a law of 25 December 1972 it became a criminal offence for a Soviet citizen to meet foreigners for the purpose of disseminating 'false' material about the Soviet Union. It appears that a sense that the Western oil crisis is likely to change the American policy of support for Israel may have taken some of the urgency out of controlling anti-Semitism, or truly liberalizing the restrictions on Jewish emigration from the Soviet Union; if as a consequence the US Congress refuses to grant most-favoured-nation treatment to the Soviet Union, this is hardly a cause for serious concern since most of her exports to the United States are likely to be raw materials on which import duties would merely add to American inflation. Even a measure that appears to be a sign of increasing Soviet readiness to participate in the normal intercourse of nations, her adherence to the Universal Copyright Convention in May 1973, also has the effect of making a manuscript a commodity in which only the state may trade, and thus gives it greater control over the flow of *samizdat* material to the West, or the publication there of the works of great writers like Solzhenitsyn.

Finally, Brezhnev has had the satisfaction of quietly disposing of his adversaries in the Politburo. In April 1973, Voronov, who had criticized his agricultural policy as being too centralized to provide incentives, and Shelest, who was too good a son of the Ukraine, and had been critical of Brezhnev's *Westpolitik*, were retired on pension. In their place came Gromyko, for twenty years the workhorse of Soviet diplomacy, Marshal Grechko, the first Minister of Defence in the Politburo since the unlucky Marshal Zhukov sixteen years earlier, and Andropov, the head of the KGB. These are not necessarily Brezhnev's own choices; Gromyko may be there from a feeling on the part of others that contemporary diplomacy is too complicated to be left to First Secretaries of the

Party; Grechko may be there at the insistence of the military that détente with the United States be not pursued at the expense of security; Andropov to oversee the process of tightening ideological conformity. But if Brezhnev is less dominant in the Politburo itself than in recent years, his record of success in foreign policy does not expose him to the kind of cabal that brought down Krushchev.

Unease in the Kremlin

Yet the beaming and friendly First Secretary who travelled to Washington in June 1973 went partly because he has many anxieties. The most obvious is the Sino–Soviet dispute with its tangled historical, territorial, ethnic, ideological and social roots yet which is primarily of the Soviet Union's own making. In four years, indeed in ten years, there have been no serious signs of its mitigation; and although there may be ideologues in Moscow or soldiers in Peking who would like to at least attempt the process of rapprochement in the name of solidarity, efficiency or security, the material with which they must work is most unpromising. Quite apart from the ideological dispute, and this remains of prime importance, at least to the Chinese, the possession of a very long land border, undefined for the most part by natural features and the product of historical acts for which the Chinese have never forgiven the Russians, is itself an endemic source of tension. (Canada and the United States are almost the only pair of countries in a similar situation who, by reason of quite different historical circumstances, have been able to master this source of tension.) If Soviet policy has been animated in the post-war era by genuine fear of attack from the West, Chinese policy is still animated by similar fear of attack by the Soviet Union even though the skilful evolution of political tripolarity by the United States may have made the possibility of such attack less plausible. If the Russians have less reason to fear direct attack, the majority of Russians have an atavistic concern for the 'yellow peril', which finds its reflection at all levels of Soviet society.

For Brezhnev and his colleagues the emergence of China creates particular anxieties and frustrations. For one thing, it has destroyed any hope that the Soviet Union could one day mobilize the whole ex-colonial world against the West as Krushchev at one stage hoped to do. If the presence now of 45 Soviet divisions and

2,000 military aircraft in Eastern Russia is more a form of diplomatic pressure or deterrence on China than indicating fear
of imminent war, China still possesses the ability to threaten
certain key areas of the Soviet Union, Vladivostok for one, or to
stir up unrest in the Asian minorities of the Soviet Union. But
beneath these obvious calculations of security lies a deeper concern, namely that if the structure of international power becomes
more diffused, if the international system becomes more plural in
character, the Soviet Union is exposed to the permanent risk that
a hostile coalition, say of Japan, China and the United States, or
of Japan and China alone, could be created to pursue a new
policy of containing her pretensions as a world power, even if not
to prosecute a shooting war. As Malcolm Mackintosh has put it,
'The Soviet Union already feels the odd man out in the East Asian
"quadrilateral" '.[1] This is one of the motives for trying to enmesh
the United States in what Henry Kissinger has described from the
American standpoint as a 'web of relations', though he has also
said, quite correctly, that such agreements are not self-enforcing
and depend entirely on reciprocal influence and confidence.[2]
It is essential from the Soviet standpoint that the other emergent
major powers have the least possible freedom of manoeuvre.

The Sino–Soviet dispute has for some years affected Soviet
policy in the developing world, and many of the Soviet moves
there have been animated by the attempt to construct a policy
that would contain Chinese as much as Western influence. The
principal country that sees the threat in the same light as the
Soviet Union is India, whose friendship is an important asset but
who is also a drain on Soviet resources; so is Bangla Desh, even
though her emergence may have tilted the balance against China
in the sub-continent. The Soviet position in Asia has its strong
points, to which I will return in chapter 10, but how far it can be
extended is still an open question. For the moment she may retain
such influence as she possesses in North Korea (made no easier,
presumably, by the process of North–South rapprochement) and
in North Vietnam (which is partly a factor of her relations with
the United States), or make a bilateral deal where a surplus
commodity emerges as with Malaysian rubber in 1971. But in the
Middle East and elsewhere the very fact of rapprochement with
the United States may undermine Soviet influence, as the chorus
of Arab disapproval there at the perfunctory references to that
area in the Nixon–Brezhnev communiqué of June 1973 exemplified.

In addition to her new treaties of alliance, the other means by which the Soviet Union has chosen to extend her influence in the developing world is the classical instrument of naval power. Throughout the late 1960s and early 1970s, she got remarkably high dividends out of a modest investment. The mixture of alarm and special pleading in Western capitals to which the appearance of a small Soviet squadron in the Indian Ocean and off Conakry gave rise was clearly a source of considerable satisfaction, as well as impressing the developing countries themselves. To see the 1971 Commonwealth Conference in Singapore brought to a standstill by an argument between Britain and the developing members of the Commonwealth on this subject was one of the more remarkable diplomatic spectacles of recent years. But as with most *tours de force* the effect of Soviet showing of the flag is likely to wear thinner with time, although the acquisition of permanent ports of call or refuelling stations like Aden has a certain diplomatic value.

But Brezhnev has other worries. One is the Soviet position in Eastern Europe, where Yugoslavia, despite closer trade relations, continues to evade Soviet control. Yugoslavia, under a weakening leader with its ethnic and historical animosities rising to the surface again, may present the Soviet Union with very difficult choices. When Tito dies, the country might move towards some form of social democracy, which is anathema, or it might break up and one republic, say Croatia, invite Soviet intervention which, if she moved, would produce a major diplomatic crisis: or it might lapse into civil war into which both alliances might get drawn, whatever the declaratory positions on non-intervention emerging from the CSCE. Rumania sought in the preparations for it, with Western support, to get the principle of non-intervention in the internal affairs of other states made universally applicable and not just in an East/West context; and on this the Russians eventually gave way. Whatever finally transpires in the Conference, it will be very much harder for the Soviet Union to sustain even the shadow of the Brezhnev doctrine, and she will pay an even higher political penalty than in 1968 if she applies it.

Over all discussions about the future of Eastern Europe looms the shadow of the Community, rich, advanced, now acting as a unit in commercial relations and demonstrating that cooperation can be nourished by internal mainsprings rather than imposed. It may be no more than a sketch of a political community at present, but the very bilateralism with the United States which the Soviet Union seeks for other reasons may inevitably accelerate the political coherence of Western Europe, while COMECON, its Eastern counterpart, is likely to remain a not very effective bureaucratic apparatus based in Moscow itself. There are signs that she is tightening her control of it, for clearly one Soviet nightmare is that over the years one Eastern European country after another will get drawn into first the commercial and then the political orbit of the Community, even though the latter may have no specific intention of balkanizing Eastern Europe. In their heart of hearts the Soviet leaders must regret the domestic necessities which might impel the United States to reduce its military and political leadership of NATO, and curse the political integrity which has led successive Administrations to encourage European integration. Nevertheless, by pursuing bilateral relations with individual West European countries, she can still hope to sow sufficient discord within the Community to prevent its political advance.

Yet what possibly causes the Politburo more anxiety than any external factor are certain internal problems of the Soviet Union. (Great nations are often most active externally when confronted with intractable problems at home.) One is the perennial question of minorities, a problem that now afflicts a great many states but on which Soviet policy appears to be moving in precisely the opposite direction to that of say Britain, Canada, India or indeed China. The Union of Soviet Socialist Republics was established on the principle of national self-determination, but this federal structure has never been honoured in more than name, and Brezhnev's Politburo seems even more determined than Stalin's to make no concessions to Latvian, Ukrainian and Asian cultural or ethnic sensibilities. In February 1972, a resolution of the Central Committee praised the Soviet Union as 'the most viable and perfected form of organization for a multinational state'.[3] But the fact remains that there are only two non-Slav members of the Politburo, though non-Slavs account for about a quarter of the population, and there have been recent purges in Georgia, Armenia and Azerbaijan.

There appear to be two forces at work. One is a new form of conservative Russophile nationalism or chauvinism that causes frictions with the many non-Russian minorities that live within the vast Russian Republic, most particularly of course the Jews.

The other is the growing self-consciousness of the national republics around the Russian periphery, and their reaction to the way in
which Moscow overrides their nominal autonomy, especially as
it becomes necessary to ignore ethnic boundaries for purposes of
economic planning.

To the process of cultural self-consciousness, which particularly affects peoples like the Crimean Tartars who were brutally
deported to Uzbekistan by Stalin, or the Latvians and Lithuanians,
have been added two other problems. The first is that as the Soviet
economy continues to flounder, it has become necessary to concentrate resources and to abandon what Brezhnev called 'levelling
off' and what we would call a regional policy of assistance to backward areas. If as a consequence of Soviet deals on raw materials
with Japan and the United States, Siberia becomes an area of
high investment while the Ukraine and the Moslem southern
republics are left to their own devices this could cause real trouble.
The second is that the population of the more backward republics
has been growing faster than that of Western Russia though the
discrepancy may diminish in the next decade. In 1970, the
national growth rate (net births per 1,000 of population) was over
30 for Uzbekistan, Kazakhistan, Azerbaijan, Kirghizia, Armenia
and Turkmenia as against an overall figure of 17·8 for the country
as a whole, and the same disproportion goes back at least a decade.[4] These areas are on two sensitive frontiers, with Turkey and
Iran, or with China; as the population of the Asian republics rises
either they will have to be given a greater measure of independence
and support, which seems improbable, or their surplus population
must be allowed to emigrate to the industrial areas of European
Russia, increasing the problems of racial friction that already exist
there. Russians, who were still in a majority at the time of the
1970 census, may by now be in a minority, while a fifth of the population is now Moslem.[5] Consequently, to the normal suspiciousness
of the Russian character has been added the sense of sitting on a
cauldron which increases the elite's sense of insecurity and makes
any conception of the Soviet Union as 'a country like another',
able to assimilate normal contacts with the outside world, harder
than ever to contemplate despite the vast external strength of the
state.

This problem is linked to the general sluggishness of the Soviet
economy, and not just to bad harvests or low agricultural productivity alone. National income in 1972 grew by under 4 per

cent as compared with Rumania's 10 per cent and Poland's 9 per cent. The Soviet Union is only about a quarter of the way towards its planned growth under the Five Year Plan that began in 1971, while Poland and Hungary are nearly half way there. Investment projects in the Soviet Union have now been cut back from 700 to 460 in number.[6] And the official statistics conceal grave weaknesses and bottlenecks in the technological sectors, projects begun and then abandoned, shortage of scientific or technological manpower, which are a consequence either of bureaucratic incompetence or in many cases of the demands of the strategic weapons programmes. If President Nixon has budgetary and political reasons for trying to stabilize and reduce American defence expenditure, Brezhnev has compulsions in terms of absolute shortages, particularly of knowledge. It is this which has sent Soviet officials out into all the technological market places of the world, and has made the propaganda organs of a state that for fifty years preached the importance of self-sufficiency talk of the benefits of free trade and economic interdependence in terms that might have seemed exaggerated to Richard Cobden and John Bright.[7]

This is not to argue that trade barriers solve anything, but the new image of the Soviet Union as an interdependent member of a world economy is largely bogus. Only 5 per cent of the Soviet GNP is accounted for by foreign trade, and before the Soviet–American grain deals one-fifth only of this was with the developed West. The main Soviet interest was until recently in acquiring Western technology for consumer industries, for many Soviet citizens still have a lower standard of living than their grandfathers. But after Brezhnev's visit to Bonn in the spring of 1973 it became clear that, abandoning Krushchev's aspiration that his country should lead the world in science and technology for the slogan that 'science has outgrown national boundaries', she wished to import many kinds of capital goods as well as encouraging Western investment. But Germany does more trade with Luxembourg than with the Soviet Union and, despite a desire for good relations, the level is not likely to increase significantly. The Soviet–American trade agreement is a major step forward for the Soviet Union, but even if it reaches the level of $1,000 million a year this will still represent only one and a quarter per cent of American foreign trade, and it is not clear how even that level is to be financed, for the Soviet Union has been running a hard-currency deficit, and will probably continue to do so, until the considerably more distant date when Soviet natural gas and other raw materials becomes available to the West.

It is unlikely that the Soviet Union would have become converted to any form of Cobdenism if it had not been for the crisis in her agriculture. This is not simply a consequence of two or more bad harvests but of low productivity. In 1970, a year when the harvest was relatively good, the Soviet Union, whose population is 30 per cent larger than that of the United States, also had 30 per cent more land under cultivation; yet its output was only 80 per cent that of the United States. According to the analysis of the FAO, if one compares the number of people in farming in each country against their production, an American farmer produces enough to feed himself and thirty-nine others (official American figures put it at forty-nine), while his Soviet counterpart produces only enough for himself and five others, and on a diet lower in protein than the American.[8] In addition to the inherent inefficiency of the *kolkhoz* system and the bureaucratic top hamper through which minor practical decisions must be processed, there is still a considerable shortage of agricultural machinery and even more of fertilizers. The Nixon Administration's agreement in June 1973 to back the development of a large fertilizer plant in the Soviet Union must have been one of the most popular prizes Brezhnev won from his visit to Washington, though bad distribution of fertilizers is apparently as significant a reason for low productivity as the failure to meet fertilizer production targets.

Finally, there is the problem of the succession. Brezhnev was sixty-seven in 1973 and is not in good health; Kosygin, Grechko and Podgorny are older. The two senior party figures, Suslov and Kirilenko are respectively four years older and the same age as Brezhnev. Of the Politburo members in their late fifties, Polyansky is believed to have poor health, Shelepin has dropped out of the public eye, and Mazurov is a Byelorussian. There is no national figure in his forties, as both Stalin and Malenkov were when they emerged to power. If Brezhnev should collapse in the near future it is probable that the other old men would somehow carry on until they could agree on an heir apparent. If he should live for another four or five years, and he is a popular and respected figure and so is unlikely to be brought down by human opposition, one can expect to see him push forward some of the group of younger men who have been gathering around his private *cabinet*.

One of the difficulties, therefore, in forming any judgement about the course of international politics later in the decade is having any sense of who will be leading a country whose interests may be unchanging but whose tactics are profoundly influenced by the style and priorities of its leadership. If both Nixon and Brezhnev are gone from office by the end of 1976, what firm assumptions can we make, for instance, about the Soviet–American relationship in the late 1970s?

The resistance to a plural world

Nevertheless, one can get no sense of the possible courses that international politics may follow unless one does make some assumptions about the way in which the world's second most powerful state will conceive and pursue its interests.

First, while relations with the United States have been for over twenty years the focus of Soviet foreign policy, the events of recent years have sharpened this focus still further. This is partly the consequence of a growing community of interest. Both powers have looked into the abyss of accelerating expenditure in the strategic arms race if they allow innovation to pursue its course unchecked and now that there is an emerging community of understanding on the requirements of stability in deterrent strategies, I would expect the Soviet Union to be ready to forswear certain strategic options despite the fact that she has developed MIRV and intends to deploy it, provided a formula can be arrived at that produces an apparently symmetrical bargain: to do otherwise risks placing even greater strain on her limited technological resources to the detriment of economic growth and the satisfaction of popular pressures, without advancing her prestige in the international community as a whole. But despite the lip services to disarmament in the Brezhnev–Nixon communiqué of June 1973, despite the specific agreement on the avoidance of nuclear war, it seems improbable that the time has yet come when she will respond to a dialogue on how foundations of world order or even of strategic stability might be permanently strengthened. Despite her greater sense of security she has only recently arrived at the status of a world power, everyone in the *apparat* has been educated to view the world in ideological and national terms, and new domestic reasons have been added to traditional ones for refusing to behave as 'a country like another'.

More than that, the present moment offers a good opportunity, as well as creating the incentive, to involve the United States in a network of special agreements beyond the strategic field which a more confident or more militant successor to Richard Nixon, a John Connally or a Henry Jackson could only abrogate at the risk of raising international tensions.* Since her leaders are, in George Kennan's words, 'power-snobs', their minds are not readily open to the argument that an increasingly close relationship between the two super-powers, between two countries who have each a diminishing number of close or confident supporters, also diminishes the broader political influence of both, and tends to accelerate that very diffusion of power which the Soviet Union opposes.

But the pursuit of good relations with the United States serves other purposes. It mitigates the nightmare of an anti-Soviet entente between the United States, China and Japan (perhaps also with European technological assistance to China) which would isolate the Soviet Union in Asia. Clearly she now sees the risks of attempting to destroy China or do more than check her influence in the developing world.

Soviet–American rapprochement also serves its purpose in Europe, where Soviet external interests are still mainly focussed, and where she believes that, as the strongest European power, the balance should be weighted in her favour. There she may feel somewhat as many Americans do, that military force is now something to be used for the purposes of diplomatic bargaining rather than for overt pressure. We shall know more about this when the CSCE and MBFR conferences are further advanced. But of the two political options she has always tried to keep open, that of dividing the individual Western European countries from each other and dividing them from the United States, the advance of the Community and its expansion plus her own choice of détente in Europe, may induce her to give preference to the latter for the time being, though she may still hope to exploit social tensions in Western Europe, and to kindle somewhat different expectations in different capitals, especially Bonn. If she can further undermine what is left of the notion of Atlantic Community, and help transform the European–American relationship from a friendly to a sour one, then she has nothing greatly to fear from the develop-

* Evidence of the priority given to Soviet–American relations was the embarrassed reaction of the Soviet press to Watergate.

ment of the European Community itself for a long time to come. Indeed, her alternative option of working for its dissolution would become once again a realistic one.

It is difficult to write about Soviet policy objectively without sounding like an old cold warrior. By reason of the wholly different conception of stability that she holds from that of other nations, because of the continuous undercurrent of ideological cant that flows beneath such reasonable declaratory positions as 'peaceful coexistence' or her new espousal of economic interdependence, because of the arbitrary treatment of her citizens, and for many other reasons, it is very difficult to accord her the benefit of the doubt where her intentions are obscure. The most difficult problem is to know whether her leaders, brought up as they are in a closed elite system, have any true sense of the context of change, or whether, with their crude attitudes to power, they may not again misjudge the temper and the objectives of other societies, as Stalin thought Europe and China could be browbeaten, Khrushchev that decolonization could be exploited to Russian advantage, or the earlier Brezhnev that force could be employed against Czechoslovakia without penalty or that a new sphere of Soviet influence could be created in the Middle East.

Sooner or later, of course, a leadership with a different kind of background will emerge. If there is a man of fifty-five at the head of the Party or the government in 1980, he will have only a child's dim memory of the Second World War and none at all of Stalin's purges. He will have grown up in an atmosphere of expanding Soviet influence and responsibility, with little material hardship (for him), and in which his contemporaries have tended to pay only perfunctory respect to Marxist orthodoxy. He may have travelled more than his predecessors and he will probably speak and read English. At that point, especially if little headway has been made with domestic, economic and social problems, we may see a less striving Soviet policy, more conscious of the costs of power, a Russia that is more content to rest upon its laurels, to accept its place as one power among others in a constellation of great, middle and lesser states endeavouring to frame norms of international conduct in the light of common problems of interdependence and scarcity. But until such a species of Soviet leader does emerge, we must expect the kind of hard definition of the Russian national interest to which we have become accustomed.

Peking Prospect

Chinese realpolitik

The 'image' of China which Mao Tse-tung and his colleagues have so successfully thrown upon the screen of world opinion is one of calm, consistency and order. By comparison with the hot debates of the open societies or the harshness of Soviet actions and reactions, a picture has been projected of a country governed by a band of old, wise men, of a society infused by the irenic ethos of Confucianism, heirs of two thousand years of wisdom, resuming gravely and without rancour the leading position in the family of nations from which it had been unjustly excluded for a generation.

While there are elements of truth in this, much of it is romance. For one thing, the present leadership has pursued a much more devious course over the past generation than that of any other major nation. In 1945 Mao and Chou En-lai were attempting to get to Washington to express their friendship and admiration for the world's leading democracy;[9] five years later China was a full ally of the Soviet Union; eight years after that the relationship between Peking and Moscow was beginning to become one of adversaries and in another three years, that is by 1961, had ruptured; by 1969 China was once again putting out feelers towards the United States for a new relationship which was cemented in the spring of 1972, though at the same time she was warning the allies of the United States against the danger of undue dependence on her. In 1955 she swore friendship with India, seven years later they attacked each other. In 1967 the British Mission in Peking was burnt down, in 1972 China was ordering aircraft from Britain and choirs in Peking were singing the Eton Boating Song in honour of her visiting Secretary of State.

The list could be extended, and the point is worth making simply to emphasize the flexibility that Chinese attitudes display by comparison with the slow-moving shifts of emphasis in Soviet policy. It does not mean that China is not a revolutionary power but that the two revolutions are, as William Griffiths has suggested, out of phase:

'The Soviet Union is in a Thermidorian period but China is still ruled by its revolutionary elite. Formally, Mao is a Chinese nationalist, a revolutionary intellectual-in-arms, and an ascetic.

He has usually insisted, at the cost of purge and turmoil, on a radical, anti-bureaucratic state. The post-Stalin leadership, conversely, has favoured a technologically oriented, bureaucratic model of development.'[10]

There is an unresolved, and indeed irresolvable, argument as to what really animates Chinese policy in the world. Is she the truly revolutionary power that she seemed to be a decade ago, intent on rallying the world's 'countryside' against the rich countries of 'the cities', prepared to make sacrifices if not of blood at least in terms of aid, support and precept to create a wholly new world order under her own leadership in a way that the bourgeois Soviets no longer are? Or is she simply an ordinary great power on the make, as her recent acts of *realpolitik*, her sowing of dissension in various UN conferences, her veto of UN membership for Bangla Desh, her continuous denunciation of rapprochement between the super-powers or her encouragement to the West Europeans to stand up to the Soviet Union, would suggest?

The answer surely is that she is both, but for the time being *raisons d'état* must take priority over more long-range revolutionary objectives by reason of the precariousness of her position. A triangular political relationship has developed, partly at her own, partly at American, instigation of which she is by far the weakest member; she deploys only minimal deterrent power, she is not yet an industrial nation in the true sense and though her agricultural growth rate improved her industrial growth slowed down in the 1960s; her trading assets are modest, she is feared by many other Asian countries; she is flanked on the west and north by a hostile super-power and on the east by a very powerful and dynamic industrial nation, Japan. Moreover, her friendship has only the limited diplomatic value for the United States – especially now that the Vietnam war is over – of making the Soviet Union more amenable to certain kinds of agreement, though on a different level it also eases American consciences about the past and reanimates a traditional American Sinophilia. She must, therefore, exploit the assets that she does possess, the magnetism of her culture, the West's sense of guilt about its past behaviour towards her, the sense of identification that a big developing country can attain with smaller ones, to strengthen her political independence while her physical security and material strength gradually augment.

The Soviet Union is fighting a rearguard action to maintain a primarily bipolar structure of power and influence in international politics. China's interest for the foreseeable future is the opposite: to accelerate the diffusion of influence and initiative, whether by a balance-of-power diplomacy or by using the established mechanisms of international cooperation and consultation in order to assert the equality of states. By an irony of history a nation that has had little or no part in the development of the modern state system, or in the evolution of its norms of conduct, that is by no means 'a country like another' and has a deep sense of its moral and cultural mission, has yet become one of its most enthusiastic supporters. At some later date it may become possible for her to claim the status of a super-power, to insist on participation in some kind of great-power condominium of a more effective kind than the UN Security Council, or in some other fundamental reorganization of the international system. For the foreseeable future, the Chinese interest is to minimize the pretensions of the super-powers, and in particular any claim that they have to a special responsibility for world order. Her interest is in restoring the conception of great powers, several in number and including herself, and demolishing any notions of diarchy.

One question that constantly recurs is whether the Sino–Soviet rift is a permanent feature of late twentieth-century politics. Before the 1970s are over, Brezhnev and Kosygin, Mao and Chou En-lai, the men deeply involved in the polemics of the 1960s, are likely to be gone. Big states constructed on the principles of Marxist–Leninism are rarities and should find it easier to communicate with each other than with capitalist states; powers on the Asian mainland inevitably have certain common interests as well as inherent conflicts. When the polite, middle-aged Chinese officials who now thread their way through the agenda of UN agencies meet the new breed of *mondaine*, middle-aged, Soviet bureaucrats in the corridors of international power, may they not find common ground which was denied their elders? It is possible, but the probability of rapprochement is still low unless the Western powers and Japan make very serious mistakes. For the Chinese despise the Russians as well as at present fearing them, and the border is a source of tension to her (in part because Sinkiang is an important source of uranium and became a significant oil field). Above all, each has little to offer to the other. If China wishes technological skills it is easier and politically more useful to get them from Japan; both China and the Soviet Union are deficit agricultural producers but there is no equivalent to the energy–wheat relationship that the Soviet Union is so assiduously pursuing with the United States; and both, moreover, are fundamentally autarchic societies. The Chinese leaders prefer the autonomy of a relationship of balance with all its risks to one of partnership.

This does not mean that Sino–Soviet relations need remain embittered for ever. The cost to China of switching her main defensive line from her coasts to her west and northern frontiers and of building up a strategic nuclear force at the same time is very considerable; so is the cost to the Soviet Union of maintaining over forty divisions and a large tactical air force at the end of long lines of communication on her eastern borders. Moreover, the Sino–Soviet estrangement in its present form has opened up new areas of manœuvre to the United States and at some point it may be in the interests of both powers to circumscribe them; such is the logic of a triangular balance. What may eventuate, therefore, is simply a relationship that is cold but not violently hostile, in which the military confrontation on the border is somewhat reduced and the strategic stance of both parties becomes increasingly one of deterrence rather than active confrontation. Certain accommodations may even be reached in Central Asia that limit, for instance, the present attempt to subvert each other's minorities. But both will insist on their independent access to the world and will continue to compete for influence in East Asia, in the developing world, and in Western and Eastern Europe. Certainly a less violent hostility is very much a Western interest; otherwise we may risk a continuous increase in Soviet armaments and a frenzied, Hitlerian outlook on the world.

In the meanwhile the conflict continues at the level not only of invective but also of a gradual build-up of China's strategic power. By June 1973 the United States government was satisfied by its surveillance techniques that China had achieved a dependable missile that could reach Moscow or targets in European Russia and was beginning to build hardened silos for its emplacement: the conception of strategic stability, the need to build a force that could survive a disarming strike and thus obviate the danger of pre-emption in a crisis, with which the other nuclear powers had wrestled in the earlier years of the missile age, has apparently been assimilated without difficulty by the Chinese. Even so, it now takes a formidable degree of hardening to protect a land-based missile against the Soviet SS9 with its three five-megaton warheads or even more modern types with MIRV, and the Chinese are clearly aware that their protection for the time being lies partly in Soviet uncertainty about the American reaction to an attack on her. Hence the evolution of an orderly relationship with the United States has equal if not higher priority than the Sino–Japanese relationship.

The invitation of Henry Kissinger to Peking in February 1973 and the subsequent decision to set up a high-level mission in each other's capital, a development that had not been envisaged after the Nixon visit of a year earlier, was an index of the need which the Chinese felt to make much of this relationship. Their difficulty is that there is not a great deal of substance in it, once barriers to cultural and other exchanges have been swept away. By the middle of 1973 there were only two concrete problems to be solved directly between Peking and Washington, the future of Cambodia and of Taiwan. The refusal of Congress in June 1973 to grant funds for continued American air support of the Lon Noi government in Cambodia after August pointed to the eventual restitution of Prince Sihanouk who has been the protegé of China for several years. Although this represents a formal reversal of the Nixon–Kissinger policy of insisting on political status quo in Indo-China, it is doubtful if the Administration is prepared to confront both Congress and Peking in actively supporting Sihanouk's opponents. Otherwise, China seems to have little wish to disturb its general relationship with the United States by making trouble on other aspects of the attempt to achieve some subsidence of conflict and anarchy in Indo-China.

Taiwan is a quite different matter. In the communiqué that followed President Nixon's visit to Peking in February 1972 Taiwan was recognized as part of China, which was not only a reversal of the position of the Eisenhower and Kennedy–Johnson regimes, but disposed of any suggestion that the United States might back a Japanese claim to Taiwan. At the same time the Chinese said nothing of the twenty-year-old American–Taiwan defence treaty. Both parties face, in fact, a difficult problem: the Chinese in convincing the Taiwanese that becoming part of the People's Republic will not jeopardize their prosperity and liberty, the United States in persuading herself and her other Asian allies that she is not tearing up a treaty simply for the sake of a quiet life. What appears most probable is that Peking will offer Taiwan, presumably after the death of Chiang Kai-shek, the status of an autonomous province, free for the time being to organize its economy and conduct its own external trade, and becoming only gradually subject to its own governance. It seems that it may envisage a period of some twenty years of transition, possibly aiming to consolidate Taiwan fully within its framework of authority at the same point in time when the lapse of the lease of the New Territories to Britain will make it essential to face a revision of the status of Hong Kong. The United States appears ready to dovetail its own policy with this, withdrawing its military assistance to Taiwan and eventually its defence treaty with the old 'Republic of China', while still maintaining strategic bases elsewhere in the Western Pacific and encouraging Taiwan gradually to look towards the mainland. Very possibly the timetable may be a much shorter one than either party is prepared to acknowledge at this time. But any sudden rejection of the Taiwanese who, after all, have only spent five years under the rule of the mainland out of the last seventy-eight, could do considerable damage to the American diplomatic position in the rest of Asia, while any retreat from the position that Taiwan must eventually be reunified with the mainland would come face to face with Chinese determination that it shall.

New partners for Peking?

Of equal importance to China is the development of a stable relationship with Japan, for it is she, not China, who possesses the economic and technological foundations to become a third superpower in the near future. Until the visit of Mr Tanaka to Peking in the autumn of 1972, there was a continuous drum fire of Chinese propaganda about the dangers of Japanese militarism, and even now such a fear cannot be totally allayed, for the Chinese are aware of the manner in which sudden shifts of policy have occurred historically in Japan, while any Chinese over forty remembers the devastating effects of Japanese aggression. However, the Sino–Japanese treaty did make considerable concessions to Chinese fears of 1972 and European visitors to Peking during the ensuing winter noticed that emphasis on this danger no longer figured significantly in the conversation of Chinese officials. Instead, Chou En-lai in his conversations in January 1973 with Mr Nakasone, Japan's Minister for Trade and Industry (and former head of the Japanese Defence Agency) emphasized the necessity of maintaining the Japanese–American Mutual Security Treaty and of Japan's deploying an adequate Self-Defence Force to ward off any Soviet threat to her integrity. She has also endorsed Japan's claim for the return of the Kurile Islands.

This does not mean that the Sino–Japanese connection has become one of sweetness and light. One difficult aspect of the national relationship is that while the Japanese have an admiration and respect for Chinese culture and civilization of which their own is historically an outgrowth, this is not reciprocated, and Japanese goodwill tends to come up against the basic arrogance of the Chinese outlook. In more concrete terms, the Chinese are unready at this stage to permit Japanese business the kind of investment facilities which it has been granted elsewhere (including probably in the Soviet Union) even though Japan is her largest trading partner and the level of trade increased by nearly a quarter in 1972 over 1971. Mr Nakasone was also told that China would not be needing Japanese capital for joint exploitation of the oil reserves on her continental shelf, and there are signs that China will, if she can, exact a high price for her limited exports of crude oil. As the problem of energy comes to play an increasingly dominant part in Japan's preoccupations, her desire to exploit the much larger Soviet resources in Siberia inevitably creates stress in the Sino–Japanese relationship. In addition there are large Japanese investments in Taiwan, and, on the horizon looms the relationship of both countries with Korea if the American military presence there is withdrawn completely.

Elsewhere in the world, Chinese policy has three prime motives, to contain Soviet influence, to use her position in the developing countries as the counter-weight not only to Soviet but also to Western influence in international organizations, and to diversify her trading relations. The first involves maintaining such influence as she can in the internal balances of the Indian sub-continent which for the time being have shifted to her disadvantage; developing her relations with Western Europe and encouraging the Community's constituent countries to stand up to the Soviet Union in negotiations such as CSCE and MBFR, warning them about letting down their guard; and trying to get a foothold in Eastern Europe. The latter policy has not been very successful despite the signature of a number of commercial or minor agreements with most of the COMECON members, except with Rumania which has for a number of years found relations with

China a useful stick with which to beat the Russians. The other East European countries tend to fear her diplomacy as an un- settling factor in a European order which they hope is moving toward greater stability; and the level of relations with one poten- tial friend, Yugoslavia, has never really moved beyond the formal by reason of China's acquisition many years ago of Albania as a client and propaganda base in Europe.

Her influence in Western Europe is not great despite diplomatic visits, editorials, table tennis teams, exhibitions. It is interesting for West European politicians to be warned so repeatedly and with so much vehemence about the dangers of doing business of any kind with the Soviet Union, or to have such explicit encourage- ment from the other side of the world for the development of the European Community. There has been a European school of thought, which found its strongest official support in France, that Western Europe should develop much closer ties with China for the same basic reason that the United States has reopened its channels to Peking, namely to increase leverage on the Soviet Union. The difficulty is (and it is one of the reasons that invali- dates the conception of a pentagonal balance of power) that Western Europe has little to offer China in political terms, with the possible exception of the delivery of Hong Kong, a gift which China does not seek at this stage because it is so valuable as a trade outlet, and which the British government would not in any case consider offering unless there was a clear majority of the colony's Chinese inhabitants in favour. By the same token, China could afford no real help to Western Europe if the European–American relationship were to degenerate or if it were to come under some new form of pressure from the Soviet Union.

The West European countries find it useful, it is true, to have a new outlet for their exports, especially in the field of high- technology goods where the American market is virtually closed to them, where even their own markets tend to be dominated by the United States, and where either strategic considerations or Soviet autarchy make the prospect of such a new nexus with the Soviet Union a dubious one. Contracts have been signed for aircraft, locomotives and much else besides. But though China has moved beyond the stage of a subsistence economy, she also is an autarchic state; and she feels neither the compulsions that now inspire the Soviet Union to expand her high-technology industries nor does she have the means, such as gold and major raw materials (except such exotics as tungsten, antimony and wolfram), to pay for major import programmes of capital equipment. Her exports are still primarily her traditional ones, textiles, tung oil and the disagreeable components – frozen egg melange or frozen rabbit – which are the basis of some cheap foods. Moreover, she has hitherto refused to incur other than short-term debts to accelerate her development or to import foreign capital on a long-term basis; though this policy may be in process of modification, Chou En-lai in talking to Western visitors reserves his particular scorn for India in this respect, as in others. Although the Chinese economy may now be accelerating again, it is probable that her foreign trade with the OECD countries will grow only slowly from its present level of $2\frac{1}{2}$ per cent of estimated GNP and that Japan will continue to account for about 40 per cent of this and Germany, Britain, and France together for some 30 per cent.[11] The factor that would alter this situation markedly would be if she were to find oil in really large quantities, and at a low cost of extraction.

The containment of Soviet power

But if China can exert only marginal influence over the unfolding drama of American–Soviet–European relations, she has urgent priorities of her own, deriving primarily though not entirely from the need to contain Soviet influence in the developing world. The Russians may be a clique of revisionist swindlers, but China despite her new *realpolitik* is a revolutionary power with a sense of *mission civilisatrice* not unlike that of colonial powers in their hey-day; her leaders obey Marx's great dictum that the point is not to understand history but to change the world. Her relative weakness in relation to the major industrial powers presents her both with the necessity of calling in the new world of ex-colonial and poor states to redress the balance of the old, and also the opportunity of doing so by talking the common language of low living and high thinking, of 'relevant poverty', with them. Yet in the nine years since Chou En-lai toured Africa and declared that it presented an excellent revolutionary situation, two things have happened: China has had to recognize that her resources are too limited to permit an active diplomacy everywhere and that it must be concentrated in defined areas that affect her interests as a state; second, like the Soviet Union before her, she has had to deal

increasingly with governments and less with revolutionary movements even where governments are based on their support.

The official delegations pour into Peking and by March 1973
China was in official diplomatic relations with eighty-six states (as
compared with about twenty, two years earlier). But those from
Latin America and West Africa, where a few years ago it seemep
she might be a major supporter of radical movements, for the most
part get politesse and trade agreements and little more. In South
East Asia she is not particularly active other than in Indo-China,
through her patronage of Sihanouk, though her re-emergence as an
active diplomatic power inevitably increases the national self-
consciousness of the overseas Chinese communities; she does not
need to be very active to be influential there, for her sheer size
weighs upon the consciousness of small Asian states far beyond
her ability, or it may be her will, to dominate the area. The principal focus of her diplomacy is an area bounded by Malta (to
whom she has made a substantial loan) in the West, Islamabad in
the East, Dar es Salaam in the South and Bucharest in the North.
The prime but not the only function of her activity in this area is
to undermine Soviet influence there, and to create a belt of
friendly states along Russia's southern border (she has even
praised the value of the Central Treaty Organization).[12] Her aim
is to make it harder for Russia to establish an exclusive sphere of
influence in the old Near and Middle East, that would permit
Moscow to treat the Black Sea, the Eastern Mediterranean, the
Persian Gulf and the Indian Ocean as a strategic unity. Until a year
or two ago that meant supporting Fedayeen and revolutionary
movements with arms and propaganda in the Middle East and the
horn of Africa, but as Russian credit in the area declines and as
more and more governments enter into relations with China, her
activities are becoming more conventional.

But her attitude to this area also serves other purposes than a
purely anti-Soviet one. Friendship with Iran may enable her to
shift some of the load of supporting Pakistan on to the shoulders
of the Shah and thus strengthen the containment of India's influence, as well as ensuring that the Western presence in the Gulf
is not replaced by a Soviet one. Her financing of the Tan-Zam
railway and her strong position in Tanzania and Zambia is in
part a tactic of wresting influence over anti-Portuguese and
anti-Rhodesian resistance movements from the Russians; but
it also probably has the much longer-term objective of enabling

her to play the dominant part in the eventual overthrow of white supremacy in southern Africa, which, if it succeeded, would have profound political and social repercussions around the world.

No country has assimilated so completely Palmerston's dictum that a great power must have neither permanent friends nor enemies. But is she really a great power in the sense of having universal interests? Her commerce is limited and will remain so; the cult of Maoism in the West is only the intellectual fad of an unhappy student generation; she can project military power at only a few hundred miles from her borders; her activities both in Europe and in the developing world are merely the extension of a quarrel with a powerful neighbour. Is she not really a regional power, as for most purposes the European powers which only a generation ago bestrode the universe, are now regional powers (though they like she have broader interests)? In calculations of force and of the crunch in any commercial or strategic negotiations, this is possibly the case. Japan is probably the only major state whose policy she can influence significantly, and East and South East Asia are probably the only areas where her views could not be ignored, as they could be elsewhere, if the other major powers of the world were in broad agreement. Nevertheless, in a situation of détente rather than entente between the West and the Soviet Union, in a plural world of many states in which significant middle powers are emerging who do not fit into neat patterns of alignments and where crude calculations of relative military or economic strength are giving way to more immaterial considerations, China must at least be credited with a unique ability – in a useful American phrase – 'to change the name of the game'.

One can make a respectable argument that China, at any rate since the Cultural Revolution and as long as the present leadership survives, has a better perception of the nature of late twentieth-century international politics than has the Soviet Union, despite such crass actions as the explosion of a multi-megaton hydrogen bomb in order to register her disapproval of the Nixon–Brezhnev Summit of June 1973. She is ready to adapt her diplomacy and her interests to a more plural structure of power than existed during the Cold War years, while her resistance to the conception of super-powers, let alone any form of super-power condominium, accelerates such pluralism since her view is shared by the majority of states. The Soviet Union by contrast seems intent on trying to create a new bipolarism which, if it succeeds, may simply diminish the authority of each of the two super-powers, even with their traditional friends, and also assist in the acceleration of multi-polarity. But this is not to argue that China is now an irenic force in world politics or by any means committed to upholding the status quo. The fact, for instance, that there is only a modest agenda of Sino–American business may make her obdurate on certain issues such as Taiwan simply in order to increase her leverage over the United States.* Her role in some of the inter-national conferences in which she has participated so far, such as the 1971 Stockholm conference on the Environment, or the pre-liminary meetings on the revision of the Law of the Sea has been largely one of playing to the gallery. The Chinese conception of stability, like that of the Soviet Union assumes the continuous assertion of her influence and the undermining of that of others.

I was in the process of sending this book to the publishers when the Tenth Congress of the CCP was held, and with it the emergence of Wung Hung-wen of Shanghai as the second figure in the Polit-buro, and therefore third only to Chou En-lai and Chairman Mao himself in the whole hierarchy of power. Not a great deal is known about him including the amount of party support he commands, except that he is from Shanghai and was a leading figure in the Cultural Revolution. But the striking thing is his age, thought to be between thirty-two and thirty-eight, some forty years younger than his new colleagues. Assuming the higher figure, he would have been a schoolboy at the end of the Civil War and he has lived most of his life in a metropolis. Surely the values that a man of this age and background will bring to the formulation of China's perspective in the external world must be profoundly different from those of the veterans of the Long March, mostly from peasant backgrounds? Have Mao and Chou deliberately decided to devolve the succession upon the kind of more *mondaine* figure I have mentioned, a man who presumably might rule for a very long time?

* In his Report to the Congress of May 1973 on *US Foreign Policy for the 1970's*, President Nixon has said 'Together we have revived our historic association. . . . We are under no illusion, however, that its development is inexorable.'

7
The Framework of
American Choice

The state of the nation

I will not waste the reader's time by emphasizing a point of which his newspapers remind him of every day, namely that American society has been and still is passing through a crisis of self-confidence. Much of the credo that an American boy or girl has for three generations absorbed at school about his country, that it is the fount of liberty and tolerance, the nation where 'the people' can most directly control actions of government, the protector of the weak and the respected leader of the world has been under challenge for the past decade, most particularly from articulate Americans themselves. It would be false to suggest that they despair of the republic, although there have always been some who have; but no one who knows the United States well can fail to be impressed by the lengthening agenda of urgent and difficult problems that now confront the American polity.

Since the United States is of all the major powers the one where public opinion makes the most direct impact upon the evolution of official policy, one must, in discussing the future of American attitudes towards the world at large, give first consideration to the problems with which the ordinary American citizen now feels himself to be surrounded. And, at first sight, they appear to be much more domestic, even parochial, in their nature or possible solution than related to considerations such as national security or the external influence of the United States.

One can choose different orders of priority but the agenda of domestic difficulties is hardly in dispute. First, I would put the question of race relations, the American counterpart of the probem of minority self-consciousness with which the Soviet Union and other countries have to grapple. But a minority problem that raises the issue of race and colour is much more difficult to confront than one that involves differences of culture or tradition, both for its internal and its external implications. Other countries like the Netherlands and Britain have coloured minorities: the difference is that the American black community is so very much larger, over 10 per cent of the population as against about 3 per cent in Britain. The fact that racial tension has been more quiescent in the early 1970s than in the late 1960s, may not mean that 'benign neglect' has made any serious headway towards overcoming white prejudices; the issue is simply latent, with a leaderless and more silent black minority but one whose expectations are not fulfilled, especially in the northern cities. This is one aspect of a host of problems attendant on the fact that the United States is no longer a land of farms and small towns with a few big cities here and there, but primarily a series of interlinked and sprawling conurbations, which still often have the administrative structure or the public resources of a group of villages. This plus the decay of the inner city, and very often its conversion into a black ghetto, has been one of the contributory causes in the rise both of racial tension and of crime and disorder of the past decade.

To this must be added a source of tension that defies the kind of practical redress for which Americans have a deserved reputation once a problem has been identified and analysed, in the way that organizations like the Urban League, or Common Cause are directed to the new problems of megalopolis. I mean the change in values and concerns that are implicit in phrases like 'the quality of life', 'the problem of the environment', or 'global humanism'. To apply a catch-phrase like 'the generation gap' to what is process as much as problem is misleading, for many middle-aged as well as most young Americans feel that in the past quarter century many of the most cherished aspirations of American society have become subordinated either to gross calculations of enrichment and economic expansion or to the dictates of national power, at the expense of the dispossessed, the crowded, the hungry, and of themselves. But this sense is particularly strong among the younger generation and, as an interesting study of American opinion in 1972, *State of the Nation*, observes, after commenting on the rise of hundreds of voluntary organizations, many of them semi-religious in character, 'For all the signs of fragmentation, youth in general appeared to remain solidly monolithic in one fundamental respect: the desire to work for social welfare, justice and reform.'[1] And with the entry into force of the Twenty-sixth Amendment, lowering the voting age to eighteen, the political influence of the young is not to be disregarded.

A similar process of changing values is taking place in other countries, most notably Japan; a similar phenomenon of youthful disillusionment with the political and social framework in which they find themselves is also observable elsewhere, particularly in Japan, France and Germany. The point is that by reason, first, of the size and influence of the United States in world politics, the fact that it is the core state of a network of international relationships, and, second, because it is also the world's great experimental society whose social failures and achievements eventually affect many other countries, changes of this kind are also of international significance. In every major democracy one can observe a growing distaste for 'power politics', especially among the young, a growing concern with the problems of the developing countries and with domestic and social questions. The point is that the American disillusionment with national power has been given an added impetus by the war in Vietnam (in which over four million young Americans served) and its consequences, which other countries lack. Another phenomenon which perhaps strikes a non-American who knows the country well more forcefully than a native son is the remarkable change in the role of the Federal Government. Gone are the last traces of Jeffersonian caution, which the Republicans espoused after the Civil War, about big government. From Roosevelt's New Deal to Johnson's Great Society, the expenditure of the Federal Government, its regulatory powers, and its social responsibilities increased steadily despite Eisenhower's attempt to stem the tide. President Nixon's 1973–4 budget, even though it attempted to arrest the steady growth of Federal expenditure and responsibility by cutting out minor welfare programmes and attempting to devolve some responsibilities on the States, was $269 billion or nearly a quarter, when a few years ago it was a sixth, of the national income and this despite decreasing expenditure on the form of 'showing the flag' that was popular in the 1960s, namely the exploration of space. The United States is inevitably becoming a social democracy in the way that the European countries became social democracies in the post-war years, irrespective of the label of the party in power.

But this quiet revolution in social and political attitudes to central government has gone hand in hand with the disorganization of American politics. The standard calculation of the first two-thirds of the century that national politics did not divide along ideological lines since the two parties were coalitions of interests, the Democrats uniting those of the South, the urban working class or organized labour and the intellectuals, and the Republicans those of the farmer, the small towns and the urban middle class, has not survived the last few presidential elections. The defection of the South to the Dixiecrats or to Republicans, the transformation of the urban poor into an industrial lower middle class, the declining numerical importance of the farm vote and other changes have undermined traditional calculations. As television has transformed the Presidential election into a personal contest of competing 'images', less and less related to party organizations or programmes, it is no longer a question of the successful candidate capturing the middle ground, for no one can be sure where it is to be found nor what is the established base from which he is to travel towards it. The assumption that the Democrats are the natural majority party whom it takes an unusual combination of circumstances (as first Korea and then Vietnam did) to unseat from the White House seems to have gone the same way as the assumption that the Tories are the natural majority party in Britain; yet the Republican ranks are also now in serious disarray.

Another aspect of the same process of change lies in the relations between the President and Congress. The position of presidential dominance which Roosevelt established has fluctuated throughout the past generation, but it has been sustained partly because the exigencies of the Cold War years imparted greater authority as well as responsibility to the Executive, partly because radio and television have for forty years made it possible for the President to appeal to the public over the heads of the Senate and the House. But Congress has been increasingly assertive since about 1966, and the Nixon landslide victory of 1972, which was a personal, not a party, triumph has left him confronted with a legislature which has a significant Democratic majority and a Republican minority which feels no great sense of gratitude or obligation to its party leader.

On top of this has come Watergate which, whatever the rights and wrongs of it, and whatever its eventual outcome – unknown at the time these words are written – is the most extensive and diversive political scandal in a democracy since the Dreyfus case. On the assumption that President Nixon does not resign but that his public standing is seriously impaired for the rest of his period of office, the prospect is of an Administration that may have little authority to take a major initiative, either in domestic or foreign policy, until 1977, and of a President who will then have no influence over the choice of his successor. Consequently, if we are trying to make assumptions about the actions and interactions of the major powers over the coming decade, the succession question in the United States presents much the same mystery as it does in the Soviet Union and China. What sort of man will emerge from the debates of the next few years to place his imprint on the years after 1976, to what forces and emotions will he appeal, from what constituency of established interests will he operate? Ought we to think in terms of an energetic nationalist like John Connally, even though he is only a recent recruit to the Republican party; a conservative internationalist like Senator Henry Jackson; the last member of the royal family of the 1960s, Senator Edward Kennedy; or some relatively new figure, Senator Mondale or one of the Republican governors from the Middle West? Twice in the last ten years men with an ideological motivation from the far right and the far left have contested the Presidency and been heavily defeated, Goldwater in 1964, McGovern in 1972. But if, as a good deal of newspaper reporting, American and non-American, would suggest, a national debate that is of a more ideological character is developing, can we be certain that the years after 1976 will be dominated by a figure from the middle of the spectrum?

Since we can make no certain clear assumptions about the kind of leadership which the political system will throw up, and since whoever the contestants are in 1976 and beyond 1980, they will be sensitive to public attitudes, it becomes important to try and find out as much about these attitudes as we can, especially as far as international problems are concerned. The study to which I have referred and which is based on a complex sampling system does establish one point that often gets overlooked: American public opinion is not as mercurial as the tactical victories and defeats in Washington might suggest. In 1972 those who regarded themselves as strong internationalists represented 13 per cent, those whose views were predominantly internationalist represented 41 per cent, those who had a mixed reaction to American commitments and responsibilities represented 33 per cent, while those who were wholly or partly isolationist in outlook represented only 13 per cent of the total interviewed. It is interesting that when the poll is compared with similar ones taken in 1968 and 1964, even though the proportion of enthusiastic and reluctant internationalists varies considerably, that of the small isolationist minority has remained virtually constant.[2] As other indicators have corroborated, the Nixon realignment of policy towards China and the Soviet was popular with seven out of ten Americans, and the danger of war, which in 1964 was considered by nine Americans out of ten to be the country's principal international anxiety, is now considered so by only two-thirds of the public. But whereas eight years ago international problems in general, defence, combating world communion, nuclear proliferation, maintaining international respect for the country, headed the list of public concerns in general, now they are clearly subordinated to a wide range of domestic anxieties, prices, drugs, crime and violence, pollution, medical care, consumer protection, unemployment and so on. What is most interesting is that, though fear of war or of communism has sunk considerably in the scale of public priorities and domestic preoccupations have risen, the foremost international priorities – peace in Vietnam apart – are given as 'maintaining respect for the US abroad' and 'maintaining close relations with our allies' (though this also elicited greater support for the European than the Japanese alliance).[3]

The proposition that 'the US should mind its own business and let other countries get along as best they can' found 35 per cent of the respondents in agreement and 56 per cent in disagreement, while 72 per cent were opposed to the proposition that American power made it unnecessary to worry whether other countries agreed with her. On issues of defence, including maintaining the overseas deployment of American forces, national opinion appears in 1972 to be divided broadly in half, and the same was true on international economic issues, half the sample favouring free trade, 43 per cent supporting a restriction on imports and 7 per cent having no opinion, the free traders coming from the cities, the blacks, the west, the professions and business.[4] Business executives, other research has shown, remain keenly interested in overseas investment, but are less certain about political commitments.

Priority to adversaries

It is worth noting these orders of magnitude if only to dispose of any assertions about the inevitability of a resurgence of American isolationism. By the 'Klingberg cycle' from which it appears that American history since 1776 has been particularized by alternating periods of introversion, lasting some twenty years each, and of extroversion, lasting about twenty-seven to twenty-eight years each, the United States should have become an introverted society again in about 1967 or 1968;[5] indeed this was about the time when popular preoccupations did begin noticeably to alter. But with a very high level of popular education and communication American public opinion is a good deal more sophisticated than those who generalize about it sometimes suppose. So that quite apart from the personal preoccupation of the incoming president with international affairs, it was apparent to the public at large that a country that was a strategic super-power and which was importing, even in 1969, over $50 billion a year worth of goods and services could make no simple choice between withdrawal from or continuing commitment to the world. Nevertheless there is a great deal of disillusionment, not only about American omnipotence but also about what American goodwill, power or participation in the international system can achieve in terms of a more stable and less crisis-laden world. Consequently, a narrower and less abstract definition of the national interest has inevitably taken precedence over commitment to broad principles, the defence of democracy, the rule of law, the containment of Communism, or maintaining the authority of the United Nations.[6]

This is evident, for instance, not only in the sharper attitude which the United States now adopts towards conflicts of interest between herself and Europe or Japan, but also in the more selective attitude she has adopted towards the developing countries. Just as the Soviet Union has developed a more stringent list of priorities in her external policy and China is forced, for the time being, to limit her activities to a particular geographical area of the world, so American policy has become more carefully defined in terms of either economic or strategic interests. In Africa, for instance, she has decided to concentrate her primary attention on a short list of countries which include Ethiopia (for its strategic significance), the Côte d'Ivoire, Zaire, Nigeria and one or two others. In the Middle East, for reasons already discussed, she is becoming increasingly preoccupied with her relations with the Gulf States rather than with the Arab world as a whole. The breakdown of relations with India after the 1971 war or India's new ties with the Soviet Union seems to occasion no particular grief in Washington, though ten years ago or less the economic and social progress of India, as the largest democracy in Asia and the world, was high on the American priority list. In South East Asia a low American profile is deliberate for the time being, but she has also adopted one in Latin America, her old sphere of influence, as the European countries, and to a limited extent, the Soviet Union, have become more involved there and anti-Americanism has increased. Brazil has become the focus of her interests. In the past few years, the Latin American countries have imported six times more, by value, of their armaments from Europe than from the United States.[7] The developing world as a whole drew nearly twice as much of its exports in 1970 from the enlarged EEC as from the United States.[8]

Henry Kissinger in May 1973 very considerably modified earlier assertions of President Nixon about the desirability or the actual emergence of a penti-polar structure of power, a balance between five power centres; he accepted what his critics had pointed out, that the existence of nuclear weapons and the emergence of strategic super-powers, coupled with the fact that economic and strategic power no longer go hand in hand, made the analogy with classical balance-of-power relationships misleading.[9] Nevertheless, there is no argument that it is the future of American relations with the Soviet Union, China, Western Europe and Japan which are the prime focus of both official and public concern. If the particular problems which they present, the strategic relationship with the Soviet Union, the political relationship with China, the economic relationship with Japan and Western Europe, can be maintained on a basis of mutual comprehension and restraint, then the United States will continue to enjoy greater freedom of action than her partners; in the Sino–Soviet–American relationship by reason of the mutual hostility of the mainland powers; in relations with Japan or Europe because the American economy is still the most powerful of the three and because she possesses a degree of strategic power and other resources which her partners do not. If these relationships can be sustained without either worsening or conflicting with each other, then problems in American dealings with, for instance, the major middle powers,

India, Canada, Australia, Indonesia, Brazil, Iran or with areas like the Middle East or South East Asia, can be managed also. But if her relationships with any one of her major partners degenerates seriously, not only would this produce wider international repercussions, it would also affect substantive American interests, in reducing her balance of payments deficit, keeping defence expenditure under control, or assuring her energy supplies during the coming one and a half or two decades. This, as I see it, is the central justification of the Nixon–Kissinger *realpolitik* in which the United States has become a largely independent actor in world politics as a whole (differing thus from the Johnson–Kennedy *realpolitik* in which American independence of allied consensus manifested itself primarily in relation to South East Asia) rather than presenting herself as the leader of a coalition, of 'the West' or 'the free world'. But do the necessary domestic foundations of such a policy exist?

In order to judge the extent to which this conception is a tenable one, one must examine each relationship in turn, and attempt one's own judgement not only on the extent to which one can be reconciled with another, but also on the extent to which its substance can satisfy the requirements of American safety, pride or wellbeing. Since we are attempting to see the problem through American eyes, it is better to start with problems rather than with partners.

The most urgent questions of external policy, the questions that will continue to dominate public and official debate, whether or not President Nixon becomes politically immobilized and whoever may succeed him, are five. First, there is the strategic relationship with the Soviet Union; second, and related to it, the maintenance of adequate military force to sustain a variety of external commitments; third, the protection or assurance of the country's energy supplies; fourth, the reversal of an adverse balance of trade and an ever larger deficit in the overall American balance of payments; fifth, and related to this, the evolution of a new international monetary system of which the dollar is not necessarily the central pillar.

The reason why I believe that the Soviet–American relationship will continue to govern other aspects of American foreign policy relates only partly to the Soviet attainment in the later 1960s of parity with her in long-range striking power. If it had become simply a one-for-one relationship which had been accompanied by a decelerating pace of technological change, the outcome of the SALT negotiations of 1969 to 1972 with its attainment of mutual restraint on the number of missile launches might have succeeded in establishing a stable basis for 'the adversary partnership' for a long time to come, perhaps until that still unknown point in the future when China becomes a sufficiently formidable strategic nuclear power to insist on some new agreement with the old super-powers. But the fact that it was impossible to begin even the preliminary SALT negotiations until MIRV had become tested and was therefore a practical proposition has involved a political price whose payment has been impending for the past four years and is likely to become actual in the next one, two or three. The American official judgement is that the development of MIRV by the Soviet Union, which has now been admitted by the Secretary of Defense, coupled with the increasing accuracy of long-range missiles, could, if unchecked by a mutual self-denying ordinance, give the Soviet Union the capacity to disarm the 1,000 American land-based *Minuteman* ICBMs, in other words a 'first strike capability'. Allies like Britain and France who have only submarine-based missiles may point to the very considerable submarine retaliatory force that the United States also maintains which could destroy a large part of Soviet civilization. Other allies and students of the strategic relationship of the super-powers may point out that American ICBMs with MIRV, which are now actually being deployed with *Minuteman* III and *Poseidon*, may already endow the United States with a disarming capability against Soviet ICBMs and for the Soviet Union to develop MIRV would merely restore parity. It is believed that American missiles in single or multiple war heads are more accurate than their Soviet counterparts.

To this, the official response is first, that Soviet intelligence about the exact location of American ICBMs is better than American intelligence about the location of Soviet ICBMs; Soviet reconnaisance satellites are less often frustrated by cloud than their American counterparts and the gathering of intelligence by other means is much easier in an open than in a closed society. Second, the invulnerability of the nuclear submarine, which will become the backbone of deterrence if the deployment of MIRV continues unchecked cannot be taken for granted over the indefinite future, given the massive research that the super powers and countries like Britain and France continue to direct to the problem of underwater detection. And, third, American officials sometimes point to the contrast in the constitutional and political positions of the President and of the Soviet leadership which endows the latter with a freedom of action – moral considerations apart – in a crisis which the former might not have.

One may reply that this represents simply the tendency to argue from the worst case that was an important factor in the strategic arms race of the 1950s and 1960s. But the situation has changed profoundly in that President Nixon, though not noted for his sensitivity to changes in the *timbre* of the domestic debate, is fully aware of the intense and growing reluctance of Congress to support even the present level of American defence expenditure, let alone increase it. He has, therefore, the strongest possible personal incentive to conclude further agreements with the Soviet Union which will limit the deployment of MIRV by both parties, lest the United States be faced with the necessity markedly to increase the size and to diversify the deployment of its land-based strategic forces, or, more likely, to accelerate the deployment of the very expensive *Trident* submarine, at a time when rising cost of military manpower is making it difficult to keep general defence expenditure stable, and the demands for other forms of public expenditure are insistent. Despite his achievement in realigning great-power relationships, in achieving a considerable measure of détente with the Soviet Union, his achievements could be undone, both in his own and in the public eye, if the upshot was to put the United States at the mercy of Soviet strategic power, or to make her the weaker bargaining partner in a crisis. And the considerations that scare Nixon would be felt with equal force by any successor except one who reflected a public readiness to see the world's strongest power become of secondary importance in world politics, a change of sentiment of which there are no real signs at present.

It is legitimate to assume that there is a coincidence of interest on the part of the two super-powers to limit the development of MIRV, for in the Soviet Union the sluggishness of its general technological expansion is clearly related to the heavy demands of its strategic programme on scarce skills and resources. But MIRV has ever since its inception presented a baffling problem to those charged with negotiations to control it, in that being a cluster of warheads within the nose-cone or final stage of a standard ICBM, it defies inspection by surveillance satellites or indeed by any means short of taking the missile apart.* But the Soviet Union remains as adamant as it has always been in earlier arms control negotiations in refusing ground inspection on its territory; indeed neither power is prepared to give the other the kind of intimate access to its missile sites that would be required completely to satisfy its partner that it was honouring a self-denial agreement. Consequently, the control of MIRV presents a problem that was not present in the negotiation of the Atmospheric Test Ban Treaty of 1963, for such tests can be monitored by seismic means over long distances, nor in the ABM Treaty of 1972 which can be effectively monitored by national surveillance. It did not arise in the Non-Proliferation Treaty since inspection could be limited to the activities of the non-nuclear powers. It was present, it is true, in the Soviet–American agreement not to use the seabed for emplacement of underwater missiles but this was only a theoretical and not a very interesting strategic option whereas MIRV already exists. The only way in which either power could monitor the activities of the other would be to survey its flight testing of MIRVs, but this is chancy and would give only a partial indication of its later deployments.

The consequence is that President Nixon, who made his reputation as a stern anti-Communist, must now feel that he has little option but to convert the adversary-partner relationship with the Soviet Union, that Kennedy established with the initial Soviet–American arms control agreements of a decade ago, into one in which the element of partnership takes precedence over that of confrontation or competition. The fact that Brezhnev feels much the same compulsions, to which the intractability of the problem of controlling MIRV seems to offer little alternative, increases the plausibility of the argument; the two powers have got to reach a position in which they can trust each other's word, and develop a diplomatic and political intimacy which enables each to convince the other that it is honouring its troth, a level of mutual confidence moreover, that can survive changes of leadership in each country. The grandiose statements of principles which characterized the Summit Meetings of May 1972 and June 1973 are an attempt to feel their way toward such a position of trust.

But this sense that there is now no alternative to trusting each

---

* The assurance with which Mr Schlesinger, the Defense Secretary, spoke on 17 August 1973 of a Soviet breakthrough in the development of a MIRV must rest on traditional sources of intelligence.

other applies only to one level of their relationship, the one most fraught with danger and therefore in one sense the highest. If it is not to have a wholly destablizing effect upon the whole structure of world politics, they must be prepared to honour their commitments or defend their own interests on other planes of interaction than that of strategic confrontation or deterrence. For the Soviet Union the maintenance of large conventional forces presents no insurmountable problems, though as I have suggested in the previous chapter, maintaining forces in both Europe and the Far East represents a general economic burden which she has an incentive to reduce. But for the United States the problem is more acute, partly because of the rising cost of equipment (which the need of increase expenditure in strategic forces may exacerbate), partly because one legacy of Vietnam has been the political necessity of turning from armed forces that were partly volunteer, partly conscript to a wholly volunteer force. In 1972, that is after the effective end of deployment in Vietnam, the US armed forces totalled 2,350,000 men; and in January 1973 President Nixon set a figure of 2,230,000 as the target for volunteer forces. However, by the summer of 1973 there was considerable doubt that such a target could be attained, still less sustained throughout the second half of the decade, especially as the number of eighteen-year-old American males will begin to decline after 1977; to do so might involve levels of remuneration which would again inflate defence expenditure above the 7 per cent of GNP which appears to be the limit of Congressional tolerance. Manpower experts in the Pentagon have suggested that a figure of 2 million may be the best attainable after 1975 and Dr Morris Janowitz, who is a distinguished authority in this field, has proposed 1,750,000 men (about half those under arms in the Soviet Union) as the basis of realistic thinking about the future.[10]

Figures as low as this imply the development of the Nixon doctrine to the point where there would be virtually no substantial forces deployed outside the United States except those committed to NATO in Western Europe, and it is unlikely that these could be maintained at their current level of about 300,000 men. There might, for instance, be virtually no American military presence west of Pearl Harbour; even if these recruiting estimates are too low, the unpopularity of American bases or garrisons in Asia implies a considerable reduction in any case – probably air units only in South Korea, one or two bases in the Ryukus, and three air and naval bases in the Philippines plus one or two ports or airfields in Micronesia. In the Pacific the United States seems likely by the second half of the decade to be broadly in the same strategic position as it was earlier in the twentieth century, that of one great power among several, and no longer in the same position to act the guardian of peace in the Pacific in the sense that she conceived that role for over twenty years after MacArthur's occupation of Japan. This has important implications for the future of her alliance relationship with Japan, but not only Japan, for Taiwan (from which she is now committed to withdraw), South Korea, the Philippines, Thailand, Australia and New Zealand have over the post-war era regarded the United States as the principal guarantor of their security. This she will undoubtedly continue to be in terms of the improbable contingency of nuclear attack. What is now open to question is the political content of these alliances, or the role that she would be prepared to play if the assumption that Sino-Soviet hostility will prevent either mainland power from attempting to exert serious pressure on her Asian allies should prove false; for on their confidence in her partly depends her influence with the mainland powers. There are indications that China would be unhappy at the prospect of total American withdrawal from the Western Pacific. Proposals for the establishment of an American naval presence in the Indian Ocean are being discussed again. But despite the considerable naval power she will continue to deploy in the Pacific, any idea of intervention in Asian guerrilla conflicts would be hotly opposed. Yet the provision of sufficient potential force to maintain a stable adversary-partnership below the level of nuclear threats in East Asia and the Pacific may present itself in a new guise over the long term.

The problem as it presents itself in NATO is familiar and of long standing. Senator Mansfield now probably speaks for a majority of his fellow Senators and a substantial proportion of public opinion in asserting that the post-war era has definitely ended, and in demanding to know why there should still be 'hundreds of thousands of US troops and dependents in Western Europe, most especially Germany, 27 years after the end of the Second World War'.[11] President Nixon has reasserted unceasingly, both in his first and in his second Administrations, the necessity of maintaining an adequate American contribution to countervailing power or deterrence in Europe below the strategic level. But, Watergate apart, if the total size of the American armed forces, most particularly the army, cannot be sustained at the level at which he has set his sights, then to the Mansfield arguments about equity will be added practical arguments about the wisdom of tying up about 30 per cent of an American army that might be no larger than 700,000 men in one overseas area, however strategically significant. In such circumstances a considerable reduction in American forces in Europe will be virtually inevitable, irrespective of whether it is unilateral balanced by Soviet reductions, or part of a multilateral agreement.

Consequently, to the virtual necessity of establishing a relationship of mutual confidence with the Soviet Union in order to prevent MIRV and technological innovation from destabilizing the central strategic balance, has been added the more complex and uphill task of trying to persuade the Russians to lower the level of deployed forces in Europe. As the Vienna negotiations on Mutual Force Reductions have shown, it is a task that is more complex because it involves the concurrence of a group of NATO allies who have not the same motive for achieving an intimate relationship with the Soviet Union as the United States, who are more sceptical that it can be achieved, and who are more vulnerable to Soviet pressure if it cannot. It is a more uphill task in that the Soviet forces serve a different purpose in central Europe than do the American, to maintain Soviet ascendancy in Eastern Europe and to offset German influence there, as well as to protect the Motherland or ensure European stability. It is made doubly difficult by Soviet knowledge that either Congressional pressures or recruiting problems or both are virtually certain to lead to reductions in American forces in Europe during the 1970s whether they make any reciprocal concessions or not.

The end of autarchy

The other contemporary preoccupations of American foreign policy, energy, trade and money, have already been examined in chapter 5. But it is worth giving them a brief second glance to see how they present themselves specifically through American eyes.

The problem of energy elicits a conflict of view, that now runs deep into the American foreign policy debate, between what Zbigniew Brezinski has called 'power realists' and 'planetary humanists'.[12] Both accept the increasing interdependence of the international system, but the former still see the world as dominated by international politics while the latter see it as beset by many common problems which, in addition to that of energy, include the protection of the human environment and the ecology, poverty, population growth and the demands of social justice. An extreme attempt to formulate planetary humanism failed in the hands of Senator McGovern in the 1972 Presidential election but it unquestionably appeals to the strain of idealism in the American national character which in an earlier era showed itself in the support of the churches and their missions, and then became the foundation for the internationalism which sustained the United Nations in its fledgling years, the evolution of functional techniques of international cooperation, the Marshall Plan, and development aid. It is an aspect of a tradition of concern with the problems of mankind as a whole of which the United States may be 'the last best hope' rather than the American national interest which stretches back at least to William Jennings Bryan and through Herbert Hoover, Wendell Wilkie and Adlai Stevenson. It can be dismissed as sentimental, even humbug, and as never having guided the actual policy decisions of the United States any more than Marxism has guided those of the Soviet Union. Yet a national leader who ignores this sense which education and the national tradition inculcate in young Americans that theirs is 'not a country like another', risks also failing to mobilize a broad consensus for a difficult decision or for a policy that must endure for a long period ahead. Kennedy succeeded in eliciting just such a consensus for his ambitious conception of a world order of which the United States would be the main policeman but would not aspire to dominate: it broke in the hands of his successor over the frustration of Vietnam. Nixon's skill in defusing the Vietnam issue and pursuing the conception of a plural world order by seeking détente with both China and the Soviet Union seems to have had the effect of turning the idealist–realist debate away from issues of peace and war or of great-power relations to issues that are more functional in character.

It can be argued that the problems which the United States will confront in maintaining its supplies of energy over the next decade present issues that are weighted heavily in favour of the realists, that Americans, even young ones, are used to warm houses in winter and cool houses in summer, to big cars and bright lights. Moreover, to arguments from personal convenience – the American way of life almost – can be added strategic arguments that as long as the United States remains the core state of a large network of alliances, she must have the oil for her ships, the kerosene for her aircraft, and the gasoline for her tanks and trucks; that her needs override those even of her friends. But, although this may be an argument that appeals to a large section of Middle America, one can detect also a distinct uneasiness, and not just on the part of the young or radical, at a situation in which a nation that comprises only 6 per cent of the human race consumes 33 per cent of its available energy (and the disproportion is growing). Uncomfortable as may be the revolution in personal habits that may be involved in curtailing energy consumption, especially at a time of general inflation (for presumably only drastic increases in its prices will effect such a change), difficult as it may be for Detroit to convert to the production of European or Japanese-sized cars, the prospect of continuous breakdowns in supply, still more of some form of gunboat diplomacy to assure it, is even more distasteful, at any rate to an articulate minority of American opinion. As Professor Carroll Wilson, who is no stump orator but one of those most deeply involved in the development of the American atomic energy programme, has written:

'On any rational look at the production and consumption of energy all over the world, the United States represents not only a statistical discrepancy and target for the role of villian . . ., but a potential disruptive force in almost every market day by day; only if this is brought under control can the United States play any responsible role in the effort that may have to be undertaken within the next decade, or at least by the end of the century – to balance and distribute world energy supplies much more fairly and reasonably than nature or men have ever done to date.'[13]

One must hope, therefore, first for a change in the general American attitude to the use of energy, a change that will have to be largely inspired by American society itself or at best by local leadership, since the national leadership to confront the American people with their true predicament or to inspire modifications in scores of millions of personal habits and preferences may not be forthcoming in time. Greater American autarchy in this field, the acceleration of research and exploration in domestic sources of energy, which President Nixon finally decided to initiate in

July 1973, is likely to be less destabilizing than a quantum jump in American dependence for energy on the outside world.

The trade negotiations present a rather different problem, though one that is related to the energy question in the sense that even if the United States does accelerate its nuclear and other domestic resources of power, it will inevitably be spending increasing sums on oil imports over the next decade and a half. This is a grim prospect when the country's trade balance was in deficit by $6·8 billion in 1972 with even higher deficits in its current and long term capital accounts, and with an overall deficit of $10·2 billion despite a marked retrenchment over 1971 in overseas investment.[14] The recovery of 1973 which is partly a consequence of Japanese forbearance is not necessarily permanent. An observer cannot fail, moreover, to see a certain justice in American complaints about the restrictive practices of her main trading partners, though as I have mentioned the United States is almost equally guilty of violating the letter or spirit of GATT. In particular it would seem to me a tragedy if the Community's somewhat offhand record of developing a preferential bloc in the Mediterranean and Africa – like the creation of the British Empire in a fit of absent-mindedness – cannot be solved by the generalization of preferences, not only in the interest of the United States but also of the developing countries: the American desire to see tariffs eliminated in the industrialized world seems to me inherently reasonable provided the United States is ready to draw the logic of its own argument.

For what is apparent to even a non-expert in this field is that the American position has weakened over the past five years partly because of a cultural lag in American opinion. The United States is a low-cost agricultural producer for reasons partly of skill, partly of climate. She also dominates the world's markets in high-technology projects such as long-range aircraft, computers and many forms of capital equipment. But she is no longer competitive abroad in such consumer goods as cars (except those made by Detroit's overseas subsidiaries) or a whole range of durable household goods either at home and abroad, including small cars. Since this has become apparent, the general reaction has been to press for freer trade in agriculture which is a reasonable objective,* but

* Even though the American position, at least as far as her own interests are concerned, was somewhat weakened by the prohibition on the export of soybeans and other foodstuffs in the summer of 1973.

to nourish protectionist impulses for other industries. What one misses in the American debate is any widespread recognition that if the United States is to remain the core of the Western economic world, whose balance of payments does not continuously complicate the prospect of monetary stability, she must become competitive with Europe and Japan over a wider range of goods than she is at present; to produce toasters and textiles and small cars that can hold their own in the world's markets (she accounts, for instance, for only 1 per cent of OECD trade in shoes and 2 per cent in watches). The high American wage level is often given as a reason for doubting the feasibility of such a change of policy, but the fact is that European and Japanese wage levels are rising to meet the American, and the competition of many of their products is a consequence of efficiency, not low wages. The real reason is, in my view, that for five generations, since her own industrial revolution, her businessmen and labour leaders have had little reason to concentrate on anything but her large and growing domestic market, regarding exports as no more than a bonus. The United States in the 1970s is not unlike Britain in the 1870s, suddenly conscious of the fact that her dominant industrial position is under challenge, as Britain's then was becoming challenged by Germany and the United States itself. This is a question where a change of public attitudes and priorities may be as important as the outcome of any international negotiation. Is the leadership there to produce it? The only alternative might be an artificial division of labour within the industrial world and an agreement on the part of her trading partners to forego certain forms of industry, e.g. aircraft or computers, in the interests of international stability, which would involve serious industrial dislocation locally and the swallowing of much national pride, and so would be very hard to negotiate.

Certainly the American imbalance will not be effectively remedied if one particular delusion is allowed to affect American foreign trade policy. This is that the Soviet Union, Eastern Europe and the centrally planned economies as a whole present a serious alternative outlet for American exports to her principal trading partners, Japan, Europe, Canada and the major countries of the developing world. Quite apart from the diplomatic repercussions of some of the statements of Mr George Shultz, the Secretary of the Treasury, and others, which have implied that the United States is out to beat the Europeans in the game of East–West trade, the fact is that trade with the Communist powers represents only a fraction of American exports, and there is little prospect of balancing it, let alone using it to redress imbalances with Europe or Japan, even though at a much later date and after vast American investment, the Soviet Union may be able to offer oil and natural gas as a *quid pro quo*. No one can challenge the American claim for closer trade relations with the East. The point is that it will solve few of her problems which are those of the structure of the American economy itself and of the attitudes which underlie it. Walter Laqueur has recently pointed out the illusion that prevailed at the end of the Second World War when the US Bureau of Commerce in 1943 estimated that a third of America's post-war exports would go to the Soviet Union, and Eric Johnston, then head of the US Chamber of Commerce, stated in 1944 that 'Russia will be, if not our biggest, our most eager customer'.[15] Brezhnev would like to rekindle this belief but it is an illusion.

On the related issue of monetary reform it seems to me, as a layman, that the American position is more coherent than that of her partners. She welcomed the Community's attempt to create a parity of its diverse currencies, but as that prospect has become more remote and as the shift of vast sums across the exchanges has continued to create anarchy in the world's money markets, her weight has been placed behind a strengthening of the IMF, the expansion of SDRs and the establishment of agreed criteria about parity changes based on the changes in a country's reserve position, a position that can be monitored over a period of time so that changes in par values are not sudden and conspiratorial acts which throw the system into crisis. It is true that such a permanent solution depends on dealing with the 'dollar overhang', the vast store of dollars held by her trading partners, but to solve this is a European and Japanese interest also, and it has recently been suggested that it might be met, that many of these dollars might be repatriated, by a marked increase in foreign investment in American companies whose shares have become relatively cheaper with the successive devaluations of the dollar.[16] The United States has a desire, as well as a strong incentive, to restore order to the monetary field, for the dollar cannot cease overnight to be the chief international currency, and if she is prepared to honour a new agreement that places obligations as severe on her as on her partners, then, in a period when they have come to fear her tendency to unilateral action in other fields, this may be an opportunity not to be neglected.*

The failure of American diplomacy

There remain three broader questions to be asked about the American position in the world. The first concerns the relationship between the American public and its leadership; the second the relations between the United States and her principal allies; the third her relationship with her smaller allies and to the developing world.

It is no derogation of President Nixon's real achievements, the courage needed to send Henry Kissinger to Peking in 1971 and to go himself in 1972, the tough, clear-headed bargaining that has characterized the American approach to the SALT negotiations, Kissinger's patience and energy in pursuing a peace settlement in Vietnam, to say that they were taking advantage of a unique opportunity or series of opportunities. China's proffered olive branch of 1969, the pressures on Brezhnev to stabilize the arms race and to get American food and technology, the war-weariness of Hanoi were opportunities that a man not committed to the positions of the Kennedy–Johnson years could hardly fail to perceive. But it would be mistaken to argue from Nixon's adroit seizure of these opportunities, that an American Administration can pursue wholly flexible policies designed merely to protect or promote its conception of the American interest, one of no permanent friends or adversaries. The American policy debate is the most open in the world; its press really is a fourth estate; the third and second estates, the House and Senate, have an entrenched role in the formulation of a large area of foreign policy; and its society is the most permeable in the world in its hospitality to the views of foreigners. Even more important, the fact that the United States is to a significant degree an ideological society, however much its achievements may fall short of its aspirations, imposes upon the President the restriction not only of being, for the most part, unable to indulge in sudden shifts of attitudes or alignments, but of having to formulate policies that elicit the basic idealism of articulate American opinion, even though the leadership of that

* The aspect of the American position which her partners in the Group of Twenty find unacceptable, however, is that countries in chronic surplus should have the 'discipline' of import surcharges imposed on them by their partners.

opinion may change from time to time, as it appears at present to have moved out of the hands of the East Coast educated class. Henry Kissinger once wrote an excellent essay on Bismarck, who is clearly one of his heroes, but Nixon is not a Hohenzollern prince and his Secretary of State enjoys little of Bismarck's domestic freedom of action. All this might seem a statement of the obvious had not the Watergate scandal revealed the existence of men around President Nixon who patently despised public opinion and its representatives in both houses of Congress, and who conceived it their sole duty to protect their boss from outside advice and contact. I will not dwell on Watergate whose final adjudication is not clear as I write, for it is primarily an American tragedy; there is no pleasure to be gained from it for either the friends or adversaries of the United States, for it seems certain to weaken the Administration's hand in relation to Congressional or sectional pressures in the multiplicity of multilateral negotiations from which a successor to the post-war international order will emerge. His diminished public standing might also encourage the President into external initiatives that are popular rather than wise. But I must return later to the question of American decision-making for this is crucial not only to the domestic authority of the President, but to the basic structure of contemporary international politics.

Although two successive Presidents have over the past ten years given only secondary attention to the country's principal alliances, one preoccupied with fighting a hopeless war, the other with establishing a new basis of relations with old adversaries, nothing fundamental or fatal has occurred to undermine the European–American or the Japanese–American relationships. A mutual perception that an interdependent economic and security relationship is essential to the security and wellbeing of both is still anchored in the mind of all but the hoariest Gaullist, the most radical young Japanese or the most disillusioned and introverted American environmentalist. It is interesting that a recent book by a distinguished American political scientist which makes a case for a total withdrawal of American forces and political commitments from Asia and elsewhere, rejects the case for isolationism in relation to Europe.[17]

It is best to deal first with the European relationship which has always been a difficult one to sustain in terms of confidence and common action. For one thing, however often American or

European political leaders may speak of European–American partnership, they are not partners in the sense that Germany and Austro–Hungary or even Britain and France were partners in the years before 1914, nor will they be in the foreseeable future. The United States is an enormous unitary state exerting power and influence of every kind while the European Community at present 'is no more than an economic animal and a sketch of one at that – a customs union, a managed farm market, and little else',[18] and its individual countries exert only limited political, and even more limited strategic, influence in the world – though this is not the same thing as saying that their interests are purely regional. More-over, on political and security questions they are bound to the United States in a multilateral relationship, and will continue to be, so long as NATO lasts, even if the kind of functional European cooperation on defence production and logistics that I and others have sketched (and to which I will return in the next chapter) comes into being. Yet on economic and monetary questions the United States has lost its hegemonial position and feels threatened by and competitive with Europe. The consequence is a sense of mutual impotence and suspicion that has led to a transatlantic slanging match.

A certain degree of mutual tension is inevitable in a relationship of this kind. In the later 1950s and through much of the 1960s there was a continuous undercurrent of concern in Europe that the United States would become so deeply involved in the politics of Asia that it would either cease to promote and protect the interests of Europe or else land the Europeans in an Asian war. That fear has gone and another has returned, namely that the United States is developing a special relationship with the Soviet Union from which some package deal that affects Europe's vital interests may emerge. On the American side patience has run out with the pro-tectionist devices that were once accepted as necessary to build up the European Community, and this is accentuated by a belief that Europe is building a system of preferences in the Mediterranean area and in Africa, which is either the basis for a future political sphere of influence, or else just an attempt 'to take the cash and let the credit go, nor heed the rumble of a distant drum'. Europeans see the United States as Macchiavellian, the Americans see the Europeans as get-rich-quick men; it is an exact reversal of his-torical suspicions and attitudes.

Now there appears to be substance in both these accusations.

Every serious person in Europe admires the way in which President Nixon with the assistance of Henry Kissinger has altered the whole course of American foreign policy; no one wishes to see the United States return to a wholly adversary relationship with the Soviet Union: SALT One was a triumph of hard bargaining of which European governments were kept reasonably well informed. Moreover, in its more considered statements the Nixon Administration has made quite clear its continuing sense of commitment to its allies and the priority it gives to its relations with them. Take for example the description of Soviet–American relations from the President's 1972 *Foreign Policy Report*: 'We are ideological adversaries, and will remain so. We are political and military competitors, and neither can be indifferent to advances by the other in either field. We each stand at the head of a group of countries whose association we value and are not prepared to sacrifice to an improvement in Soviet–American relations.'

But there was a grinding of teeth in every European chancellery at their apparently deliberate deception about Kissinger's visit to China in July 1971, at the high-flown Declarations of Principles that Nixon and Brezhnev signed in May 1972 and June 1973, at the way in which the United States unilaterally decided to separate negotiation on MBFR from the European Security Conference, and in general with the increasing unilateralism of American diplomacy – at what has been called American Gaullism. Yet in the years immediately ahead lie three East–West negotiations, SALT Two (which may involve the NATO allies to an extent that SALT One did not),* CSCE and MBFR each of which necessitates very careful coordination of allied positions if they are to achieve any results. In the MBFR negotiations in particular the Russians have tried to bilateralize a multilateral organization, and it has been difficult for the United States to avoid the temptation to respond.

The decline in the confidence and cordiality of Japanese–American relations is even more marked than in the case of Western Europe. There are a number of reasons for this: American economic relations with Japan, with whom she runs a heavy trade deficit, are under more immediate strain than with Europe, though Europe being a larger market is more important to the United

---

* This derives partly from Soviet insistence on including FBS (Forward Based Systems) – many of which use aircraft – in the hands of NATO allies, and possibly the British and French nuclear forces) in any reciprocal bargain.

States in this respect; there are not the same amount of cultural and personal links as with Europe, the United States and Japan are much more foreign to each other as cultures and societies than the United States and Europe; and there is a risk that Sinophilia and Japanophobia may become two sides of the same coin again. The Japanese–American alliance is a bilateral one which is in many ways more difficult to manage than a multilateral one such as the Atlantic Alliance in its present form; and the fact that Japan is even more dependent than Europe on the American nuclear strategic guarantee while being also a fiercer competitor in the American domestic consumer market compounds this difficulty.

Nevertheless, the Nixon Administration's relations with Japan have been characterized by what gardeners call black fingers, the opposite of green ones; almost every major initiative it has taken has exhibited, by bad luck or bad management, a minimal concern for Japanese susceptibilities. The lack of consultation on the Kissinger visit to Peking in July 1971 or on the imposition of a domestic surcharge and the suspension of dollar convertibility a month later, the President's failure to make a visit to Tokyo, though he has travelled extensively to other capitals, the cancellation of the Emperor's visit to the United States are cases in point. Henry Kissinger's attempt in his speech of 23 April 1973 to drag Japan by the heels into an attempt to formulate a new conception of European–American relations was similarly maladroit.[19]

Indeed this speech with its emphasis on the evolution of 'a new Atlantic charter setting the goals for the future – a blueprint that ... creates for the Atlantic nations a new relationship in whose progress Japan can share' illustrates one of the principal weaknesses of the current American approach to foreign policy.[20] Kissinger is rightly animated by a fear that relations between the United States and her allies may get bogged down in the details of the impending trade, money and security negotiations, and so by the necessity to rekindle a more imaginative vision of their common future than the communiqués of individual meetings with heads of governments or of expert negotiators tend to produce. Hence his reference to a new Atlantic Charter (despite the vacuity of the original one signed by Roosevelt and Churchill at Placentia Bay in 1941) and his emphasis on fresh summit meetings to produce a new definition of 'western' objectives.

One point to be made in passing is that the emphasis of this speech, the only significant one on allied relationships in what was billed as 'Year of Europe', on 'the West', was in conflict with the President's earlier statements about the emergence of a five-sided balance of power. But too much should not be made of this: statesmen often float a *balloon d'essai* which they are entitled to forget when they see it punctured. And Henry Kissinger went on to restate the American fidelity to its alliance commitments, in terms no stronger, it is true, than those used by other officials but clearly carrying the direct mandate of his President.

' – We will continue to support European unity. Based on the principles of partnership, we will make concessions to its further growth. We will expect to be met in a spirit of reciprocity.

' – We will not disengage from our solemn commitments to our allies. We will maintain our forces and not withdraw from Europe unilaterally. In turn, we expect from each ally a fair share of the common effort for the common defence.

' – We shall continue to pursue the relaxation of tensions with our adversaries on the basis of concrete negotiations in the common interest. We welcome the participation of our friends in a constructive East–West dialogue.

' – We will never consciously injure the interests of our friends in Europe or in Asia. We expect in return that their policies will take seriously our interests and our responsibilities.

' – We are prepared to work cooperatively on new common problems we face. Energy, for example, raises the challenging issues of assurance of supply, impact of oil revenue on international currency stability, the nature of common political and strategic interests and long-range relations of oil-consuming to oil-producing countries. This could be an area of competition; it should be an area of collaboration.

' – Just as Europe's autonomy is not an end in itself, so the Atlantic community cannot be an exclusive club. Japan must be a principal partner in our common enterprise.'[21]

If it is really the case that the United States is prepared to maintain this degree of emphasis on its alliance relationships, if it is really prepared to confront the responsibilities of remaining the core power of a wide system of alliances and the mainstay of a great many non-aligned powers as well, then certain consequences follow. The first is that declarations of principle are not enough, however many presidents and prime ministers may make them, and that a significant change must take place in the way in which the Administration deals with its allies on day-to-day issues, particularly if the major allies are to be encouraged, as Kissinger has suggested elsewhere, to develop their own policies and initiatives in relation to the mainland powers, Eastern Europe or the developing world. If Washington is to remain the centre of the western system, if the political headquarters of the West is to remain in Washington, rather than be divided between it, Brussels and Tokyo, then the present techniques of American diplomacy, policy and decision making must be overhauled. It has never been easy even for allied governments to have a successful relationship with the United States, and in so far as it has been possible, Washington is the only place where it can be pursued. With the best will in the world she cannot make effective use of her own diplomatists or of multilateral institutions like the NATO Council or OECD by reason of the fact that the process of in-fighting, among the great departments in Washington or between the two ends of Pennsylvania Avenue, whereby American policy is evolved, is so complex that American ambassadors overseas rapidly lose their effectiveness as an instrument for the influential communication of the views of other governments.* Governments, allied and adversary, have recognized this for many years, and have maintained strong embassies in Washington. (The Soviet Union has kept its ablest diplomat, Mr Anatol Dobrynin, there for over twelve years.)

Moreover, from the mid-1950s onwards successive American Administrations, recognizing this fact, devised instruments to lend a helping hand. The State Department until 1968 had the characteristics of a normal foreign office though its influence in the policy-making process varied; its Policy Planning Staff as well as its regional bureaux were a recognized channel of communication with governments and influential individuals; the Office of International Security Affairs in the Pentagon, founded in the late 1950s, enabled allied governments to keep in touch with the

---

* This happens particularly soon if their distinction is merely their ability to contribute to political campaign funds, but has also been true of professionals or distinguished academics: the failure of Kennan, Bohlen, Galbraith or Reischauer to have any effective influence from Moscow, Paris, Delhi or Tokyo on the policy of their government contrasts with the European tradition, with the careers of, say, Oliver Franks, Harold Caccia, David Ormsby Gore in Washington or Rene Massigli or Hans Herwath in London.

development of military and strategic policy; the Arms Control and Disarmament Agency enabled them to have a dialogue on the subjects with which it dealt. Essentially allied governments fought their policy battles informally with the United States in Washington, reached concordats during the visits of their foreign or prime ministers, and their outcome was then reflected in the formal instructions given to the representatives of both parties in the NATO Council, in OECD, the IMF, and other multilateral bodies. This did not, of course, prevent crises in alliance relations, over *Skybolt* with Britain in 1963 (which was partly a classic mix-up between ISA, the Joint Chiefs of Staff, and Whitehall), for instance, nor Adenauer's increasing suspicion of Kennedy's intentions (for which his own embassy in Washington was partly responsible) nor de Gaulle's contention that Washington should not be the headquarters of the alliance. But I think it is fair to say that without implicit recognition of this fact, that Washington was the effective centre of the alliance, it would have been impossible to work out the contingency plans in 1958 to 1961 which gave the major allies (including France) confidence that they could face a Soviet *promenade militaire* over Berlin. It was an untidy system but in dealing with a country that is not only the world's most powerful state but one possessed, for a mixture of constitutional and behavioural reasons, of the most complex decision-making process since Byzantium, it was the best available.

Gradually this system began to erode in the mid-1960s as far as the European allies were concerned, as Lyndon Johnson, McNamara and Rusk became increasingly preoccupied with Vietnam (involving for instance the redeployment of 50,000 American troops from Europe in 1966–7 without consultation). But the mechanisms for sustaining allied confidence remained and in some cases, on strategic planning for instance, were strengthened. But with the Nixon Administration a structure of government that had hitherto been organized in such a way as to keep the American decision-making process permeable and intelligible to other governments, became replaced by one designed primarily for the formulation of American national policy only, the National Security Council system, dominated by the White House with tentacular ramifications in other departments. By its nature, the fact that it is a system of inner government within the bureaucracy, it is avowedly impenetable to allied governments. ISA has ceased to have any influence, the Arms Control Agency has been partly disbanded, and only certain portions of the State Department that are related to the NSC system have much relationship with or knowledge of the formulation of high policy; the rest of it is concerned with areas that are of only secondary importance to United States policy. More and more of the discussion that precedes the evolution of an American position in the international field has become concentrated in the White House, to which allied embassies in Washington – especially those of smaller countries – have no regular right of access, with the consequence that they have come to feel increasingly ignorant of what is in the mind of the Administration. Consequently when Henry Kissinger spoke of 'a dramatic change in bilateral relations between the US and the USSR', what should have been a source of comfort was clouded with an aura of collusion.

This is not simply an aspect of the fact that President Nixon is a man whose political fortunes have led him to trust few people but himself, nor of the fact that Henry Kissinger is a man of great skill as a diplomatic operator but who at the same time does not work easily with colleagues. It is partly a consequence of the disappearance, through the passage of time and the bitter disputes of the Vietnam years, of the old foreign-policy establishment that emerged after the war, who manned the key jobs in the different departments and knew and trusted each other, or their counterparts in other governments. It is partly an aspect of the fact that, since 1969, the agenda of American external business, SALT One and the evolution of more normal relations with the Soviet Union, the opening of relations with China, and the ending of the Vietnam War, has been an extremely demanding one.

But a question remains which no amount of declarations or summits can dispose of: has there been a permanent change in the American approach to the making of Western policy as a whole? Does Washington, as part of its modification of the American position as the trustee of world order, now simply envisage itself as one Western actor among several, bargaining with its allies by methods more stringent than those it uses with adversaries, so that in Raymond Aron's words 'it appears as if the United States had as adversaries, if not as enemies, allies only'.[22] If this is not the case, is it prepared to reconstitute old or discover new techniques of consultation on the development of both American and allied policy? American policy statements of recent years point in both directions: the demands of Mr Connally and his successors

at the US Treasury suggest the former; the general approach of
the President's Foreign Policy reports of 1972 and 1973, namely
that the structure of world politics is now one in which the United
States expects its allies to take initiatives of their own in East–West
diplomacy, without losing their intimacy with the United States,
points to the second.

Henry Kissinger is now the Secretary of State, but what gave
the assurances I have quoted a mixed reception in Europe was an
earlier phrase in his Atlantic Charter speech: 'The political,
military and economic issues in Atlantic relations are linked by
reality, not by our choice nor for the tactical purpose of trading one
off against the other.' It has been clear for some time that this is
the American position (though on at least two occasions between
the end of 1971 and the spring of 1972 the White House and the
State Department spoke with different voices on the subject). In
fact it was acknowledged five months before Kissinger's speech
when Dr Ralf Dahrendorf of the European Commission said at a
meeting in Brussels in November 1972, that 'since we are not all
deaf, we have also realized that, in developing this dialogue, the
United States will no longer be prepared to deal with sectors of
policy-making separately'.[23] And though there has been grumbling
in Europe at this 'linkage', it is accepted by most Europeans as
inevitable: the United States cannot be expected to devote the
same level of military resources to NATO or diplomatic resources
to maintaining a unified position in negotiations with the East or
the developing world, if the Community is not prepared to tackle
the impediments which both its tariff and its non-tariff barriers
create for an expansion of Atlantic trade (provided, of course, that
the United States is prepared to consider the impediments that its
own legislation have created) or if the Community is not prepared
to generalize some of its preferential arrangements with EFTA,
and the Mediterranean and African countries with whom it has
various treaties of association. The case is somewhat different as
regards Japan because although protectionism is a more serious
difficulty there and the American balance of trade adverse with
Japan to an extent that it is not with Europe, there is not the same
close interrelationship between security and trade negotiations at
present in the Far East as in Europe. Similarly, a European
monetary policy that simply concentrated on developing and
maintaining stability within Europe itself with no relation to the
health of the dollar could not only make the trade negotiations

more difficult but would directly affect the cost of the American contribution to European security.

The weakness in the doctrine of 'linkage' – in the assertion that trade, money and security are all one 'ball of wax' – is that the means of reviving confidence in the European–American relationship are different in the three fields. As Ian Smart has pointed out, '. . . an effort to negotiate a comprehensive plan, covering all sets of interconnected issues, is vulnerable to failure to resolve any of them'.[24] For in the trade field, a strong matrix for negotiation still exists in GATT which no one wishes to abrogate though it may need revision, and within that matrix the Community as a community, the United States, Japan, Canada and other countries can conduct a kind of economic peace conference. On monetary relations, although a multilateral framework, provided by the IMF or the Group of Twenty exists, there was not the same sense of urgency until oil prices shot up. Even today the prospect of conducting a successful multilateral conference against a formal deadline may be less promising than in the trade field, especially as monetary reform is linked to prospects in trade patterns. Nevertheless, the difficulties are not insurmountable and there are incentives on all sides to reach an eventual concordat.

On security and diplomatic questions the situation is quite different, not only because the United States still disposes of much greater relative strength than in the other two fields, not only because as yet she possesses no single European partner with whom to conduct a dialogue, but also because they involve not just intra-Western bargaining but also three current negotiations with the East, one of which is purely Soviet–American and in all of which it is a Soviet interest to divide Europe from the United States. Moreover, we have to think beyond the immediate future. Nothing solid can be built on the accident of current personalities, such as Kissinger's personal skill as a diplomatic operator. Linkage works both ways and if the trade and monetary negotiations are to succeed on the basis of mutual concessions, it is essential to recreate an atmosphere of mutual political confidence that will survive into the Presidency of a Connally, a Kennedy, a Percy and beyond. Otherwise, as Miram Camps puts it: 'The danger is not so much that a situation will be created which invites Soviet military probes as that the transatlantic confidence that is essential for a successful policy of détente will be eroded.'[25]

If both the Europeans and the Americans wish to pursue the

reorganization of the political aspect of the Atlantic relationship on a broad front, they are faced with a choice of three alternatives. (I deal with the military aspect in the next chapter.) The first is to enhance the importance of the NATO Council, so that it becomes what the Pearson–Martino–Lange report of 1957 suggested that it should, namely the central focus of Western diplomatic consultation and coordination, not merely on questions of the defence of Europe but in negotiations with the Soviet Union and Eastern Europe, on problems where European and American interests are equally involved such as the Mediterranean, the Middle East, Africa, the Indian Ocean, and on functional problems such as energy. President Nixon's request to NATO in 1970 to concern itself with environmental questions was a modest and not very successful step in this direction. In parallel, greater emphasis could be placed on OECD, as the economic cabinet of the developed powers. The second course is for the United States to behave towards the European Community on such questions as if it were more politically developed than it is, and by thus acting as *demandeur* to accelerate its emergence as a fully fledged political actor.[26] The third course is to refashion the techniques that made it possible for Washington to act as the political clearing house of a multilateral system of alliances, many of which have been rather carelessly dismantled in recent years.

The first course seems at this stage to offer little promise; NATO is a very large alliance; it contains countries like Portugal whose association is a positive disadvantage in discussing the broader themes of world politics. France is at present only an observer; NATO has never had a Secretary-General who has acquired the initiative of a Mansholt or a Hammarskjöld; and there are few signs that, despite the occasional appointment of able men as American ambassadors to the NATO Council, its deliberations have any significant influence on the policy-making process in Washington during its formative stages (even though it may be a useful means of keeping its allies informed of what American policy is once it is decided upon; in this latter function the Nixon Administration has been scrupulous).

The prospect of progress seems to lie down the other two avenues, namely of encouraging the political mechanisms of the Community as rapidly as possible so that a more powerful dialogue occurs between Community Europe and the United States,* while

* This does not necessarily require some new form of European-American

at the same time returning to a less conspiratorial method of policy-making in Washington. Without the latter reform, the linkage of trade, monetary and security issues may backfire on the United States in the sense that diminishing European political confidence makes it harder to achieve compromises in the trade and monetary fields.

I agree with Karl Kaiser (and Henry Kissinger) that 'since the problems are fundamental they cannot be settled by a technical approach but require a thorough assessment and policies that look beyond the immediate future'.[27] My point is that sporadic summitry and windy declarations of principles will not produce the framework that makes the alignment of perspectives or its maintenance possible, for it involves adjustments in the way in which Brussels, London, Paris, Bonn and a number of other capitals go about their day-to-day business. But of all the capitals it is in Washington that the machinery for conducting complex multinational diplomacy is in greatest disarray.

One footnote should be added to this question. The fact that Japan has become almost as important an economic partner of the United States as the European Community, the delicacy of great-power relations in East Asia, and a guilty conscience at the American neglect of Americo-Japanese relations, has led to discussion of 'trilateralism', of the development in new techniques of consultation between the American, Japanese and European governments.[28] This may be of value: though the overlap in European and Japanese interests is not extensive it exists in questions such as energy; it is important to mitigate the tensions caused by the import of Japanese exports to the European consumer market; together they may be able both to explore new avenues of mutual cooperation and also play a more weighty role in influencing these aspects of American policy that affect all three partners. But trilateralism is not a solution in itself, for it ignores the fact that the United States is allied to forty-four countries, not fifteen, and has growing relations with countries like Iran, Saudi Arabia and Brazil, let alone Canada, Australia, New Zealand,

---

council. At this stage it requires that European embassies in Washington know that they are reflecting a Community viewpoint in their dealings with the various departments of the Administration, and that foreign ministers and heads of state explicitly and with knowledge speak in the name of the Community when they visit Washington. Both processes would be assisted by the advances in European political, industrial and defence cooperation that I have dealt with in the next chapter.

Indonesia, Pakistan, Israel and others, which she cannot sacrifice to the interests purely of her main industrial partners. Unless she deliberately rejects the achievements of a whole generation, she must remain the hub of a great arc of international politics of which Europe and Japan are only the most important sectors. In the developing world, moreover, too close an affiliation of the United States, Japan and Europe assumes the same overtones of collusion that Soviet–American intimacy arouses in the developed world and in China. What is needed is a healthy dose of the internationalism that animated American foreign policy in the immediate post-war years. For what is at issue is a much more far-reaching reform of American diplomatic practice than just forming new special relationships. It involves the reconstitution of the State Department as an effective foreign office, a preference for experienced men over merely rich ambassadors, restoration of the morale of a largely demoralized foreign service, and the evolution of more professional and orderly conduct of a government whose responsibilities are by no means contracting.

How empires fall

I first visited Washington in the years of the New Deal and have seen it undergo profound changes, of size, atmosphere and responsibility. The black McCarthy years were as different from the euphoric atmosphere of the mid-1930s as the confidence of the Kennedy years was different from the doubts and recriminations of recent years. But there has been one consistent thread throughout this whole epoch, the increasing power of the President at the expense of his Cabinet, his party, Congress and indeed of the people. Many writers have commented on the almost monarchical position of modern presidents; his personal staff is 500 strong, of which the National Security Council accounts for 100, quite apart from the Executive Office of the President which numbers four and a half thousand officials and includes such key agencies as the Bureau of Management and Budgets. As a British student of the American system has noted recently, 'Where policy-making is concerned the President is more than ever before autonomous, able to get his own information, free to consult, free to ignore, free to annex, as it were, to the White House whatever segment of the huge administration he desires to honour with his personal attention.'[29] That such a position of Presidential dominance has advantages, especially in a crisis, no one would deny. The realignment of American policy on China might have been difficult to manage if pursued through departmental channels; Henry Kissinger's firm control of all aspects of the SALT negotiations, including his personal dealings with Dobrynin, when the delegations in Vienna and Helsinki became deadlocked, was probably an advantage.

But over the long term it makes for neither external nor internal confidence in the government of the United States when so much more power and discretion is in the hands of one elected official than he can possibly wield effectively, however hard he works. This centralization and personalization of authority, which is in marked contrast not only with parliamentary and cabinet systems of government (for talk of prime ministers becoming presidential figures ignores the real difference between individual responsibility to the nation and corporate responsibility to parliament) but also with the collective leadership systems of the Soviet Union and China. Presidential dominance is often justified by pejorative references to the second-rate quality of 'the bureaucracy' in Washington which, it is true, is more noted for its size than anything else. The problem was to a certain extent masked for much of the post-war era by the ability of the lawyers, bankers and academics who were prepared to serve in its key jobs. But the dissolution and discrediting of the old Establishment by reason of the mistakes of the 1960s makes it no longer possible to ignore the disagreeable fact that the United States does not have an executive bureaucracy of a quality that measures up not only to its own needs but to those of other nations, adversary or friends alike. The issues that confront us in the ensuing decade are of an order of complexity, twining as they do a number of strands which it has hitherto been possible to keep separate, that cannot be solved by a series of *tours de force*. For one thing, there are few Kissingers and it is essential that there be no more Ehrlichmans. The reconciliation of the different views and interests of the great departments, State, Defense, CIA, Treasury, Commerce, as well as those like Agriculture and Interior that are increasingly involved in foreign policy or affected by the external world, has been attempted either by pitting them against each other as Roosevelt and Kennedy tended to do, or letting them fight out issues among themselves without leadership as Eisenhower did, or operating above their heads as Nixon has done. No modern President has done more than toy with the fundamental problems of administrative and executive reform in Washington. And the European complaint that the United States government is very ill organized to participate in the wide agenda of multilateral diplomacy that lies ahead is unfortunately fully justified.

In the mood of chagrin and frustration which must clearly be President Nixon's today, one great service he could render his country and the world would be to capitalize on the desire of the younger generation of Americans for public service in order to launch a thorough and dynamic reform of both the structure of executive government and the quality of its entrants and members, in the knowledge that able people will not make public service their life's career unless they are eventually going to wield proper influence on policy. (At present, the only Americans who commit their lives to the public service and reach positions of great influence are professional military men, and many American decisions are explained by this fact.) Unfortunately, the fact that Nixon is a 'loner' makes it unlikely that he will give this high priority, and we may have to wait both for a new man and for a sharper public sense that an arbitrary monarch at the head of a dim bureaucracy was the situation at the fall of the Roman, the Spanish, the Hapsburg and the Russian empires.

What I am suggesting is not a fundamental process of constitutional amendment or reform, although, as the United States approaches the bicentary of the founding of the Republic, a constitution evolved for a small group of states whose writ ran across no more than a third of their own continent, might repay scrutiny in the wholly changed conditions, external and internal, of today. What is immediately at issue is whether the United States can modify and modernize attitudes to decision making and techniques of diplomacy and administration that are more suited to a small, fifteenth-century Italian principality than that of the most articulate and still the most influential state in modern history.

In a useful study of the diplomatic history of a bygone age, Henry Kissinger committed himself to the judgement that 'The spirit of policy and that of bureaucracy are diametrically opposed. The essence of policy is its contingency; its success depends on the correctness of an estimate which is in part conjectural. . . . The effort to administer politically leads to total irresponsibility, because bureaucracies are designed to execute not to conceive.'[30] Yet ten years later he wrote, 'A system which requires a great man in each generation sets itself an almost insurmountable challenge, if only because a great man tends to stunt the emergence of strong personalities.'[31] Now that he is in charge of the Great Seal of the United States he will have to find a reconciliation of these two largely conflicting views.

8

The Promise and Limitations of Europe

The end of provincialism

No geographical term is used more loosely, or has more diverse political connotations, than 'Europe'. For some it stretches from the Urals, for others from the Elbe. There are twenty-nine sovereign states (nearly a quarter of the total membership of the United Nations) who answer to the name of European. For the past generation it has been divided into two antithetical political sub-systems, and a growing degree of contact and business between Eastern and Western Europe has not eliminated the difference. Although more than a third of the European states belong neither to the Warsaw Pact or to NATO, the interests of say Cyprus and Sweden, Austria and Ireland are so different that they form no coherent non-aligned group in European relationships. And, as I have emphasized earlier, there is no symmetry between the position of the two blocs. The Warsaw Pact and COMECON are the security and economic organs of an imperial system. Thirteen of the Western and Southern European countries belong to a multilateral security organization, NATO, which is still largely dominated by a North American power, while nine of them form an Economic Community which is now to a certain extent in an adversary relationship with it on trade and could become an adversary on energy problems. Only one organization, apart from the UN itself (which has, however, played no role in European politics and conflict since the later 1940s), attempts to serve the interests of both Europes, the Economic Commission for Europe, and this has been confined to an analytic role only for many years.

So any consideration of the effective ending of the postwar era in 'Europe' raises a number of different questions. To what form of Community have the nine countries of Western Europe committed themselves and what are its limitations? Has it the makings of another super-power, as some European and some American writers and politicians have tended to suggest? This must now be one's starting-point because it not only comprises the wealthiest European countries, other than the Soviet Union, but those with the greatest autonomy. Is it likely to develop into more than an economic union or extend the scope of communal action to fields not envisaged when the Treaty of Rome was signed? If West European unity was a product of the Cold War will the one survive the demise of the other? To what extent is the Community the master of its own destiny? How is its enlargement likely to affect its relations with the United States, hitherto its strategic guarantor? If the prospect of military conflict in Europe is receding, has the need for such guarantees receded also? If the Soviet Union's objective of breaking it up has been modified, to what extent can the Community negotiate its own *modus vivendi* with the Soviet Union and the Eastern European states? If it can, are pan-European institutions or systems of collaboration now close enough to our horizon to merit serious study and negotiation, and, if so, in what fields? What role should the European Community play on a wider stage, in the developing world, or in relation to far away countries like Japan or China? Can it make a positive contribution to a new world order or will it be doing well if it can protect its own interests?

A scholar of comprehensive learning using a long time perspective, a Toynbee or a Myrdal, might well choose another starting-point for a discussion of Europe and its future place in the international system than the Community. Someone who has been asked to assess the political interactions of the immediate past, and the way in which they may affect the foreseeable future, feels compelled to concentrate first on the Community because it appears to be the most dynamic focus of change both within Europe and in Europe's relations with the rest of the world. It is significant, however, that ten years ago he would have started with the Atlantic Alliance.

The situation of the European Community, regarded either as a series of central institutions or as a group of states is now very different from what it was during the decade or so after its expansion in 1958 from a Coal and Steel Community into a generalized system of free trade and economic cooperation. In the first place there is the fact of enlargement itself, which involves more than technical problems of national and institutional adjustment. It also involves the adjustment of its focus of interest to embrace not only a third major industrial power, Britain, but also three countries whose external links and interests are somewhat different, and, in some respects wider, than those of the original Six. But this has happened, in the second place, at a time when the nature and the agenda of international and transnational politics are changing rapidly. So to the problems created by enlargement has been added the Community's need to develop common positions in formal negotiations with the Warsaw Pact countries in the European Conference on Security and Cooperation, on force reductions and on trade; with the United States on trade, monetary and security relationships; and with Japan and the developing world on trade. Third, enlargement has coincided with the appearance of new problems on the agenda of all the industrial states and inevitably therefore on the agenda of European cooperation, such as the control of the environment (where no serious conflicts of interest may arise) and on energy supplies where the position of the various members of the Community may differ considerably.

Andrew Shonfield has accurately characterized the atmosphere of what now seems like a bygone age:

'In the early days of the European Common Market, the Six managed to achieve a kind of illusion of privacy within the international system; they treated the often quite profound effects which the arrangements that they made with one another had on the rest of the world as if they were subsidiary matters, of no particular concern to them. They behaved for much of the time rather as though they were living inside a charmed circle bounded entirely by their own problems and preoccupations. The special circumstances of the later post-war period, when Europe finally withdrew from empire and experienced the longest uninterrupted run of prosperity ever, based on cultivating its own garden, certainly helped. The forward march of American world power which accompanied the European withdrawal was another factor. The Europeans acquired a sure military defence through the American nuclear umbrella; and American power, abetted to a diminishing extent by the British, supplied sufficient security for the movement of world trade to guarantee Europe's requirements of vital raw materials like oil. At the same time the American dollar provided an extremely effective international medium of exchange and a common reserve currency for the Europeans. Why should the countries forming the European Community have cared very much about what happened in the world beyond Western Europe?'[1]

It was in this atmosphere that France, from whose inspiration and initiatives the Community originally derived, felt able, under de Gaulle, to challenge the growth and authority of Community institutions, culminating in the crisis of 1965, when he nearly broke it up. He failed, but the difference between the French official conception of the Community as a series of specific and limited contractual relationships between governments, and that of its original architects and of the other governments who had seen the Treaty of Rome as the basis of an eventual United States of Europe, has only gradually been modified. The consequence is that, though many of the foundations of a single coherent economic system have been laid, other large areas of policy such as monetary cooperation, let alone the evolution of common foreign policy, have been tackled only recently, and largely because 'the illusion of privacy' has been dispelled by developments outside Europe's control. What might have been considered ten years ago (and actually was by President Kennedy and his associates) as the historical grand design of the later twentieth century, a United States of Europe evolving in close association with its counterpart across the Atlantic, foundered on de Gaulle's personal opposition both to the cession of state power and to the Community's enlargement. In other words, by the time the United States in 1970 was apparently ready to accord greater political initiative to her allies, the European Community was not yet in a position to accept much more than that fraction of it that concerned its own immediate economic interests. It still primarily is a supermarket, and there are now few people in Europe who believe that the Community of the 1970s either has the will or can develop the means to become either a super-power, in the Soviet or American sense, or even a great power in the sense that China is one, a country that can stand alone without allies.

For all that Community Europe disposes of a combined national income of $700 billion, two-thirds that of the United States and nearly double that of the Soviet Union, and accounts for a third of world trade, it does not dominate the international economic order. For all that it contains two nuclear powers and maintains over two million men under arms, it remains an area of high strategic vulnerability. Even if its present leaders did cherish high ambitions for European autonomy of influence in crude power terms, of the Community acting in every sense as a balancing agent in the relations of the two existing super-powers, as Chou En-lai has suggested to recent European visitors it should, the experiment is too young for them to nurse any illusion that the development of a single European polity or state is attainable in their own life times. The Community aspires to achieve and in some fields has achieved, *gesellschaft*, the ability of its constituent units to act in cooperation and to regulate their relations with each other; it cannot really at this stage hope to achieve *gemeinschaft*, the sense of patriotism, identity, social community that is to be found within a historic nation state. Moreover, a consortium of middle or ex-great powers does not necessarily feel the compulsions of a contemporary great power. Its exposure to the general winds of change, its inability to isolate itself from the world, its lack of an ideological base and the fact that it consists of already highly governed states, most with considerable history behind them, and with no hinterland to discover and tame, makes any analogy with the formative decades of the United States of America hopelessly misleading.

To say that the Community lacks an ideological base is not to discount the importance of 'the European idea' as propounded first by men like Monnet and Schuman and their respondents in the other countries, nor the degree of enthusiasm it has later aroused in men such as Willy Brandt, Edward Heath, or Roy Jenkins (who has risked his political career for it). But the European idea or the goal of European union was tied, in the minds only of a minority of enthusiasts, to a European super-state on the federal model (Jean Monnet was never one of them). Nor is the conception of Community simply tailor-made for Europe, as is evidenced by attempts to develop arrangements similar to the EEC in Central America and elsewhere. But it did seem to have particular relevance or political validity in Western Europe by reason of the fact that the populations of the Six could recall the failure of purely autarchic policies in living and vivid memory, that not only their economic but their social structure and policies were broadly similar, that they lived cheek by jowl and that they had common external problems. Their first objectives were to remove a lot of obsolete impediments to trade and capital movements between themselves and to organize on a supranational level certain functions that could apparently be better discharged there than on the national level. And as the process accelerated Britain and the Scandinavian countries – or more accurately a majority of their decision-making elites – both saw the success of this enterprise and came to feel a greater sense of identity with, than differentiation from, the countries of the Community, not just on economic questions but in their perception of broader interests.

Equally, to say that the value of the Community is no longer seen in the minds of the people most concerned with it, as deriving from the fact that it is the first step towards an ultimate federal union or super-state, is not to say that such a union may not be found necessary in some eventual combination of circumstances that it is impossible to foresee – even though federal systems themselves are experiencing considerable stresses at present in the United States, Canada, Australia and, in so far as it really is a federal system, the Soviet Union. It is more that the Community's admittedly limited experience so far suggests that supranationalism is only a partial answer to the technical problems which confront the constituent countries, while at the same time breeding new resentments between them.

Gesellschaft und Gemeinschaft

The enlargement of the Community has coincided with a number of critiques – mostly American – to the effect that it has lost its way, that it is stuck, that it is the victim of profound malaise.[2] Some of these laments have an element of truth, for the Community and its constituent countries are facing very difficult problems. But much of it undoubtedly reflects disappointment with the fact that its leaders do not at present use the ambitious language of ten or fifteen years ago, and in consequence the Community looks less and less to Americans like its own sibling and more like a selfish system of economic protection.

Before dealing with the Community's external relations, which may well be decisive in determining whether it advances or stagnates, it is worth considering the extent to which both the modification of its objectives and its enlargement are a source of strength or weakness. It is true that since the crisis of 1965 the European Commission, which was envisaged in the Treaty of Rome as an embryonic government of a United Europe and for a while behaved like one, has lost power to the Council of Ministers who meet regularly as the representatives of their governments. Moreover, the Council of Ministers has dropped any serious pretence of reaching decisions by weighted voting, so that they appear to be harder to take. In other words it appears that the new association which the Nine have inherited from the Six has more the characteristics of an alliance than a Community, that the Gaullist approach has become institutionalized and that the British have accepted this.

Against this must be set two considerations. The first is that if the Commission had been allowed to acquire increasing power, it would also have become increasingly unpopular not just with governments but with public opinion in the Community countries – 'the faceless bureaucrats of Brussels'.[3] To this must be added the fact that the Commission is a very small bureaucracy (about 1 per cent of the whole British civil service or, as Christopher Soames has put it, an executive staff about the size of Harrods) to cope with both the external and the internal problems of a number of complex states, and is subject to all the inefficiencies of an international bureaucracy which are observable in NATO or the UN agencies. It is only when it ceases to be regarded as the basis of a super-government, and more the means of identifying new problems, as it was under the Presidency of Dr Sicco Mansholt, of exercising 'preventive diplomacy' (as the UN Secretariat was in the days of Hammarskjöld, Bunche and Cordier), or of offering alternative means of solving existing ones, that its real function emerges.

The Council of Ministers is by no means an ideal body for taking Community decisions, since, although on certain specialized subjects it meets at the level of agricultural or industrial ministers rather than foreign ministers, ministers as a species are always overloaded, especially as other multilateral organizations and their own parliaments make increasing inroads on their time. Though the Council of Ministers has legislative power, it also has an inbuilt tendency to shelve difficult decisions. This jerky process of decision-making, all-night negotiations with every party leaking its position to the press, tends to alienate citizens who are accustomed to smoother and more discreet processes of national decision-making. But ministers have the great advantage of representing the dominant political view in their own countries and have a better prospect of formulating realistic medium term objectives for the Community than has the Commission. This is not to say that a great deal could not be done to improve the functioning of the Council, by allowing the Commission to play a greater role in the formulation of its agenda and in its discussions, by appointing Deputy Foreign Ministers to meet weekly or more often, or by overcoming the absurd formula by which it has to meet part of the time in Luxembourg rather than Brussels.

There is another, less evident advantage to the functioning of the Community in its enlargement. Before British entry the Commission and the Council were crucially dependent on securing the support of France on any decision. But as Andrew Shonfield has pointed out, 'a system run by three major nations is deeply different from a diarchy; no one of the three will be able to make the ultimate assumption about its own indispensability'.[4] This assumes, he adds, that it is the British aim to strengthen the Community, since two large nations acting in concert could also wreck it; at the moment, despite the formal position of the Labour Party about renegotiating the 1971 terms of entry, it is clear that such a work of construction is a central ambition not only of the Conservative government, but of Whitehall, and of British industry: even the position of the British trade unions is changing (which may pave the way for the return of the Labour Party to a more central position). The fact that Mr Heath has so far been reluctant to step out of line with President Pompidou on major issues does not mean that a French veto has been replaced by an Anglo-French one, although Britain has not been the stabilizing force in Community politics that continental Europeans had hoped.

There are, moreover, other devices for the alignment of the policies of individual countries. The so-called D'Avignon Committee, founded in 1971, consisting of the heads of the political departments of the nine foreign offices, meets monthly and has, for instance, achieved a certain success in evolving and maintaining a united position of the Nine in the preparatory discussions on the European Conference on Security and Cooperation in Helsinki. It may have to be replaced by the more high-powered Council of Vice-Ministers that I have mentioned, for the process of preparing a response to the Kissinger demand of April 1973 for a common declaration of principles was a painfully slow one. There are also a host of other specialized committees of national officials or representatives of unofficial organizations which are gradually creating the network of contact and identity between the constituent national governments and societies that is the only basis on which the confidence for uniform internal and external policies can be generated. It may be as much in acting as a skilful intermediary in such multilateral policy discussions as in propounding policies of its own that the Commission will find its more effective function in the years immediately ahead, though for certain purposes, the Nixon Round on trade, for instance, it must also act as the external agent of the Community. Although the laws and directives of the Community in theory override national legislation, there is in reality no political substitute in the immediate future for an increasing parallelism of national policies and legislation. 'The Community does not move forward by capturing power from the governments of national states and then transferring it to a separate European institution, but by exercising compulsion on the governments themselves to act together in new ways.'[5] Nevertheless, to attempt to create a political secretariat has failed, and as instruments for the taking of unpleasant decisions, the institutions of the community are not impressive.

The entry of Britain into the Community has had the effect of focussing attention on the shortcomings of the European parliament, despite the Labour opposition's initial refusal to nominate their quota of national delegates to it. The Prime Minister of the Netherlands went home from the October 1972 Summit in unconcealed dudgeon that its communiqué had no reference to an ultimate objective of direct elections. There was, moreover, in many of the countries a spate of critical comment on the fact that the heads of government had committed themselves to the ambitious objective of a full economic and monetary union by 1980, that is to say relinquishing the principal forms of leverage and influence that states normally exert upon each other, without reaching any decision on the strengthening of the central mechanism of democratic control over the totality of central European institutions. True, it is likely that within the next few years the lines of cleavage and alliance between the heterogeneous group of nominees of national parliaments, Gaullists, Christian democrats, liberals, social democrats, socialists, communists, populists, catholics, protestants, or peasant parties, may sort themselves out into broad alignments of conservative or christian democrats, liberals, social democrats with a small marxist left wing. But it is unlikely that the European parliament will acquire the coherence of a national assembly, and since we are a long way from *gemeinschaft* there is little prospect that direct elections to it will be seriously considered during the 1970s.

This need not imply stagnation or inaction in parliamentary activity. In the first place the European parliament can serve a very useful purpose if, instead of indulging in continual debates, it acts as a kind of Grand Committee or a series of more specialized ones for the scrutiny of the policies and decisions of the Council and the Commission. It is somewhat ironic that the British, who enter the Community with a longer tradition of parliamentary institutions than any other member, have been slower than continental countries, let alone the US Congress to develop the kind of parliamentary committee of scrutiny which is essential for control of complex modern bureacracies (with the exception of the Public Accounts Committee of the House of Commons). A second important development could be a growing interrelation between the research or ginger groups that stimulate the making of party policy in the different countries. A European Fabian Society, for instance, or a European equivalent of the Bow Group could be invaluable Communitarian enterprises. They could provide the spur to imaginative thinking about future steps towards unification which was originally supposed to be the Commission's task but which it has partly abrogated through preoccupation with administrative detail. A third function of the parliament, though of other bodies as well, is to act as a clearing house for ideas; it is interesting to observe how much more interest is now taken by, for instance, British parliamentarians in the success of German experience in industrial co-partnership than was the case even a few years ago.[6]

Agriculture, industry and defence

But when some of the more obvious criticisms of the functioning of the Community have been met, the fact remains that its constituent countries are faced with some intractable problems, largely deriving from the changes in the priorities of world politics, but partly self-made. I will try to deal with the latter first, though the two are hard to distinguish.

In the first place, the meeting of the nine heads of government in October 1972 drew up a list of priorities which concealed con-

and West European pressure; the abrogation of the Brezhnev doctrine may be attained yet. The Soviet Union's insistence on the immutability of frontiers made the West insist on the right of self-determination. On military aspects of security, the Warsaw Pact countries have the convenient alibi of the MBFR conference in avoiding any serious reference to the question, and the Soviet Union showed itself reluctant to permit serious study of practical means of building East—West confidence such as the prior notification of military movements although she may make concessions as to notification of manœuvres in Eastern Europe.

The economic basket was more straightforward to negotiate since it covers obvious subjects such as industrial, scientific and technological collaboration and cooperation in fields such as environmental protection, transport and tourism. But the agenda may be difficult to translate into actual agreements. On the one hand, the Communist powers demand most-favoured-nation treatment, which in the case of the United States depends on Congress, while the elimination of quotas raises fears in some West European governments of dumping in their markets. The West wants a considerable improvement in the information, facilities and guarantees that the Eastern state organizations are prepared to offer to Western businesses.

The third basket – broadening of contacts between people – is there at Western insistence (and of Britain in particular). It covers human contacts, the freer flow of information and the broadening of cultural and educational cooperation. The first Communist response was to suggest that these proposals represented an attempt to 'smuggle subversive ideas' and indeed the Soviet Union did manage to get the reference to exchange of ideas and of books deleted altogether. It is clear that they will use the principles in the first basket, to uphold the sovereign rights of states and so on, to obstruct any real freedom of movement, broadcasting, or thought in the third. The fourth basket deals with follow-on measures, in which the Soviet desire had been for a prior commitment to permanent machinery. Some Western governments look askance at such an idea, as giving the Soviet Union an excuse to intervene in Western business. The Western view, that the creation of any permanent machinery of East—West or pan-European cooperation should depend on the outcome of the specific agreements, seems to have prevailed.

Naturally, both parties in a negotiation of this kind start from a maximalist position and many compromises may be made along the way. And as with American–European negotiations, one is predisposed to ask what 'linkage' there is between the subjects in the disparate baskets. The Soviet instinct is to deny that there is any, the original American position was that unless the Soviet Eastern bloc proved amenable in the third group it would get no satisfaction in the second. But in fact the Americans themselves are increasingly interested in trade with Eastern Europe, and the Eastern European countries, if not the Soviet Union, accept that increased trade and investment cannot be achieved without relaxing restrictions in the movements of Westerners and their access to information. A gradual process of accommodation therefore seems likely.

Although CSCE no longer has the characteristics of a peace conference, the word 'security' remains in its title. There are many aspects of security that are not concerned with force levels; the management of crises; their prevention by facilitating the communication of intentions, of which notification of both military manœuvres and troop movements are only two; the creation of machinery for the identification and accurate reporting of situations of violence; for the judicial settlement of disputes between states. This has led to a discussion in the West of whether a modest superstructure could not be erected over NATO and the Warsaw Pact in the form of a Council or Commission, charged with implementing its agreements, or whether the Conference could lead, admittedly after a lot of negotiation, to a declaration not just of principles but of intent with whose gradual implementation such a Commission would be charged.[20] The Eastern European states who desperately desire a normative instrument that would relegate the Brezhnev doctrine to the lumber room have made suggestions of both kinds.

The real difficulty with such proposals is either that they are too modest or too ambitious. If, say, an all-European council were created with the same function that Western European Union had when it was founded twenty years ago, namely to prevent disputes between a group of like-minded states, it would wither on the vine unless it had much broader responsibilities for pan-European cooperation in other fields; yet this posits Soviet agreement to broader human and cultural contacts. On the other hand, if CSCE constituted itself into a smaller version of the UN General Assembly and evolved a European Security Commission or Council, it would be in many ways competitive with the UN Security Council. An influential young German writer, Karl Kaiser, has suggested that such a body should be set up and should have an institutional link with the UN;[21] but it is hard to see what it would be, and if such a body aspired to be a substitute for the UN it would arouse the violent hostility of China, to which the United States and the European countries would inevitably be responsive. There would also be considerable opposition from the large non-European majority of the General Assembly to any idea that a particular region of the world, even one particularly prone to conflict, should develop a substitute for the universal organization. Now that the two Germanys are members of the UN, it is to be hoped that European questions will reappear on its agenda and that it will no longer be completely dominated by arguments over the fag-ends of colonialism which have made European and American opinion less and less interested in its deliberations. However, if the Soviet Union refused to allow the Czechoslovak crisis to come before the UN Security Council in 1968, she is unlikely to agree to the creation of some veto-free European Security Council with real powers of crisis management. The opportunity such a body might offer her to intervene in the affairs of Western Europe would be considerable. It was against just such a concept of mutual interference without the legitimacy of an accepted central system for the governance of Europe that Metternich had to deploy all his diplomatic guile against the Czar in the European congresses of Laibach and Troppau.

What both sides should be in search of, therefore, is on the one hand a declaration of principles which would have the effect of clarifying the limits of conflict and the rights and duties of European states, and on the other a means of maintaining a permanent dialogue. As I have suggested, until we are a long way further down the road to reconciliation of what are still antagonistic political systems, part of whose security is provided by a balance of military power, there may not be enough substance to keep such a dialogue alive solely on issues of security. It therefore becomes an Eastern as well as a Western European interest to broaden the compass of the dialogue to include other subjects. It is easy enough to say that it should include trade. One difficulty with trade is that it is not very significant to the West: the percentage of their foreign trade that the OECD countries conduct with the Communist countries (including China) has run at only about

3·5 per cent of their total foreign trade: put another way, the trade of the COMECON countries with Western Europe accounted for only $7·5 billion in 1971 or 2·2 per cent of world trade.

But there are other problems in using trade as the vehicle of a political dialogue. For one thing it is now formally on a bloc-to-bloc, not a multilateral basis, with the extension of the EEC's common commercial policy, though the COMECON countries have great difficulty in reaching common positions largely because their external interests vary so much. Hungary is heavily dependent on foreign trade while the Soviet Union until recently has hardly been dependent on it at all and has used trade agreements largely as diplomatic instruments. Moreover, she still can do so, most particularly at a time when the United States is searching for fresh markets and has become increasingly aware that Western Europe does five times as much trade with the state-controlled economies as she does.[22] Nor is it easy to reach common positions in the EEC, Germany being much more optimistic on East–West trade than her partners. What is more promising in the trade field is the adherence of Poland, Rumania and Hungary to GATT in addition to Czechoslovakia. If the United States gives most-favoured-nation treatment to the Soviet Union, we shall be approaching a situation in which East–West trade is no longer regarded as in a quite different category from other forms of trade, except for a diminishing number of strategic items which now are defined more carefully than in the past. The difficulties, however, of Western investment in state-controlled economies, though not insuperable, will persist unless real progress can be made in the second and third baskets of CSCE.

But there are other aspects to the dialogue than trade. All the European states, it has been suggested, 'could examine various possible cooperative ventures such as a common energy grid for Europe, the development of new means of transportation, the establishment of a common pipeline system, common industrial ventures, cooperation on a comprehensive environmental program to clean up rivers shared by East and West as well as to save the Baltic Sea'.[23]

However, one could have no sense of assurance on the central issue of coexistence and security unless some concrete undertakings can be given about freer exchanges of information and of people. True, communiqués after the recent visits of Soviet leaders to Western Europe have spoken of improving 'contacts between people'. But how ready the Soviet Union and other governments, notably the DDR, are to translate such statements into practice remains to be seen. Yet without it, the stereotypes of what are now a largely bygone age will persist at the popular level and undermine the confidence of governments or their freedom of action. Research has shown, for instance, that young Poles still regard the young of both East and West Germany as markedly less 'peace-loving' than Russians or Americans.[24] There is a great deal to be said for the attitude of the continental New Left movements that invite their Eastern counterparts to the challenge of debate rather than sheltering behind barriers of censorship and silence.

Europe, as Jean Laloy has pointed out, 'is the fatherland of middle-sized powers'.[25] To survive they must associate as they always have in one way or another. But by the accident of history they have also become intimately associated with the super-powers, and that association is not going to disappear in the foreseeable future. However, down a long perspective of time one can envisage a world which contains two different types or groups of European medium-sized powers, yet with an increasing range of common interests which softens the sharp edge of their differences. If nothing else, they share by far the lowest population growth rate of any area of the world, and by some estimates of population increase would account for no more than 7 or 8 per cent of world population by the end of the century. But this process of amelioration will not be a purely European one, however powerful, unified and magnetic the European Community may become. It will depend to a crucial extent on the way in which the super-powers interpret their interests and responsibilities. China will attempt to influence the process, possibly without greatly affecting it. But it will also be dependent on the stability of large parts of the developing world, for in terms of the maintenance of détente, 'Europe' in effect stretches from Vladivostok to San Francisco and from the Arctic Circle to the Middle East and the Sahara. It is bound to be affected by the climate of world politics as a whole, of which Europe cannot form a sheltered enclave with rules entirely of its own.

At some point in this process of gradual change, the Community will be subjected to various forms of Soviet challenge, whether as a result of some crisis at the interface of the two systems, or from anxiety to arrest the process of political union, perhaps at the point where the Community embarks on certain forms of defence cooperation. If challenge takes a military form, then NATO is the only instrument and this both the Americans and the Europeans still accept. But it is more likely to take the form of diplomatic enticements to some countries and threats to others in order to test the vulnerability of Western European integration, or of a fresh attempt to negotiate the United States out of Europe. When this happens, what will blunt or avert it will be the diplomatic solidarity of the Community, for although the United States will remain militarily involved in Europe at some level, she has an agenda of her own with the Soviet Union and will not devote the same close attention to European affairs as in the past. And political solidarity among the Nine will in turn be a factor of the degree of *gemeinschaft*, of a sense of belonging to a cultural and political identity, that has been achieved. Consequently, in parallel with a demand for freer East–West access, it is also a Western European necessity to accelerate all those internal forms of communication between voluntary and interest groups, students, professional people, and trade unions which create such an identity, as well as constructing the political machinery for joint decision-making.

Mercantilism and its dangers

I have attempted to deal in chapter five with the general problems of trade and monetary relations among the developed powers including those issues that are most likely to engender friction between the United States and the Community. But since the Community is a great centre of economic power and a great trader, one must conclude this review of its position and policies with an examination of them from the European standpoint.

Since the Community is in a strong economic position but in a more precarious political one, it is perhaps most useful to evaluate not so much its own objectives as the demands that are likely to be made on it by other countries. Foremost among these is the adjustment or generalization of the preferential agreements which the Community has negotiated with nearly forty other countries. It is important not to lump all these together, for though some of them may have been negotiated without sufficient thought for their political implications, others are directly related to the political future of the Community itself. First, there are the six remaining members of EFTA with whom the Community has agreed to abolish all industrial tariffs, but for a small range of exceptions, for the next five years. This was both equitable and political sense, for the Community's security in the widest sense and the stability of Europe in general depends partly on the well-being of Sweden, Austria, Finland, Switzerland, Portugal and Iceland. Then there are two countries, Greece and Turkey, who, by agreement with the United States, have been regarded as eventual candidates for membership of the Community itself (though depending partly on the stability and liberalization of their regimes); they receive aid from the Community and participate in a gradual process of reducing trade barriers. The same argument applies to the agreement with Spain, though there is no formal agreement on her eventual entry into the Community. Then there is Israel, which is heavily dependent on exports, for whose birth Europe is partly responsible, and for whose security it may well also ultimately be responsible. Next come agreements with Morocco and the island states in the Mediterranean which, though compatible with GATT rules, really reflect the traditional French concern with Europe's influence in the Mediterranean. Of French inspiration also was the Yaoundé Convention with 18 countries of the French Community in Africa, a free-trade arrangement, which was followed later by the Arusha Agreements with three East Africa Commonwealth countries, Kenya, Uganda, and Tanzania and may be followed by an agreement with Nigeria.

This patchwork of agreements negotiated over more than a decade has aroused the animosity of many developing countries, who argue that the Community picks and chooses those with whom it will enter into free-trade or preferential agreements according to its own interests, and by reference to no rules or objectives other than a desire to sustain a connection with parts of the old European empires; the Asian Commonwealth countries and some African ones as well are not so favoured, partly because they produce semi-manufactured goods or textiles that are competitive with European industries. It is hard to deny the charge that there is greater interest in Africa on the part of the Latin members of the EEC than in Asia. This is not compatible with the Community's assertion that its interests are world-wide.

In addition the United States, now fighting for the value of its currency by a readjustment of its balance of payments, feels that it is being excluded from markets in Europe and Africa by preferences which open the associated countries to European. capital, or that its competitors, especially in agricultural products,, are being given preferential access to the Common Market. The fact that this assertion can be disputed by the figures, that the European balance of trade with the United States was until 1972 in deficit as it has been for decades, or that American exports to the countries of the Yaoundé convention rose by 158 per cent between 1958 and 1971 whereas they rose by only 97 per cent to the Community over the same period, does not alter the American public image of Europe as selfish in economic as well as security terms. Another prime source of American anxiety is that many individual countries in the Community still maintain high barriers against Japanese exports which have tended to swamp the Ameri-can market, partly as a consequence of the liberal trade agreements which the United States negotiated many years ago with Japan as part of the process of restoring Japanese economic health; there is a strong American demand that Europe help get Japan off Uncle Sam's back.

There are two stances which the Community can adopt in the forthcoming negotiations. One is a reactive and defensive one which insists on the legitimacy of both its protective and its preferential arrangements, which emphasizes that it has not yet fully acquired the economic cohesion which is the essential basis of political unity; that it has a moral obligation to the countries of the Mediterranean basin and sub-Saharan Africa which derives from European history, while Asia is now either a Russian, a Japanese or a universal responsibility; that Japan is an American not a European problem since the United States has political and security interests and obligations in the Pacific which Europe no longer has: or that the real problem which the United States must confront in its economic policy is its heavy outflow of capital in-vestment, not its trading relationship. Let others propose and it will dispose. There is a particular temptation for the Community to adopt such an approach because in addition to the protectionist instincts of countries like France, there is a certain kind of in-fluential Eurocrat in Brussels who sees in an adversary confronta-tion with the United States over trade, the opportunity to restore a sense of unity and the impetus towards internal progress in Europe which has been slowed down by enlargement and the intractability of problems like a common industrial or an agreed regional policy.

The other approach is to accept that the days when Europe's economic priorities could be accepted as *sui generis* are over, that a prolonged fight with the United States on trade barriers is more likely to cause political disruption in Europe than to accelerate unity, as well as increasing American isolationist tendencies in the security field: that an irredentist Japan could pose the same indirect threat to Europe as it did in the inter-war years: that the entry of Britain has inevitably widened the Community's interests in the developing world; above all that the Community cannot claim to be a power centre of world interests, even in civilian terms, unless she can play a leading part in formulating a more liberal system of universal trade and payments that satisfies the anxieties of developing countries as well as the United States.

The bold course for the Community to adopt would be to propose the abolition of all tariffs and quotas in the industrial sector over say a ten-year period for countries above a certain stage of development (which can be measured by various means such as GNP per head) as well as on raw materials. In the first instance, this means primarily Europe, including EFTA, the United States, Japan, Canada and Australia.[36] It would carry risks in that, for instance, it would expose Europe to the full blast of Japanese competition (and of competition from new mini-Japans like Taiwan or Singapore) which it is only just beginning to feel. But it would have the advantage of eliminating what in certain sectors are still high tariff barriers in the United States, including such protective devices as the 'American selling price'. These perpetuate a sense of grievance about the trade policy of the United States, which when added to the diplomatic unilateralism of the Nixon administration tends to make Europeans despair of the future of the European–American relationship.

The advantage of the radical approach would be to eliminate a great deal of haggling over individual tariff levels, and to concentrate the negotiations on more politically significant questions, the lowering of other barriers that diminish the earning power of the developing countries, freer trade in agricultural products and the thorny problem of non-tariff barriers. But clearly it is impossible to contemplate moving towards industrial free trade without individual countries, or in the case of Europe, the Community, being permitted to take measures of regional diversification that will cushion the shock for industries that may be forced out of business by foreign competition. So effective domestic policies are an inevitable concomitant of industrial free trade.

The generalization of preferences that the EEC has negotiated with the countries of the Mediterranean and Africa (and which the United States also has with certain areas like Puerto Rico) may be difficult to negotiate. But a failure to do so would carry particular dangers for Europe in opening the way – especially if no immediate solutions to monetary problems prove attainable – to a new perception of the relation between the developed and the developing world as one of spheres of influence, Europe asserting a primary interest in the Mediterranean and Africa, the United States in Latin America and certain Pacific countries, and Japan in South East Asia. For one thing, the temper of the developing countries is bitterly hostile to any such paternalistic or exclusive conception of relations with the developed world; for another, Europe is not really prepared to take political responsibility for Eurafrica in the sense of a readiness to fight Africa's battles at the UN or to mediate in its disputes, any more than Japan is ready to do the same in South East Asia; for yet another such a division would exclude Southern Asia, which would tend naturally to be considered increasingly as a Soviet sphere of influence.

In agricultural trade, which accounts for over 13 per cent of world trade, the boot is on the other foot in the sense that tariffs are not the major aspect of the problem and the real impediments stem from the domestic policies that states have pursued to protect their farmers or support domestic farm prices. Although the United States and Japan have engaged in such policies for years, it is the Community that will be the real focus of criticism because it is protecting high-cost producers by a method that is both expensive and inefficient. Moreover, as I have tried to suggest earlier, the Common Agricultural Policy is a divisive factor within the Community itself. Any modification that precedes or emerges from the trade negotiations will have to be applied only gradually because of the time it takes to absorb over-large farm populations in certain countries into other occupations. But if the Community countries do not enter the trade negotiations with some agreement on the way in which, and the extent to which, they are prepared to overhaul the CAP, from one of general levies to direct support for the poorer farmer, from a protectionist to a social policy, then the image that many people and nations hold, be they American grain farmers, Caribbean cane-sugar producers, Argentinian stockmen or Asian rice growers, of the Community as an essentially selfish system will be reinforced – and in the process the individual countries of the Community, where the cost of food is increasingly a political issue, will also find themselves increasingly at loggerheads.

In the thorny jungle of non-tariff barriers, which arise from state trading, different customs and administrative procedures, different domestic standards about hygiene, quality or a host of other factors, or else from specific quotas on imports or 'voluntary' restraint, the Community may be in a better position than the other major trading blocs. For much of its effort over the past decade has been addressed to removing such barriers among its member countries by getting common standards or removing administrative obstructions. To achieve this on a global scale implies extending the spirit of 'community' to the relations of all the developed countries (or else the improbable alternative of consensus on a supranational authority that overrode the domestic jurisdictions of the governments of all the industrial powers). Consequently, the experience of the European Community is relevant. No one can expect complete success but nothing, perhaps, will provide a surer index of the fundamental unity of interest which is seen to persist within the non-Communist developed world, or alternatively of the extent to which local pressures are undermining it, than the headway which the negotiations make on the reduction or limitation of the host of non-tariff barriers to trade which they maintain, quite apart from regional measures of support for depressed areas.[27]

The American complaint about its European allies, that they have become basically selfish, both in the trade policies of the Community and the share of the common burden of security they are prepared to shoulder, is similar to and different from the European (and Japanese) complaint about American unilateralism in the diplomatic sphere. It is similar in that its basis is that Europe in its preoccupation with its own *enrichessement*, and with the welfare of a small number of developing countries with which its member states have been historically associated, has become forgetful of the principal of universal commercial access which (with exceptions) was the foundation of the post-war international system. American unilateralism in the diplomatic field appears to be matched by European unilateralism in economic and commercial relations. The Americans have become alarmed at the prospect of a giant European trading community whose economic associations appear to spread through a wide arc from the Arctic Circle to equatorial Africa and into the Middle East and the Caribbean, yet for which the Community is unable to undertake effective measures of political protection, even if this were desirable. Europeans have become alarmed at the prospect of a United States entering into an increasingly close dialogue with a Soviet Union whose interests still contend with theirs in the sensitive centre of this arc, namely Central and Southern Europe. But it is different in that the United States still exerts influence over a greater range of issues than Europe or Japan, and consequently still carries a greater burden of general responsibilities.

The still unanswered challenge to both the United States and the Community is to negotiate on those subjects where modifications in the European–American relationship are inescapable, defence, trade, money, energy, relations with the developing world, not only with sensitive concern for the different problems of each other but also with a similar conception of the way in which East–West relations, in Europe and elsewhere, should develop. Each side could easily bring out the worst in the other, and if this happens the strength of this very powerful combination in world politics will erode. A mercantilist attitude on the part of the Community will increase the tendency of the United States to see its interests in purely national terms; while a hectoring attitude on the part of the United States, or one that seeks to achieve its objectives by sowing dissension between one European country and another will either create increasing European obduracy on material matters, or else, by weakening such political cohesion as the Community has achieved, inhibit that readiness to broaden its responsibilities which it is an American interest to encourage.

9
The Dilemmas of Japan

Political leadership and consensus

No great nation reflects, in its domestic debates, the dilemmas to which a period of rapid social, political and economic change give rise so poignantly as does Japan. At first sight she may seem endowed with many gifts and blessings which are denied to the countries of the Community or even the great powers. Not only has she a long history as an independent state but her people have a sense of *gemeinschaft*, of patriotism and of national pride which few other countries can emulate; there is also a long tradition of respect for government which can thus influence both the domestic and external environment of Japanese society more pervasively than that of many other democracies. By hard work, discipline and skill the country's wealth has advanced over seventy-fold in the post-war quarter century. Japan is an island power with none of the border problems that create a sense of insecurity in Germany, China, the Soviet Union or India; and though the unfinished business of a conflict that her disastrous intervention turned into a world war is not entirely resolved, she does not stand in an adversary relation to any other major power. The underlying strength of Japanese society and of the Japanese economy is considerable. The vertical identification of the Japanese worker with his company rather than his fellow tradesmen in other companies,[1] the high level of personal savings, the pride in workmanship, are unique.

And yet perceptive and sympathetic students of Japanese society are for the most part agreed in detecting, beneath the impressive statistics, a rising sense of uncertainty about almost every aspect of public policy, and in personal relations as well. Japan has become an anxious country with a working class that consists to a large extent of uprooted countrymen and with a consequent decline in familial and rural virtues, with a younger generation that is at the same time more hedonistic than its elders and questioning of economic growth or prosperity as the principal objectives of the nation, with daunting problems of pollution and urban sprawl, and with a political system dominated by one party, that has been steadily sinking in popularity yet to which there seems little alternative. On top of this, the end of the post-war era, most particularly the changes in American policy towards the mainland powers, has to a certain extent cast Japan adrift in an international system in which she finds it difficult to perceive her proper role or to define her long-term objectives. Is she the Pacific bastion of a western system of economic, strategic and political relationships, or an Asian power who happens also to be industrialized and capitalist?

I do not know Japan well enough to write with authority of the changing nature of Japanese society.[2] There is clearly some equivalent in her modern history to the Klingberg cycle in American history, periods of receptivity to Western ideas, as after the Meiji restoration and the two world wars, alternating with periods of introspection and nationalism. And when these changes of national mood have occurred, they have been much more rapid than in the United States. However, just as the United States was unable to withdraw into isolationism in the second half of the 1960s when the public temper may have desired it, so the Japanese economy is too enmeshed with that of others, her society is too porous to external influences, the state is too vulnerable, for her to be able to retreat entirely within her shell, even if the 'death of the past', which her fabulous and socially unplanned economic growth has occasioned, had not eroded her national traditions. Like other great mercantile societies the Japanese must come to terms with transnationalism and an interdependent international system. The question is whether they do so with prudence and with tolerance, or in a spirit of assertion and bad temper.

It is not too difficult to list the sources of frustration in the contemporary Japanese polity. First, despite the enormous success of her great corporations, operating under the quiet guidance of the Ministry of International Trade and Industry (until recently the most influential government department), a success not only in terms of growth and exports but of labour relations as well,

Japan is not yet a social democracy. Housing is bad, pollution is worse, traffic is appalling and much of the Pacific littoral has been marred.* Social security is still primarily dependent on personal savings.

The Japanese are rich and rapidly getting richer so that, in theory, a great deal of this devastation could be reversed and the chinks in their social armour mended. But the political system does not respond so easily to social stress. In the course of twenty years the Liberal Democratic Party has sunk from 380 seats in a Diet of 475 seats to 271 (losing popular support at the rate of about one per cent a year). But no alternative party has risen to challenge it; the Japan Socialist Party has remained static at rather under a quarter of the seats; the Communist Party has climbed gradually into third place but with less than a tenth of the seats of the Diet, while the remaining seats are split between the

* In his interesting and perceptive survey of contemporary Japan, *A Special Strength* (31 March 1973), Brian Beedham, the Foreign Editor of *The Economist*, has quoted some indices collated by the Sanawa Bank.

	GNP per head 1972 $	Unemployment % 1970–2	Housing[1]	Private goods[2]	Public amenities[3]	Working conditions[4]	Tension makers[5]
			Score out of 100 marks in each column				
Japan	2950	1½	14	14	9	22	−34
United States	5500	5½	24	31	24	24	−15
Germany	4200	1	21	19	20	16	−22
France	3850	2½	16	16	21	15	−15
Britain	2800	5	25	20	26	23	−14

[1] Based on number of rooms available per 100 people.

[2] Based on daily calorie consumption per person; amount of textiles used per person per year; ownership of cars, television sets and telephones per 100 people.

[3] Based on percentage of road mileage that is surfaced; percentage of houses on water supply and sewerage system; number of public libraries per million people; amount of parkland per person in main cities; percentage of 3–5 year-olds in kindergartens.

[4] Based on average number of working hours per week; lives lost in accidents per 1,000 workers in manufacturing industry; average worker's number of minutes per day spent in getting to and from work.

[5] These are the number of crimes per 100,000 people; number of victims of traffic accidents per 1,000 cars; tons of air pollutants per square kilometre; traffic congestion, in number of cars per kilometre of road; number of passengers in main city undergrounds per day per kilometre of line.

Democratic Socialist Party and Komeito (clean government).
Though many people had expected a left-wing coalition to emerge
before now, or still hope that it may emerge, the prospects are not
very encouraging, partly because of the heterogeneity of the
opposition parties, partly because in a country where TV has
tended to personalize political leadership as it has elsewhere they
have failed to produce any striking personalities.

As Zbgniew Brezinski has observed,

'The key questions, accordingly, are about what will happen to
the LDP itself – or in other words how solid will the centre-
right be – and will Japan become like France of the Fourth
Republic, where a strong left is offset by a stronger centre-
right, or like Italy, where a strong left faces a relatively in
effective factionalized centre? These are vital questions because
of the LDP's critical role in the last twenty years. The very
success of the LDP makes its future the key to Japan's political
behaviour.'3

This was written in 1971 and the answer to Professor Brezinski's
question was supposed to be Mr Kakuei Tanaka who, after the
usual interfactional manœuvring by which LDP leaders have been
chosen, emerged as Prime Minister in July 1972. Everything
seemed to be in his favour; it was his predecessor Mr Sato who
had had to endure the indignities of the 'Nixon shock' and the
American reversal of policy towards China; Tanaka by contrast
was able to make the politically popular move of negotiating an
agreement with Peking and reopening diplomatic relations with
China. More than that, he was a man of a new stamp, not a member of the Tokyo University elite which for a generation has
staffed the higher reaches of politics and the civil service as well as
the board rooms of the great corporations. But despite the fact
that he put relations with China on a new footing, his popularity
has declined, almost entirely as a consequence of his failure to be
sufficiently draconian on domestic issues (in addition to being
distrusted by what really is an Establishment as not being one of
them). He has been unable to arrest the passing of many city
governments to the Socialists, nor yet effectively come to terms
with them.

A number of Japanese as well as foreign observers have pointed
out that what really is at issue is the Japanese decision-making
process, *ringisei*, which, operating by consensus in both govern-

ment and business, is extremely slow and tentative in reaching hard and clear decisions.[4] That such a process has enormous advantages in terms of steadiness of purpose, no one has ever doubted. What it does mean is that the system is unlikely to produce a man who can sail against the tide, an Edward Heath for instance. Since this is so and since there is so little by way of a floating vote in Japan, it seems likely that the leadership will continue to be provided by the LDP but possibly by men or a man of a more nationalist stamp, someone who is prepared to be more assertive on the international scene, or to delineate Japanese interests more sharply. Political prognosis from the other side of the world is unwise, but Yasuhiro Nakasone, who has stressed the independence of Japan, and has even had to deny the charge that he is a Japanese Gaullist, would fit this particular bill, though he is not approved of by the gentler, consensus-minded older generation that, though it will soon lose it, still controls the levers of power. Conceivably, power might jump a generation to a man like Yohei Kono, son of a famous politician and still in his thirties, who is impatient with the *immobilisme* of the senior leadership.

If we are headed for a period of international rough weather, not war but acerbic negotiations and the possibility of a serious though not disastrous recession, one of the questions at issue is the future of democracy itself in Japan. On some issues – their style of management or labour relations for instance – the Japanese are wholly 'inner directed', to use David Riesmann's classification. On others they are 'outer directed' and there is no doubt that it was the appeal of American democracy, during the long period of American–Japanese intimacy, that made the Japanese one of its most fervent proponents. In this respect, Watergate has clearly done considerable damage, and if democratic government in Japan should be seen to be unequal to the country's governance, then we must expect not only more assertive but probably more high-handed forms of leadership. This said, there is clearly no question of uprooting the habits of a generation that has become accustomed to free expression or that has received a very high level of education. Democracy, moreover, as a social concept, as an expression or search for consensus, has historical roots that long antedate the achievement of democratic political institutions.

The risks of an economic super-power

The causes of Japan's economic miracle have been analyzed many times; social stability, a large and young industrial labour force, a high rate of savings, 'vertical identification', cooperation between government and industry, a ready supply of foreign technology, a low defence budget, and many other factors. But few assume that the Japanese economy will continue to grow at the remarkable 12·2 per cent that was achieved in the second half of the 1960s. The supply of labour is constricting and its cost is approaching European levels; the cost of raw materials is going up for everyone including Japan, even though American pressure has forced a revaluation of the yen; above all the government will have to spend a great deal more of the national wealth on the reorganization of the basic infrastructure of the cities and regions and the protection of the environment. The official expectation before the oil crisis was that the country's growth rate would slacken to 10 per cent, though some put it nearer 8 per cent. Now it is more likely to be 2 or 3 per cent.

Whatever the figure, it is likely to be above the average for other industrial countries during the rest of the decade. But the 'Japanese problem', that of first-class goods finding their way into their markets at prices lower than they can produce them, so that she is in surplus with the rest of the industrial world, is likely to remain. For Japan itself the converse problem, namely that as a consequence of heavy reliance on imported raw materials, her economy must be export-directed, will also remain. At the same time her instincts are still protectionist.

> 'Japan's concept of foreign trade has been one of a process whereby her industry has been fuelled and supplied, rather than one which is intrinsically desirable for the international exchange of goods. For most Japanese manufacturers home markets tend to be more important than those overseas. . . . There is no disposition to share more of this market than is absolutely essential with foreigners.'[5]

But, though this may be the national instinct, a combination of factors, the pressure of her trading partners, the potential vulnerability of her sources of raw material, the need and the desire to invest in developing countries, are inevitably making her part of an interdependent international community, and also influence her relations with the great powers.

It is best to start by looking at Japan's position as a world trader, if we are trying to gain any insight into what form the international system that will succeed that of the post-war era will assume. 'Japan', one of her most articulate academics, Professor Masataka Kosaka, has written, 'is now suffering from the after-effects of her formidable efforts at rapid industrialization, and these are magnified by the continuation of the same process. Japan, then, has an economic structure which is not suitable for a global economic power . . .'[6]

This point needs no emphasis; Japan's trade surplus, which had barely existed in 1960, was $3,650 million in 1970 and bigger still in 1972. By the estimates of the JERC, which antedated the energy crisis, her trade surplus would have been nearly $17 billion a year by 1980. One can point, if one uses this sort of projection, to a nightmare prospect in which the rest of the industrial world is in the economic grip of a relatively small Asian power, which by then would probably be producing half the world's steel, three-quarters of its shipping, most of its electronic consumer goods, and much of its capital goods. If this were really to occur, not only the United States but Western Europe, and most of Asia, would by then have become sternly protectionist and discriminatory against Japan, making her a sort of economic exile by virtue of her own dynamism.

Such figures may be an exaggeration but they are also a warning; for though many Japanese see the dangers of their country getting into such a dominant position, and although Mr Tanaka successfully reduced the Japanese trade surplus by voluntary restraints in 1973, business is still business to the great figures of the Zaikai, which controls the purse-strings of the LDP. But Professor Kosaka's point has more to it than Japan's general economic vitality. Not only is she an unbalanced exporter in that she exports more than four times what she imports in industrial goods (whereas with Germany, for example, the proportion is about two to one), but her exports are heavily concentrated in a small number of industries, which makes her seem a particularly menacing rival to similar industries in other countries, and raises the spectre of fresh quota restrictions if she is not prepared to make voluntary restraints. Yet as he and many others have pointed out, the notion of reciprocity does not come readily to the Japanese mind, for rather natural reasons; her mutual hostility with the United States excluded her from the attempt to revitalize international trade after the Great Depression; she played no part in the shaping of the Bretton Woods system; and for a decade thereafter, when most of the men who now run Japan were approaching middle age, was having a hard time keeping afloat. The cultural lag that has made the United States neglect its export industries has its counterpart in the opposite context in Japan, and will have to be redressed even more sharply.

Professor Kosaka, and other observers, have pointed also to the uniqueness of her social structure and culture which makes the smooth management of an interdependent relationship rather difficult. This explains the mysterious difficulties foreigners find in doing business in Japan. Her tariffs are not particularly high or significant, she now applies fewer import quotas than France or Germany, and she is no more protectionist in agriculture than her major partners. But the difficulties of her language, the close identity of her people and their temperamental protection-ism, create all kinds of obscure non-tariff barriers by which the foreigner's business opportunities tend to melt away.

Japan will therefore find the coming negotiations on trade and money difficult. The government has now accepted the probability that stability in exchange rates may be difficult to maintain, although she only undertook the revaluations of 1971 and 1973 under strong American pressure. But this carries the risk that at a certain point, Japanese big business might find it more economic to move much of its production and investment into cheaper labour areas in South East or East Asia or Latin America which would once again sharpen its competitive edge in world trade.[7] The answer for the next decade, as Mr Tanaka has attempted to tell his countrymen, lies in devoting a great deal more of Japanese investment, through raising her level of taxation or by other means, to the improvement of Japan itself.

If the curious mixture of pride and uncertainty that is charac-teristic of the Japanese temperament makes them wish to live in economic peace with their trading partners, but unwilling to take the steps to do so, the country's dependence on imported raw materials is bound to occasion second thoughts about limitless economic growth. She is the least autarchic of any of the world's major powers, and the search for raw materials has extended her economic relations across the world to an even greater extent than the search for markets. For bauxite, nickel, coking coal, uranium and, of course, oil, she is almost entirely dependent on imports.

This will have the effect of making her level of economic activity partly depend on the general climate of world opinion about the conservation of raw materials and on the functional measures of conservation that various governments may take, as they have already done in the case of oil.

It is true that this tends to increase the Japanese sense of frustration; having no share, for instance, in any of the international oil companies, she had no hand in the framing of the Teheran agreement of 1971, though she was closely affected by it. This sense of impotence has accelerated the attempt to make bilateral arrangements of her own, in the Gulf, in Africa and in South East Asia, but there is little prospect that she will better her own target of having 30 per cent of her oil imports under her own control by 1985.

In the 1960s, when the economic boom made her scour the world for long-term raw-material contracts, her businessmen got an unfortunate reputation for being tone-deaf to the problems and susceptibilities of her supplier nations, Peru, Australia, Canada and Indonesia, and this reputation still persists. There are signs, however, that as she becomes more involved in the fortunes of these countries, she is becoming somewhat more sensitive to the concerns of their societies, in other words that her relationship with them is becoming politicized, despite the determination of the post-war generation to keep business and politics apart. She has accepted, though reluctantly, the fact that the future of the Malacca Straits, which has been seen as Japan's jugular vein in the sense that the British once saw Suez, cannot be determined by browbeating Indonesia and Malaysia from whom she is a large importer, but must emerge out of a negotiation of new legal norms concerning straits as a whole. Nevertheless, the difficulty persists; the national sense of Japan's rising importance and influence in the world does not seem to be accompanied by a recognition that a new world is emerging in which decisions must be formed in terms broader than the national interest. 'Rather, it rests on the argument that, since an economically powerful Japan confronts a new international situation, it must determine on its own how it is to relate to world affairs.'[8]

The security of an offshore island

Modern Japan is a phenomenon hitherto unknown in history, certainly in modern history; the world's third most powerful economic state yet with very limited military capacity and still dependent for its strategic security on another great power on the far side of the world's largest ocean. She is a satisfied power in conventional diplomatic terms yet deeply uncertain about her future place in the world, and as deeply conscious of her strategic and economic vulnerability. She has no political ambitions in the sense that the mainland powers have, yet there is a widespread feeling in Japan that she has been denied the influence and the status in the international system to which her achievements entitle her. She has a sense of the unique quality of her civilization, yet Japanese are sensitive not only to any criticism of it but in racial terms as well. What resolution of these conflicting impulses can a new generation of leadership make? What opportunities does a period of détente and greater flexibility in great-power relations offer to her?

One can devise a large number of theoretical options for Japan but in terms of her actual interests, capabilities and concerns, they seem to me to reduce themselves to four: a continuing relationship with the United States on security and primary concentration on Japan's relations with the developed world in general; a new relationship with each of the mainland powers; aspiration to the status of a super-power; and an uncharted role as a new kind of international great power. Though she may over the foreseeable future have greater freedom of choice than say the European Community, each alternative, although it has its advocates, portends as many difficulties as advantages.

On the surface it would seem that the Japanese–American relationship is now on a sounder footing than a few years ago. The nightmare of the Cold War years, namely of a major Sino–American conflict, has receded; the reversion of Okinawa, whose retention by the United States aroused both nationalist and radical or ideological opposition, has been settled; and the Vietnam war, of which the Japanese strongly disapproved, though it enriched them, is over. The United States still ranks second only to Switzerland (shades of MacArthur!) as the country to which public opinion feels most attachment (even though the percentage of the public placing her at the top of the list dropped from 34 per cent to 24 per cent during the two years after October 1970),[9] and the United States is by far her largest single trading partner.

Yet it will be a very difficult relationship to sustain. Just because Japan owes so much to the United States, in terms of protection through the Cold War years, in terms of economic expansion and assistance and by providing a model for institutional reform, more and more Japanese have come to resent American influence. Though only a minority favour abrogation of the Japanese–American security treaty, the fact that Japan's essential security now seems more assured, by reason of Sino–Soviet differences and the American exploitation of them, makes her dependence on American protection seem at the same time strategically less necessary and psychologically more onerous. On the economic plane, it is similarly unbalanced in that the United States absorbs a much higher proportion of Japan's exports (31·2 per cent in 1970) than Japan does of American exports (10·8 per cent), and the former is an export-oriented economy to an extent that the latter still is not.

On top of this have come the crises of recent years; the Guam statements of 1969 and the Nixon doctrine of 1970, which appeared to be throwing on Japan much of the responsibility for the security of East Asia; the deception involved in Nixon's unilateral initiative towards China in 1971 when in the preceding months the United States had been urging the Japanese to concert policy on China; the import surcharge; and in general the increasing unilateralism of American diplomacy. In addition, the President's talk of a five-power world in 1971–2 had a profoundly unsettling effect upon Japan, since it assumed that she was being cast by another country for a role which she had not decided for herself and for which she was unprepared. As I have said earlier, the Nixon Administration has been maladroit in its dealings with Japan, and much of this relates to its style of operating; there is little value in maintaining a distinguished Japanese ambassador in Washington to maintain close relations with the State Department if the Department has little hand in policy-making; annual meetings between the cabinets of the two countries are of only marginal importance if most American cabinet officers are largely ciphers. The same malaise that affects European–American relations affects also Japanese–American relations but with the difference that European pride is not so easily wounded; the NATO system enmeshes the United States in a web of multilateral contacts with European governments from which it can less easily escape; the reorientation of Sino–American relationships has affected Japan more directly than it has Europe; while as far as Soviet–American relations are concerned Europeans, rightly or wrongly, believe that they are more indispensable to the United States than do the Japanese.

A mixture of events and deliberate actions have helped to restore some confidence to the Japanese–American alliance. For one thing, it has now become clear that the Nixon Doctrine does not mean a rapid devolution of American political and security responsibilities in Asia upon Japan. The United States is not going to abandon Taiwan with which Japan has important economic links even if she recognizes China's claim eventually to rule it. Japanese anxiety about the future of Korea also runs less high at the moment than it did; the Japanese and the Koreans have a relationship very like the British and the Irish (Koreans in my experience have a national humour rather like the Irish); the smaller power dislikes the larger though it is largely dependent on it economically; the larger power has a record of conquest of the smaller because it was strategically important to her but has little desire to get involved in its politics at present. Eventually, as American military power in the Pacific is run down, Japan clearly will have to develop a security relationship with the Republic of Korea, but for the time being the declining tension between North and South Korea removes some of the urgency from this question.

Japan and the mainland powers

Nevertheless the ambivalence of the Japanese–American alliance, the possibility that it might be overturned by some sudden crisis, or that mutual confidence might gradually degenerate if the international economic position of the United States continues to weaken, has for some years made the Japanese think of alternatives. For whatever may be said about the sense of insecurity, which both Japanese and non-Japanese regard as part of the national temperament, it has obvious geopolitical causes, by reason of the fact that Japan is separated by only narrow strips of water from two large mainland powers.

The Japanese moves towards China in 1972, and still more the American, had the expected effect of making the Soviet Union more interested in improving Russo–Japanese relations. But there seems little prospect that the outcome will be more than a limited business partnership. There is a long history of distrust between the two countries that goes back into the last century and has not been allayed by the events of the past decade or so.[10] For, in brief, the Soviet Union, after trying in the 1950s to neutralize Japan, has played fast and loose with her on the question of a peace treaty, which would settle among other things the future of the Kurile Islands, in an effort to lure Japanese enterprises into the development of Siberia. The Japanese case on the Kurile Islands is a strong one but has been resisted by the Soviet Union, partly for the strategic reason that it gives her greater control over the approaches to Vladivostok, and partly for fear of setting a precedent which China could exploit in relation to the Sino–Soviet border.

It is a sign of either rising fear of the left-wing parties, which the Soviet Union has assiduously cultivated, or of increasing preoccupation with raw material supplies, that Mr Tanaka in March, 1973, agreed to further talks during the year on a peace treaty while no longer making the return of the islands a prior condition. Yet the Soviet Union is not going to be able to solve Japan's raw-materials problem, however much the latter is prepared to invest in Siberia: at best it seems likely to satisfy under 10 per cent of her requirements for iron, coal, oil or lumber in the 1970s. And although Japan is for the time being the Soviet Union's second largest trading partner (the largest being East Germany) it looks as if Russian–Japanese trade will stabilize at a total figure of about $1 billion a year, broadly the same level as the United States expects to attain with the Soviet Union: put another way, the Soviet Union will account for a little more than 2 per cent of Japanese foreign trade where the United States accounts for 30 per cent. The prospect that one sometimes heard in the 1960s of the hosepipe of Japanese exports getting diverted from the West to the relatively high consumption mass market of the Soviet Union has faded before the prospect of continuing Soviet economic autarchy.

One clear reason why Japan is anxious not to become too deeply involved in the development of Siberia, apart from dislike of Russians and the financial risks involved, is that she must on no account become embroiled in the Sino–Soviet dispute. This essential principle derives not only from anxiety about her own security but because China exerts a lure which the Soviet Union never could. Hers is in a sense the parent culture; she is the twin state, however alien her contemporary ideology: and many Japanese see the two countries as complementary in economic terms, an advanced island power and a developing agricultural land mass. Added to this there is, or was until very recently, a lingering sense of guilt at Japan's earlier behaviour towards China.

This does not mean that the new relationship between Japan and China is devoid of friction or will necessarily blossom rapidly. Though the Chinese have ceased to harp on the dangers of Japanese militarism, as long as Japan leases bases in Okinawa to the United States which are used primarily to assure the defence of Taiwan, the warmth of the Tokyo–Peking relationship is partly dependent on that between Washington and Peking. But even though the Taiwan issue has now been partly defused, there is the problem of the continental shelf around the Senkaku Islands to which Japan, China, Taiwan and Korea all lay claim: indeed the fact that almost the whole of the China Sea is continental shelf creates potential trouble between China and all the Pacific littoral states, especially if it shows signs of bearing oil in large quantities. It is impossible, for instance, to envisage the kind of international division of exploitation areas that was negotiated for the North Sea.

After a year in Japan, Zbgniew Brezinski concluded that 'in the back of their heads, many Japanese, right as well as left-wing, carry the aspirations of a grand alliance with China', but concluded also that China would prove 'a bigger temptation than an opportunity'.[11] Trade is rising to a level a little higher than that with the Soviet Union and China has begun to accept some Japanese credits, but the hope of a dramatic increase is likely to be disappointing, despite the nominal complementarity of the two economies; and this is unlikely to be affected by whether the LDP stays in power or is replaced by a left-wing coalition. Japan must walk warily, moreover, for too close a relationship with China must in the foreseeable future arouse Soviet hostility, which could not only jeopardize Japan's Siberian investments but might bring her into an adversary relationship with a super-power who can bring every level of pressure to bear upon her. China, like the Soviet Union, is moreover, an autarchic state, determined to avoid dependence on any external power.*

Japan has an interest shared by very few other countries in the modification of Sino–Soviet hostility. For the United States the conflict has been an opportunity, for Western Europe a convenience, for India a godsend, for some developing countries a useful way of extracting additional resources or support. Japan

---

* There is also a fear of the power of the Japanese example, which is apparently the reason why new Chinese films still have Japanese villains.

has no wish to be faced with a monolithic mainland bloc but the present level of hostility between the two mainland powers increases the national sense of dilemma about her future policy. Unfortunately, there is virtually nothing she can do to adjudicate between them or lower the level of their hostility. She is not the apex of an Asian political triangle.

An independent super-power?

Japan has another alternative, however. She is an economic super-power and one of the dynamic large economic powers of the world. The way in which the UN charter was drafted denies her the place to which many Japanese feel she is entitled, namely as a permanent member of the Security Council.[12] Though she is a respected member of many international organizations, her economic strength is as much a source of envy or embarrassment as of prestige. Though her crafts and increasingly her arts win acclaim, many Japanese feel that she is regarded as a second-class civilization. But if the present international system in all its aspects treats her too lightly, why should she not embark on its reorganization? Why not translate her economic strength into military power and develop her own sphere of influence in the world? If nuclear weapons are the ticket of entry to the top table, then why not Japanese nuclear weapons? Is there no one who will do in Asia in the 1970s what de Gaulle did in Europe in the 1960s?

There are practical arguments to support such a change from a low to a high posture. The United States in the later 1970s will be only one Pacific power among several, as I have suggested earlier, rather than the guardian of its peace, and a case can be made for a strong Japanese navy to replace the Seventh Fleet and to protect her trade routes. The Brezhnev–Nixon declarations make the future of super-power guarantees to allies look a little dubious, and there has been discussion in Japan for at least a decade of the eventual necessity of her developing nuclear weapons. China despite her political influence or cultural or revolutionary magnetism has a much narrower technological base than Japan and her strategic strength is augmenting only very gradually. The Soviet Union can deploy nothing like the power in East Asia or the Pacific that she can in Europe or the Atlantic area, especially if she remains in an adversary relationship with China. In a period of growing raw-material shortage, it is the countries with the largest aid or development programmes that may get the most favourable treatment. There is no need to resurrect the spectre of the Greater Asian Co-prosperity Sphere, to envisage a Japan that is as asser- tive on her own plane of strength as de Gaulle was on his a decade earlier.

This could happen. Japan has, in the words of Masataka Kosaka, 'been playing what can be called "a potential power game" – using her potential power to refrain from a real power game. . . .'[13] At some point, as a consequence of a crisis in Japanese–American relations, of a collapse or steady degeneration of the Western trade and payments system which made Japan feel that she had to fight for her existence, or simply one of those changes in national mood that have occurred before, she might decide to play the real power game.

But one has only to posit the idea to be aware that its risks would far outweigh any gains Japan might reap in terms of prestige or influence. To take the nuclear option first, Japan is developing considerable stocks of plutonium as the result of a large civil nuclear programme and has imported or developed the basic technology for every aspect of missile development. In the late 1960s about half the Japanese public appeared to think the nuclear option should be exercised though the figure has dropped to 35 per cent since the opening to China in 1972.[14] But if it were, in the form, say, of a decision to build six or ten second-generation nuclear submarines, the country would traverse a period little shorter than ten years, while warheads and delivery systems were being designed, tested and produced, of great danger, in which she would have no allies and no indigenous system of deterrence either. For I do not see how the Japanese–American Security Treaty could survive such a decision, most particularly in the light of Soviet–American relations. American Japanophiles hope that the United States could maintain a relation of some sort with Japan if she went nuclear; but in reality the United States would bring down the whole edifice of the 1960 Non-Proliferation Treaty, one of the few constructive acts of the diplomacy of the past decade, not only if she were to offer any assistance to a Japanese nuclear programme, but even if she stayed in a security relationship of any kind with a Japan that had withdrawn its own signature. More- over, if Japan did successfully traverse this dangerous period, her position would remain intrinsically precarious, because, as Kiichi Saeki has pointed out, '32 per cent of Japan's total population is concentrated in the three separate 50-kilometre-radius areas around Tokyo, Nagoya and Osaka, in which important political, economic and military functions are concentrated as well. Of all major countries Japan is peculiarly vulnerable to nuclear attack.'[15] In addition, her dependence on imported raw materials, including uranium, means that no level of strategic power could guarantee her autarchy.

A Japanese fleet? Certainly the present modest naval element of the Self-Defence Force could be built into a powerful fleet more rapidly than any other power could do it. But what purpose would it serve? If relations with China or Russia were bitterly hostile, then it might help to assert Japanese interests. But in the present international climate Japan's interest is to normalize her relations with them, and her economic strength is her principal bargaining card. Moreover, may not the Russians have made a serious mis-calculation about the nature of contemporary international politics in building up her naval strength? How great a diplomatic asset is it, once the novelty of ships with unfamiliar flags in faraway ports has worn off? Certainly Japan's anxieties about Gulf oil or about the Malacca Strait cannot be solved by the assertion of naval strength against the littoral states, with whom she has other incentives to remain on good terms.

This leaves the question of a politico-economic sphere of influence. Japan is an Asian country with a large surplus to invest, and although the scars of thirty years ago still remain, especially in Malaysia and Singapore, they are fading. Asian countries are hungry for development capital and many big Japanese enterprises are moving major production operations overseas. But there is no 'sphere' to be carved out that would meet Japan's economic interests as well as satisfying a desire for influence. Indians and Japanese simply do not get on. Australia is prepared to be an intimate trade partner but not to accept Japanese leadership. In the poorer countries of South East Asia, the difference between their own and the Japanese standard of living creates a cultural barrier. Though Japan's share of the Asian market seems likely to double between 1965 and 1975 from about 17 per cent to about 35 per cent, in terms of investment and raw material supplies Japanese investment in Central and South America is almost as large as in South and Eastern Asia. A more generous Japanese policy on aid and development loans would be welcome but a global economic power can make no good use of a limited geographical sphere of politico-economic influence. (I will return to Japan's position as a member of a community of Pacific states in the next chapter.)

'Idealism is realism'

Japan possesses the power to 'change the name of the game' of international politics to an even greater extent than China does, though for different reasons and objectives. She can entirely alter the classical definition of a great power. For her fourth alternative is to place her considerable weight behind the effective functioning of an interdependent economic and political order through its institutions. A Japanese scholar, Kei Wakaizumi, who has thought deeply about the problems of Japanese foreign and security policy, has suggested recently that 'in contemporary Japan idealism is realism'.[16] If Mr Tanaka's government can succeed in achieving the objective he has set it of more than halving Japan's trade surplus in the next few years, then she will be negotiating from a stronger hand in the multilateral western trade, monetary and energy negotiations. If she is prepared to raise her level of development aid from its present figure, 0·23 per cent of GNP, to the Pearson figure of 0·7 per cent then by 1975 it would be running at a level of between $2·5 and $2·8 billion or nearly three times that of the United States and her influence in the developing world would grow accordingly. If she uses her potential as a nuclear power to insist on greater restraint in the development of strategic weapons – and her outpoken criticism of the French and Chinese nuclear tests of 1973 is a new departure in her diplomacy – then her influence in the United Nations will grow.

A policy of such practical idealism might enhance Japanese standing in the world more than any other form of diplomacy. The danger is that power may get confused with status, that she may be angered by the difficulty of making her a permanent member of the Security Council. A year before writing this I tried to address this question in speaking to an audience that included a number of Japanese.

'There is the question of some formal acknowledgement of the important role that Japan now plays in world politics. It has been suggested . . . that Japan should become a permanent member of the Security Council. I sympathize with this though it must be recalled, first, that the Charter refers to five powers by name and Charter revision is something from which the international community, and not just the Soviet Union, has recoiled on several occasions over the last quarter-century; second, that essential as the UN and its agencies are for a hundred different purposes, the Security Council has really been the least successful aspect of it – witness the Middle East since 1967. To quote Dr Waldheim, 'The Organization has proved to be of limited value as an instrument of collective security, not least because that concept was based on ideas and situations from the past which are not applicable to the very different political realities of our world today.'* The fact that the five permanent members of the Security Council are also today's five nuclear powers is the blindest chance and has no bearing upon world order. It is possible that over the next decade or so a mass of transnational pressures, political or non-political, problems of demography and ecology, of raw materials and energy, of arms control or the control of crime and violence, of commerce and movements, problems of poverty and regional conflict, may force the governments to modernize the Charter and the structure of the United Nations. Until that day comes, it seems to me that there are many other international institutions of which Japan is already a member, the General Assembly, the UN agencies, OECD, the Group of Twenty, UNCTAD, ECAFE, where Japan can as effectively shape the course of world politics as in that shadowy Council on the East River.

This is no longer a hierarchical world order, except in the limited case of strategic weapons. Japan is a power of the first rank economically and therefore politically, and everyone's diplomacy must and does take account of this fact. To argue that she will never be treated as a great power unless she is self-sufficient strategically, to use von Ranke's definition of a great power as one that can stand alone without allies, is to misuse the lessons of history in much the same way that chatter about a five-power balance does.'[17]

How Japan resolves her dilemma depends partly on her own policy. One important contribution at this time would be to divert investment away from her export industries to her social infra-

* Report of the Secretary-General on the Work of the Organization (Document A/8701/Add 1).

structure so that her partners in the developed world lose their current sense of being menaced and can catch their breath; it would also enhance respect for Japanese society. Constructive Japanese initiatives on the new problems of international society would enhance her influence considerably. Since there is no real alternative to the Japanese–American security relationship, much depends on the United States, partly in fostering détente as she has done, partly in refusing to be stampeded by Japanese imports as by and large she has done, and partly by making Japan certain that she is an important contributor and valued adviser in the general evolution of great-power relations, which she has not done. The Japanese–American Security Treaty will require continuous modification so that it ceases to be one wholly of guarantor and guaranteed, to one in which either American bases in Japan are run down to a minimum or new forms of joint decision-making for the use of the forces of both countries in the area are evolved. But much also depends on Western Europe and countries like Canada and Australia, not simply in terms of trade and technology, but also in terms of interest in and concern for Japanese problems. Britain, the other island industrial power, with very similar security and strategic interests, can perhaps do most. Part of the answer, though perhaps less than many Japanese think, will be provided by her relations with the mainland powers, neither of whom now wishes to break the Japanese–American nexus and with each of whom she can only pursue a relationship that is secondary and bilateral.

10
The Great Powers and Asia

The focus of a multilateral balance

Before we can attempt any conclusions, however tentative, about the ways in which the relationships of the major powers with each other, and with the rest of the international community, are changing, of the difference between the climate of world politics in the fourth quarter of this century and the third, it is essential to examine the development of their relations with some of the hundred or so states of the developing world. But it would be unscholarly and misleading to do so in relation merely to an abstraction called 'the third world' whose unity of problems and objectives had largely disappeared, as I have earlier suggested, by the end of the 1960s. Equally, to attempt to do so in detail would require a separate book, and if I concentrate this chapter on Asia, it is not from any sense that Africa and Latin America are backwaters but simply because Asia comprises so much of humanity, and is an area where the interests of the major powers have conflicted most directly.

The states of Latin America have immense problems deriving from the combination of population pressure and economic and social backwardness. Latin America is also a heterogeneous international sub-system which comprises governments of considerable stability like Mexico as well as many unstable ones, plus one aspirant to the status of a major power, Brazil. It is, moreover, no longer either an economic or political dependency of the United States since Japan is becoming rapidly more influential in the economies of many Latin American states and Western Europe steadily more influential in both economic and cultural terms. But though most Latin American societies are faced with endemic problems of social instability, which have made them the breeding-ground of urban guerrilla movements, the Soviet Union's strategy there remains what it has been for a decade, namely one of slow and peaceful penetration only, while China has abandoned an earlier policy of encouraging sectarian disputes among left-wing movements and now concentrates, as elsewhere, in cultivating good relations with governments. The fact that the rise and fall of the Allende regime in Chile has occurred without its becoming truly an international issue confirms other evidence that the great powers do not regard Latin America as a focus of their competition. This situation may change in twenty years but for the moment Latin America – except for the Caribbean where the United States remains sensitive to even minor external involvements – has the good fortune to be outside the ambit of high international politics, though its links with the rest of the world are becoming rapidly diversified.

Africa, similarly, is fortunate that its component states can pursue their own development and association without being, for the moment, the object of high politics. It is true that the fact that most of black Africa has affiliations of one kind or another with Europe makes for disputes between the Community and the United States where they are close, and for American interest in them where they are not, that China has established a strong diplomatic position in East Africa, and that the Soviet Union pursues quite successfully an opportunist policy in North, East and West Africa on state trading and the supply of arms. But no African leaders now show the interest that Nkrumah and Sekou-Touré did in playing off the great powers against each other in order to enhance the prosperity and importance of their countries, nor is it likely the great powers would respond if such policies were tried again. The Nigerian civil war saw both super-powers upholding legitimacy. Africa may yet generate the greatest crisis that the international community has faced since the Second World War when the African powers gain the strength, the confidence and the backing to attempt the overthrow of white rule in the Portuguese territories, Rhodesia and South Africa. But this crisis is beyond the horizon of the next decade, and might still be averted by external pressure on or internal change within Portugal and the white-supremacy countries. For the moment the tenor of relations between the major power centres of the world is not likely to be affected by the relationship or the objectives that any of them pursue in relation to Africa.

Asia is different for many obvious reasons. It is an enormous area, for those who live beside the Euphrates and those who live on the northern Japanese island of Hokkaido alike consider themselves Asian; it comprises two-thirds of the world's population; two of the world's major powers are Asian and a third, the Soviet Union, has vast Asian estates and a rising Asian population; it comprises countries of great and rising wealth as well as areas of great poverty. But most important of all it is in Asia that the great conflicts, of force, of diplomacy and alignments, of ideology, have occurred in the past quarter century between and among the local and external powers. And it is in Asia that chancelleries believe, rightly or wrongly, that such equilibrium as has been attained between the major powers could be overturned even more easily than in the other focus of great power interests, Europe. This is so even though the sense, that was apparent in Washington, in London and in Paris in the 1950s, that the Communist powers were engaged in a vast, concerted effort to undermine western influence in Asia, has largely disappeared.

This said, it is impossible for either governments or scholars to consider 'Asia' as one entity. For in fact Asia in political and strategic terms consists of four interrelated sub-systems: the Islamic states of South West Asia; the Indian sub-continent; South East Asia; and Pacific Asia. In each the interaction of the local powers follows a logic of its own and excites the interests of the external powers to a different extent, for different reasons and in differing degree. There is a certain relationship between developments in Europe and those in the Middle East; there is an increasing interrelationship between the politics of the Middle East and those of the sub-continent; there is a diminishing relationship between those of the sub-continent and South East and Pacific Asia but a close relationship between those of the two latter groups, and there are innumerable cross-currents.

Since these interrelationships derive partly from the policies or interests of the local powers and partly from those of the external powers the most useful approach may be to examine the international politics of Asia from two different perspectives, first from that of the external powers and second from that of the four different constellations of local powers.

The interests of the great powers

The first external power centre whose interests in Asia we must consider is Europe, whose sailors, soldiers and traders were active all over the area while Japan was still locked in the self-imposed isolation of the Tokagawa era, while Russia was still a backward principality, and the United States a group of Atlantic colonies. Has Western Europe ceased to play any part in the politics of Asia? Clearly the individual countries of Western Europe have not, for France has an active policy of entente with the Arab world; Britain is still a member of a modest security arrangement in South East Asia; all of them are dependent in greater or lesser degree on Gulf oil and Britain and the Netherlands are the home of two of the great oil companies; all have a variety of economic aid arrangements, moreover, with different parts of the continent. But these may be relationships of decreasing political significance on both sides, however much Europeans may resent American *obiter dicta* to the effect that their interests are no longer universal. French influence in the states of Indo-China has largely evaporated with the dislocation of their elites. The Anglo-Indian relationship which was still significant in the late 1960s, when Britain could, for instance, mediate between India and Pakistan over the Rann of Kutch, is fast losing its intimacy. Although European culture is admired in countries like the Philippines, although Britain has many kinds of links with Malaysia and Singapore, although the Netherlands and Indonesia have a remarkably successful relationship, it is Australia, the local power, that is most involved in South East Asian politics.

European countries, one can be certain, will continue to have many different kinds of links with Asia, but their political content may be small. And so different has been their experience in Asia – and several have had little or none – that the prospect of a unified Community position on Asian politico-strategic questions is not a promising one. Still less will the Community play an active role in maintaining the various sorts of Asian balance. Most Europeans would agree with Theo Sommer, the editor of *Die Zeit*, who writes, 'I do not envisage European gunboats patrolling the straits of Malacca, or EEC paratroopers supporting wobbly regimes in faraway countries against rebellious populations. The Community will have to have a military capacity to defend its territory but not to exercise its power far from its shores.[1]* Though the Community will be concerned with the general future of the developing world, it seems likely to have closer cultural relations with Latin America and closer economic relations with Africa than with any part of Asia, except, of course, Japan and the Persian Gulf. It will be doing well if during the next ten years it can prevent its component countries from undermining each other's interests in relations with the OPEC countries, or achieve a common position in sustaining a fair contribution to Indian development, though from humanitarian not political motives. Gradually one must expect that, as the cost of European security becomes more onerous on the one hand, and as Australia acquires greater resources and inspires greater local confidence on the other, even Britain's political interests in Asia will disappear, except for a limited number of specific responsibilities which she cannot abrogate such as Hong Kong or the trust territories in the Indian Ocean.

Far more American blood and treasure has been expended over the past thirty years in Asia than in Europe, first to smash the Japanese empire, then to develop alliances that would contain the expansion of the mainland powers, and finally to attempt to assert a system of regional order. That the United States has been and will continue to be sensitive to developments around the Pacific littoral is inevitable, for she is not only a Pacific power but her fiftieth state, Hawaii, makes her in a certain sense an Asian power. But ten years ago the United States was deeply involved in the politics of the Indian sub-continent and becoming steadily more involved in those of South East Asia. Has the revulsion against Asian entanglements caused by Vietnam, or has the new entente with the mainland powers, had the effect of narrowing her Asian interests to those which she had before her rise to the status of a super-power? If one simply took the change in the level of public interest in Asia, simply noted the greater preoccupation of the Administration with maintaining a strong military position in Europe than in the Pacific or elsewhere, one might be tempted to say that this was the case. But the true answer, I think, is that the emphasis of American concern with Asia has changed rather than diminished, and that it could change again if there was a marked

* In this sense the Community is likely to be what François Duchene has called a 'civilian power'. Only in the event of a major débacle in Asia that threatened the central balance of power, the collapse of India, or a violently aggressive Chinese strategy against her neighbours, can I envisage European military re-engagement in Asia.

alteration in her relations with any one of her other three partners, Soviet Union, China and Japan in what is now a quadrilateral relationship in Asia, even if it is not a balance of power in the traditional sense.

To take the four regions of Asia separately, the American interest in the Middle East has clearly altered. Her stance over the past fifteen years has never been a simple one of Israel right or wrong, for a total débacle in her relations with the Arab states would have weakened her position vis-à-vis the Soviet Union, as well as damaging her commercial interests. Nevertheless, throughout most of the 1960s the integrity of Israel was one of her prime pre-occupations in the area. Now she must tread an even more delicate path as the Gulf States become increasingly significant for the functioning of her own domestic economy. The Arab–Israel conflict is no longer a simple subsidiary balance of the central one, and it has become an interest of each super-power to be more selective in their Middle Eastern friendships. However, they are saddled with the legacy of the past and the events of October 1973 have shown that both Moscow and Washington intend to use their new found confidence in each other to attempt to impose a settlement on the area as, after a period of mutual crisis signalling by means of military alerts, they succeeded in imposing a ceasefire on 24 October. Whether the local states will prove amenable to such control, unless the super-powers produce a microcosm of the European balance by signing alliances with each party and stationing troops in the area, I am inclined to doubt.

In the two regions that form the centre of the Asian arc, American interests and attitudes have clearly changed. President Nixon is doubtless sincere in stating in his latest foreign policy report that 'We want to join with India in a mature relationship, founded on equality, reciprocity, and mutual interests, reflecting India's status as a great free nation'.[2] But his concern with the fortunes of Pakistan in 1971, together with his clear belief that a working relationship with Peking overrides any American interests in the sub-continent, has imposed strains in the Indo–American relationship from which it seems unlikely fully to recover. With the change in the American attitude to China, India is no longer seen as the great alternative society whose success and therefore whose magnetism for other Asian societies must be encouraged.[3] By the same token, a truncated Pakistan, which has quit SEATO, which indentifies its interests primarily with Iran on the one hand and China on the other, and which has lost its strategic significance for the United States, is no longer the special American ward it once was. This does not mean that the United States has no interests in the area; she has a strong concern in denying any exclusive relationship between India and the Soviet Union, despite their treaty and their mutual interests, and she has the same non-political anxiety with the economic stability and development of India as the European powers. She has an interest which she shares with the Soviet Union and China in creating a climate of Asian politics that makes the costs of an Indian nuclear weapon programme (which might make it harder for Japan to resist a similar move) continue to outweigh the benefits. She has a strategic interest that is to a certain extent in conflict with this in deploying *Poseidon* submarines in the Indian Ocean, for they would be better placed there in relation to a range of Soviet targets than in the Atlantic or the Pacific. So the concerns of the sub-continent are not simply to be ignored in Washington or handed over to the mainland powers.

If the foreign policies of great states were determined on the basis of logic alone, it could be argued that the United States no longer has a serious interest in South East Asia or Australasia. Her twenty-year-old treaty relationship with Australia and New Zealand was largely a guarantee on her part against the resurgence of Japanese or the rise of Chinese military power, yet Australia and New Zealand now have their own links with both powers and no serious reason to fear either. The American rationale for involvement in Indo-China in the 1950s was, ideological considerations apart, that the markets of South East Asia were essential to the recovery of Japan's economic independence, and, in the first half of the 1960s, that what appeared to be a burgeoning Chinese–Indonesian axis must be averted if possible. Yet Japan is now very securely established in the markets of South East Asia, and the present regime in Indonesia is more wary of China than most Asian governments. But the preoccupations of one generation are not easily overturned by the next; for one thing, the United States remains intimately concerned in the future of Indo-China as South Vietnam's source of arms and as the principal architect of the shaky armistice there. This remains true despite the withdrawal of her forces, the political difficulties of ever intervening again, and the refusal of Congress in the summer of 1973 to permit continued American bombing support for the Lon Nol regime in Cambodia.

There is, moreover, some evidence to suggest that China would not wish to see a complete abrogation of American responsibilities in the area from her fear of the added freedom of action it would give to the Soviet Union, Japan and India. Consequently, the President need have little fear that he is jeopardizing his relationship with the mainland powers in continuing to state categorically that the United States will maintain its treaty commitments in the area, will provide a nuclear shield if either an ally or a friend is threatened, and the sinews if not the troops to deal with other forms of aggression.[4] Indeed as far as the fourth area of Asia, the Pacific region, is concerned one can say that the continuation of the American alliances with Japan, South Korea, the Philippines and even in the short run Taiwan is almost a condition of good Sino–American relations, since Peking still has residual fears of an irredentist and nuclear Japan, or of increased Soviet manœuvring in relation to the smaller powers. A continuing American interest and military presence, however modest, in the Eastern Pacific must seem to the Chinese leadership a desirable alternative to a Soviet one. There is no urgency, therefore, from the American standpoint, in terms of Sino–American relations, in revising either her bilateral commitments or even such multilateral ones as SEATO; for to the argument that SEATO was originally designed as an anti-Chinese instrument, it can be answered, first, that it has become more the legal basis of bilateral relations between the United States and Thailand on the one hand and South Vietnam on the other than a multilateral arrangement; and that, second, it is no more a Chinese interest to permit the expansion of North Vietnamese than of Soviet influence in South East Asia. Nevertheless, a defunct multilateral treaty could be a source of danger and confusion in a crisis, and it may soon be desirable to make its form correspond to its reality. In general, of the three main choices open to the United States in Asia, virtual withdrawal, the transformation of the American bilateral alliance into a multilateral system that might even include the Community powers, and what Robert Scalapino has termed 'an alliance accommodation system', the Nixon administration seems to have opted for the third.[5]

The Asian interests of Japan are harder to identify, for herself and for others, than for the United States or the mainland powers;

they are even harder to identify than Europe's, for Japan is an Asian power and Japanese have a sensitivity to the politics of East and South East Asia which European countries (though not Australia) no longer fully share. Her attempts in the 1960s to float the conception of a Pacific Community that would include the countries of both its shores met, unfortunately with little response. She is disillusioned with the fruits of the Asian and Pacific Council (ASPAC) of which the United States (and Taiwan) are members, though Mr Tanaka has said that he will not take the lead in dissolving it. She has looked warily at a proposal by Mr Whitlam, the Australian Prime Minister, for a new Asian grouping of which China would be a member, launched by a new all-Asian conference akin to the Bandung Conference of 1955; she has also been wary of Mr Lee Kuan Yew's proposal for an international task force to counter Soviet naval influence in the waters between the Pacific and the Indian Ocean. Mr Tanaka did in fact tell the Upper House on 14 March 1973 that he saw no requirement for a new Asian organization to maintain peace and foster regional cooperation. But it is not clear that Japan can sustain such a 'civilian' pose. She clearly has a short-term ambition to play a role in the rehabilitation of Indo-China, and to make this the starting-point for wider Asian cooperation; yet hesitates to take the lead for fear of being accused of 'economic aggression' in the area. In the long term, the idea of a working entente, not necessarily a formal alliance, between Japan, Indonesia and Australia, resting on foundations of both economic and political mutual interest, naturally suggests itself, on the assumption that it will be the fourth stance I mentioned in the last chapter, of a generally internationalist rather than an irredentist or balance of power policy, that continues to elicit political consensus in Japan.

The ramifications of the Sino–Soviet quarrel

Soviet interest is to exploit any vacua left in Asia by the retreat of Western power, both for the containment of China and to validate her credentials as a universal power. If it has the effect of disorganizing Western interests in the process, as a dominant Soviet position in the Gulf might generally complicate Western decisions in a crisis, even if their day-to-day supply of oil was not constricted, then so much the better. But Soviet policy in Asia is affected by her general disillusionment with the prospect of promoting revolutionary change in the developing world as a whole, and her interest in the different parts of Asia varies considerably, being lowest in Pacific Asia and highest in the sub-continent. Like the United States, her Middle Eastern interests are changing; Arab radicalism appears to offer her as much frustration as reward, the fact that the situation of Soviet Jewry has become an international issue has forced her to open discreet lines of communication with Israel, while the fact that she is an importer as well as an exporter of oil gives her a material interest in the policies of the Gulf States (Libya is beyond her reach for ideological and Algeria for geographic reasons). The fact that she has large and growing Turkish and Muslim minorities on her southern border makes her sensitive to the present power of Iran and, in so far as it is growing, of Turkey. She, like the United States, is conscious of the developing connection between the politics of the Middle East and those of the sub-continent, especially as China seeks to woo Turkey and Iran as well as Pakistan, and as Afghanistan enters a phase of crisis. She has tried intermittently to make clear that her treaty relationship with India is not an exclusive one, that it was she who brought India and Pakistan to the negotiating table after the 1965 war, and that she would be amenable to reconciliation with Pakistan. Nevertheless, as long as the Sino–Soviet conflict continues in its present form, her alliance with India, the second largest Asian state, disillusioned with the West and hostile to the Chinese, is the natural foundation of her Asian policy.

But the Soviet Union remains an ambitious power in Asia; she is determined to establish her own credentials as an Asian state, without whose concurrence no major redrawing of the lines of Asian politics can be pursued; she like the United States has legacies from the past which she cannot disregard, her relationship with North Vietnam and North Korea, for instance; and she has a high interest in dispelling any notion that the Indian Ocean is still a Western lake. In consequence, apart from capitalizing on minor opportunities, such as Malaysia's desire to diversify its trading relationships, she has attempted the same sort of broad initiatives that originally inspired her pressure for a European Security Conference.

Mr Brezhnev's first *balloon d'essai* about a new collective security arrangement for Asia as a whole goes back four years and until recently was re-floated only intermittently. Recently, however, the Soviet Union has sponsored a number of non-governmental meetings with East European help of the Afro-Asian Peoples' Solidarity Organization, the Afro-Asian Women's Conference and so on, in an attempt to widen acceptance of the idea. But when it is discussed seriously with governments it runs foul either of the general and continuing Asian preoccupation with non-alignment or of an equally widespread desire to remain detached from the toils of the Sino–Soviet conflict. The attempts of Soviet spokesmen to maintain that it would not be an anti-Chinese alliance has been greeted with silence. Even Mrs Gandhi, who presumably has better access to Soviet thoughts than most Asian leaders, told a press conference in February 1973 that it all depended on what the Russians meant; Iran has made it clear that any such general agreement must include China; Mr Podgorny's visit to Kabul in May failed to elicit any endorsement of the proposal; Japan distrusts the idea. Mr Brezhnev has said that it is up to the Asians themselves to work out the details and has hinted that it would elicit economic benefits from the Soviet Union. But if he hoped for the sort of response that General Marshall received from the Western European countries to his Harvard speech of June 1947, he has so far been disappointed. It looks as if the best the Soviet Union can hope to do is to encourage local groupings in Asia which are avowedly non-aligned.

It is probably too early to attempt any concrete analysis of Chinese policy in Asia. That she has interests there, deriving partly from a desire to minimize Soviet political and Japanese economic influences, especially in South East Asia, is obvious. But to an even greater extent than the Soviet Union, she has found a global policy, ideological or national, beyond her reach and, as I have suggested in an earlier chapter, one principle focus of interest at present is not on the periphery of the Middle Kingdom but in an area of Africa, Southern Europe and South West Asia where Soviet influence is most vulnerable, or where it is vital to China that it should not become entrenched; but the focus of rivalry may well change. However, it would be a mistake to think that the lines of stress have been drawn forever in the subcontinent; China, for instance, has an opportunity to cultivate the new third state, Bangla Desh; and just as the Soviet Union may well attempt to improve her relations with Pakistan to bring them into line with her reasonably cordial relations with Iran, so China is committed neither by ideology nor interest to an unending stance of

mutual hostility with India. In 1962, when China was still largely
an international outcast and India was the focus of Western
interest in Asia, China felt impelled to assert her power and
initiative by answering a number of border encroachments with a
strong *promenade militaire*. But a China which is now an acknowledged great power while India is not, can afford to be more
flexible, and in confronting what she considers to be an unequal
balance between herself and the Soviet Union, an intimate Soviet–
Indian relationship is a disadvantage. However, much water may
have to flow down the Yellow River and the Brahmaputra before
such a reconciliation is possible; certainly it is difficult to contemplate while Chou En-lai and Nehru's daughter still hold the reins
of power. And an amelioration of Sino–Indian relations is, in my
judgement, more likely to be a consequence of an improvement
in Sino–Soviet relations than the consequence of a diplomatic
volte-face on the part of India.

In South East Asia, as in Korea, China like her partners is
saddled with the consequences of the past. A powerful North
Vietnam was not of her making even though American involvement in opposition to it made her support inevitable; so one of her
interests in South East Asia must be to prevent the recurrence of a
situation which enhances the influence of Hanoi, and she has a
general interest in keeping a chaotic situation in the rest of Indo-
China from degenerating further, even though she can now be
reasonably sure that it would not bring American soldiers back
again. Relics of past policies still persist, support for Thai insur-
gents (when a new relationship between Thailand and China is
to be had for the asking) and radio propaganda against local
governments in a score of languages and dialects. But China, to
quote a wise Indonesian student of Asian politics,

'may well have a stake in an increased self-reliance of the
countries in that region. At some point, she may even come to
see the utility to her of some non-ideological form of regional
cooperation, aimed at enhancing regional strength and self-
confidence. And with some stretch of the imagination it may not
be entirely inconceivable that China at some point will see the
advantage to her of a system of interlocking external balances in
the region which, in combination with the increased capabilities
of the South East Asian countries themselves, would amount to an
effective neutralization she may not even be asked to guarantee.'[6]

The Middle East and the sub-continent

The development of political relationships in Asia, and the maintenance of stability and peace in an area which has engendered or been the victim of more open conflict than any other part of the world, does not, of course, depend exclusively on the actions of the external powers. Though their affiliations or disputes with different countries will affect their relations with each other, there can be no question of developing, in the last quarter of the twentieth century, the kind of 'balance of compensation' by which the European great powers sustained peace among themselves in the last quarter of the nineteenth by the carve-up of Africa and South East Asia. 'Neo-colonialism' is almost as emotive a word in the developing world as colonialism, and communications in general are too extensive, Asian opinion in particular is too articulate, for any sort of trade-offs between the great powers – of control over Country A in return for concessions over Country B – to go undetected, still less to be accepted. All the states and regimes of Asia, as of Africa and Latin America, are struggling to develop their own persona, and would willingly forego short term economic or security advantages if it appeared that they were not the masters of their own destiny.

The exception to this judgement may prove to be the relations between Israel, Syria, Jordan and Egypt where the super-powers appear likely to attempt to control local relations directly. But even if they should succeed there will now be a second centre of gravity in the Middle East in the area not only of the Nile and Jordan but also of Oxus and Euphrates. At this point one can do no more than speculate to what political ends the oil-rich states will devote their spare resources. First, will their regimes remain stable, and conservative as, with the exception of Iraq, they now are? Or will the conflict between a customary society and the modernizing forces in its midst, that accompany great extractive operations and the import of advanced military technology, lead to the same kind of internal upheavals, the overthrow of established regimes, as has happened elsewhere? Despite the efforts of the Shah and King Faisal to forestall this by being more radical on oil policy than their neighbours, the prospect is at best uncertain, and if the government of one Gulf state is overturned it is likely to happen in others. Second, what differences would this make to their external attitudes? I think one can say if the Gulf states continue to be ruled by kings and emirs, they will have a prime concern for the development of their own countries and the maximization of profits while trying to conserve their precious resources. This means that they will remain primarily Western oriented, though cultivating their relations with the mainland powers, and ready to help finance other Arab governments, not only against Israel but for their own development. If governments pass into the hands of more radical men, presumably of the Ghadafi breed rather than men oriented towards Moscow, not only may they attempt to drive a harder bargain with the West; but they may be more ambitious to extend their influence into West as well as East Africa, Pakistan, South East Asia, wherever Islam flourishes.

How significant an effect this might have upon the politics of Asia would depend upon the corporate unity of action that either traditional or new radical regimes in the oil-rich states could develop and sustain. It is one thing for the Shah to lead OPEC in negotiating new arrangements with the Western oil companies; it is quite another for a non-Arab monarch to sustain leadership of what is primarily a group of Arab states. And the history of attempts at Arab unity is not an encouraging one. However, if the oil states can develop the characteristic of 'community' then they will have more disposable wealth than any entity in world politics except the European Community itself and the other major powers. And although the total population of the Gulf States is less than Britain they will be a force to be reckoned with in every level of world politics except the nuclear. A combination of ambition and unity, coupled with the fact that Europe, Japan and the United States and even to a limited extent the Soviet Union are their customers, might create a certain identity of interest among the external powers in containing this new centre of power and wealth.

But if they do not achieve unity then the key country is likely to be Iran, a state with a population of 30 million and $3 billion worth of armaments on order; located between South Western and Southern Asia; able if it chooses to make its outlet in every sense the *Persian* Gulf; and with a strong central government. Though sharing a common border with the Soviet Union, Iran is linked to the Western alliance systems through CENTO yet it has been careful to preserve its autonomy. The Shah is now a significant figure in the politics of Asia, and has been wooed by Japan and China as well as his traditional allies and his neighbours. It is possible that a desire for greater status in the world, without risking new contractual arrangements, on the part of countries like Iran, Japan, Brazil and the new middle powers may restore vitality to the universal political power, namely the UN. Whether this is so or not, it is clear that Iran is going to play an increasingly influential role in the politics of the Indian sub-continent. If India, for instance, made its peace with China but not with Pakistan, Teheran would be Rawalpindi's only close and effective friend. Conversely, if Pakistan moves closer to the Soviet Union, Iran could be an important friend for India in resisting any Soviet pretensions to a hegemonial or exclusive relationship with the countries of the sub-continent.

Iran at this time possesses a freedom of action denied to India despite Mrs Gandhi's triumph in converting the blunders of the Pakistani generals in 1971 into an extension of Indian power, which has disposed of any question of which is the dominant power in the sub-continent. But the future of India as a polity or as a united country is still not fully assured, despite Mrs Gandhi's success as a political leader and her skill in shifting the centre of gravity of the Congress party to the left in order to outflank the CPM, the Moscow oriented wing of the Communist Party in Bengal, and to contain and destroy its Naxalite rival. The Congress party looks stronger now than at any point since independence, but because it still is as much a movement as a party, predictions about the future course of Indian politics are unwise. For one thing experience has proved how difficult it is for a developing country to make rapid social and economic strides on the basis of political democracy; it is an unpalatable conclusion but there is no doubt that those countries which have progressed, economically and socially, are those with a strong central government that need not make short-term promises, as democratic politicians must, and can make plans and execute them over a considerable period of time.

But the last few years have also clarified an important aspect of India's interests, namely that, if she cannot afford the luxury of non-alignment by reason of her size and her relations with her neighbours, the Soviet Union is her most natural ally, though Communism as an ideology is most unlikely to make serious headway in India as a whole. Not only has a position of influence in India been a Russian aspiration for generations, but there is now no other major power which shares India's strategic concerns, has a motive for assisting India, that would be in a position to come to her aid in an emergency, and has an interest in assisting India that transcends humanitarianism. Both are land masses, both have the same ambivalent attitudes of respect and contempt for the West. Britain and Europe have lost both the means and to a large extent the incentive to sustain a close relationship with India; so also has the United States which is seeking to narrow its responsibilities; and since China is a rival she cannot be absolved of a desire to break up the still by no means unified Indian federation. The Soviet Union, it is true, could break up India if she chose more easily than any other major power; a cold-blooded decision on her part to deal directly with the governments of, say, West Bengal, Kerala or Madras could start an unravelling process which Delhi might be powerless to stop. But the fact is that a united India is a clear Soviet interest.

Moreover, India has too long a history of contact with the West, is too much affected by its economic, monetary or energy policies, for her elite to be content with one overriding bilateral relationship. So that she seems ready within limits to accept the conception of mutual access between herself and the major external power centres with, for the moment, the exception of China. But though India is Asia's second largest state, she possesses little external influence there (except with her immediate neighbours); she is a static power in diplomatic terms at present, and the evolution of local relationships elsewhere in Asia is unlikely to be greatly affected by her conceptions or initiatives, even though her relations with China may become less hostile and those with the United States less sour.

Neutrality and regionalism

No area of the world represents a greater challenge to the principles of peaceful coexistence than South East Asia which, excluding a Burma that has successfully opted out of world politics, consists of eight states, six of them weak, one of them militarily strong (North Vietnam) and one of them a potential major power (Indonesia). But each country has one or more serious minority problems and the authority of government is limited (except in Singapore). Above all, it is an area which has been an object of great-power politics for a long time and is inherently porous or exposed to the influence of outside governments, for political influence apart, it is a rich area that is deeply involved in world trade and affected by its fluctuations. First Japan ousted the colonial powers by force in 1941; then after the war the United States sought to fill the vacuum left by the retreat of European influence in order to prevent China from becoming predominant there; subsequently the Soviet Union has displayed increasing interest in the area, largely also to contain Chinese influence but with its own economic and political interests also in mind. Japan has now become the major economic influence in the area. Only China's interests there remain unclear, though the existence of Chinese communities in almost all the South Eastern countries means that she cannot be indifferent to its politics, even if she no longer fears that it may be used as an American bridgehead that threatens her own security. No major power, it is clear, is prepared to see South East Asia become the exclusive province of another.

This has led to recurrent discussion of the possibility of negotiating some formula for the neutrality of South East Asia. But the more one contemplates the prospect the more difficult the conception is to apply in practice, since, if all its countries are embraced within such a formula, neutralization offers cold comfort to the small states, caught between the actuality of North Vietnamese power and ambition to the north and the potentiality of Indonesian power to the south. To maintain stability and prevent conflict in so heterogeneous and populous an area would appear to involve an elaborate convention agreed to by both the local powers and the external powers, which gave the latter rights of intervention and surveillance to which no other group of sovereign states in the world is subjected. It is very unlikely either that the external powers would undertake such commitments or that the local powers would accept some sort of international commission to regulate their affairs.

Consequently, the avenue down which local discussion has been travelling, namely to evolve a distinction between the Indo–China area and the rest of South East Asia, is obvious common sense. At the moment the most hopeful development is the Association of South East Asian Nations (ASEAN) which embraces Indonesia, Malaysia, Singapore, the Philippines and Thailand. It has made some headway in the creation of confidence between the member governments and the coordination of their policies. But the question arises how far the evolution of this little community can be carried even if it does successfully evolve communitarian habits and institutions. The Malaysian Prime Minister, Tun Razak, has seen it as a group of neutralized states pledged to respect each other's territorial integrity, whose external security would be guaranteed by the great powers. But this presupposes that Thailand and the Philippines would be prepared to reject their alliances with the United States, and Malaysia and Singapore their security relationship, modest though it is, with Britain and Australia. The Indonesian Foreign Minister, Mr Malik, moreover, has rejected both the practicality and the desirability of neutralization as a general solution to the security problems of South East Asia.[7] The new Australian government of Mr Whitlam and the New Zealand government, while generally seeking to establish the principle of 'hands off' as far as the great powers are concerned in South East Asia, would like to foster the cohesion of ASEAN rather than see its component states neutralized.

ASEAN as a Community in embryo commands the support of all the external powers except the Soviet Union with its more grandiose design, and Chinese silence on the subject may perhaps be taken for consent. But Indo-China presents a different problem. Not only is it a more conflict-ridden area where the final lines of armistice are not yet determined, but the position of the external powers is governed in theory by the international armistice agreements negotiated at the beginning of 1973, even though two of them have legacies of direct obligations which they are reluctant to abandon; the Soviet Union has a stake in the success of North Vietnam, and, until Watergate and Congressional revolt robbed him of much of his freedom of action, President Nixon was prepared continuously to use air power to prevent the overthrow of the Cambodian government. How the situation in Indo-China will eventuate no one can guess: the Nixon–Brezhnev communique of June 1973 expressed only *banalités* on the subject. One straw in the wind since then has been the patching up of an agreement between the Pathet Lao and the Laotian government with concessions to the former. One can only venture the generality that Indo-China will be an area of endemic conflict throughout much of the next decade; but gradually the external powers, the United States from public revulsion, the Soviet Union because continued conflict militates against her broader objective, China because armed conflict on her southern border still raises fears, Japan (though she has no direct involvement) because she wishes to get on with the economic development of the area, will reach a tacit consensus to isolate conflict in Indo-China and to accept a diminishing scale of involvement there. In this situation a gradual consolidation of North Vietnamese dominance over the rest of Indo-China seems the most likely outcome, though if Thailand plays its cards intelligently, and establishes a dual relationship with Washington and Peking, such dominance need not extend to her.

The other area of potential conflict in Asia, now that conflicting Japanese, Chinese and American attitudes to Taiwan have become at least partially reconciled, remains Korea. In this divided peninsula the interests of the four major actors meet and conflict. The United States is weary of military commitment to South Korea, a commitment which she has reduced by one-third, to 20,000 soldiers and a tactical air force, and clearly intends to reduce further. Yet she can never be indifferent to the fortunes of the country because of the effect that North Korea's domination of the peninsula would have upon the security of Japan. Both halves of Korea, moreover, are united in resisting the possibility that a dual American–Communist hegemony over a divided country be replaced by a Japanese one. Japan, more sensitive to the memory of her past aggression in Korea than in more distant lands, is naturally concerned with the future of the peninsula but has no desire to accept responsibility for the defence of the South. But Kim Il Sung, a fierce nationalist, feels threatened by the divisions of the mainland powers, since North Korea is situated at one of the interfaces of their confrontation. It is a clear Chinese interest that North Korea, with important industrial assets and situated on the Manchurian border, should not become the same kind of Soviet satellite that Mongolia has. The Soviet Union can point to the risks and sacrifices she has made for the independence, security and development of North Korea.

It has been assumed for some time that peace in North East Asia depends on the acceptance by the external powers of a divided Korea for the time being and on their restraint of both governments. There has even been discussion, emanating primarily from the Communist powers, of the possibility of a four-power guarantee of the sovereignty and integrity of the two Koreas pending their peaceful reunification.[8] But it is characteristic of the effect that détente between the major powers is having upon the perceptions of the smaller ones that the two halves of Korea decided to take matters into their own hands. In 1970 and 1971, North Korea began to put forward proposals for peaceful reunification. In July 1972 emissaries of the two sides met secretly, and emphasized their mutual commitment to such peaceful reunification. A phrase in their communiqué is interesting in that it is in flat contradiction of the ideological positions that have been taken by, say, East Germany or North Vietnam, 'As a homogeneous people, a great national unity shall be sought above all, transcending differences in ideas, ideologies and systems.' Korea is of course a more homogeneous entity than Vietnam. But clearly Presidents Pak and Kim have no intention of letting the great powers determine their future, however distant the reality of Korean reunification may be.

'Cogniscence' and access

I think it is clear that the time is not yet ripe for any Asian equivalent of the Conference on European Security and Cooperation. The area, even if one excludes South West Asia, presents too great a diversity of problems, the scars of conflict are still too recent, the redefinition of the interests of the major powers has not gone far enough, to make such a negotiation possible, not only for the present but most probably for a long time to come. Yet no other group of countries, no other area of the world, is so directly affected by the end of bipolarity. In no other continent do the risks, as well as the promise, of moving out of an era of clear-cut confrontation between East and West, manifest themselves so clearly. The African, and even to a large extent, the Latin American states can, by reason of their geographic contiguity, their regional institutions and the similarity of their problems, present a common front on many issues to the major powers. The Asian states, varying as they do enormously in size, wealth, race, tradition and relative autonomy, have no such opportunity, and are more subject to diplomatic manipulation by the major powers, two of which are Asian and one of which claims to be.

Yet with the possible exceptions of some Arab radicals at the one end of the Asian arc, there is a strong desire for peace across the breadth of Asia and the Pacific, and no obvious incentive on the part of the major powers to incite conflict. There is insurgency in the Philippines and in Thailand, continuing civil war in Cambodia and a confused situation that is neither peace nor war in South Vietnam. But compared with the situation of only a few years ago, the two Koreas have entered into a dialogue, the irredentism of

Indonesia disappeared with Sukharno, Pakistan is in no position to make war with India and India has no incentive. This situation of relative tranquillity may not last. A decision on the part of India to develop nuclear weapons would not only have major local repercussions but would raise the debate in Japan to a new level of intensity. China may yet seek to strengthen her position, admittedly weakened, with the dissatisfied and unhappy populations of Bengal and Bangla Desh. The revolutionary ardour or local ambitions of North Vietnam may prove insatiable.

But for the moment Asia is sufficiently free of crises for the Asian powers to take stock of their longer term interests. At the moment also they are all the beneficiaries in one way or another of the greater polycentrism of the international system. Just as Thailand can calculate that she can retain her links with the United States and still improve her relations with Peking because China does not wish to see the Soviet Union step into American shoes, so the Philippines can calculate that if American investment there should decline Japanese investment will take its place, or Pakistan can calculate that if she loses China's friendship she can turn to that of Iran; one could multiply the examples indefinitely. The local powers, moreover, as the storms of first decolonization and then of great-power intervention exhaust their force, are developing their own systems of cooperation, frail though these for the most part still are.

Nevertheless, the fact remains that peace of any kind will not persist in Asia without tacit undertakings on the part of the major powers. There seems to be no question of a grand design for the Asian–Pacific region, some great collective security arrangement that would embrace all the interested powers, including not only the Asian states, great and small, but the Soviet Union, China and Japan. For one thing, it raises hopeless problems of definition. Is Australia an Asian state, as her preoccupations now suggest, is New Zealand, is Iraq, above all is the United States who has done most to colour the map of contemporary Asia? But even if this problem could be overcome it is hard to envisage an effective collective security organization that embraced both so powerful and so mutually hostile a pair of nations as the Soviet Union and China.

If formal systems of collective action for the purpose of containment in Asia are dying because no one major power now raises sufficient or sufficiently widespread fear to make them acceptable, or are stillborn because Asia as a whole has no one leader, what is required is a more elastic system of great-power interaction in Asia in which the relationships of the major actors are not necessarily identical at the different levels of strategic, political and economic power; a system in which, for instance, the Soviet Union and the United States maintain their current concern for the stability and safety of the overall strategic balance; in which China and the United States have a certain level of political relationship, one of reasonable diplomatic intercourse and adjustment, without attempting to hedge in the Soviet Union by the appearance of a more intimate bond; in which Japan is neither frightened nor encouraged into an active military role in Asia and develops its asymmetrical role as the strongest economic Asian power with generosity and restraint.

But for such a series of overlapping relationships to remain stable involves two important conditions. The first is a reasonable degree of communication between the four capitals of the Asian quadrilateral – what Leonard Beaton described as 'cogniscence'.[9] The line between Washington and Peking is now open, so is that between Peking and Tokyo. But stability will be hard to achieve if Moscow and Peking attribute the worst motive to every action that the other takes. Whatever its effects elsewhere, the Sino–Soviet conflict complicates the politics of Asia in a way that must continue to create crises. No one would ask for intimacy, still less collaboration, simply intelligent diplomatic intercourse. Whatever may be thought in Delhi or Hanoi or elsewhere, the Sino–Soviet conflict is not a factor making for the stability of Asian relationships in general.

The other condition may take even longer to establish; it is nothing less than the recognition by all four capitals of the principle of mutual access in third areas – on the one hand, acceptance of the fact that, in Asia and indeed the developing world in general, the various powers have acquired certain areas of primary interest, dictated by economic or historical affiliations but, on the other, acknowledgement that this endows none with the right to a hegemonial sphere of influence. The United States may legitimately argue that she has a primary interest in, say, the Philippines and Australasia; the Soviet Union, in India; China, in the Asian Balkan states immediately south of her; Japan, in Indonesia; the European countries, in Malaysia and Singapore. But the difference between primary and exclusive interests must be recognised; all

the indigenous powers must be able to pursue political, ideological, or economic relations with all the major powers; the one
that claims an exclusive relationship with an Asian country des-
troys the balance.

While it remains true that the United States is in many ways
still the most influential Asian power, since she has access to all its
different areas in a way that none of the other three have, her
position has been considerably weakened by over-involvement in
one corner of the continent. She has, I think, drawn her lesson
from this, a lesson which hopefully has not been lost on the other
major powers. It is this: Asia cannot progress and cannot confront
its formidable economic and social problems without the support
and interest of the external powers. But their involvement can
only avoid becoming politicized and militarized again if there is an
implicit agreement among them, both to generalize their relationships and to maintain a principle of mutual access. 'Such an
implicit consensus', as Soedjatmoko has emphasized, 'should be
based on a realization that over-involvement of one major power is
bound to lead to escalation by others without assurance that the
political objectives of such over-involvement would be attained'.[10]

11
Looking Forward

The differing impact of change

If this analysis of the process of change which we are experiencing in the patterns and priorities of international politics has any validity, the time has come to try and draw the threads together for the purpose which interests us most, namely to comprehend where it is leading, despite my own reservations about attempts to predict the future with any degree of confidence, even for a decade ahead, in an era of such dynamic change.

What I propose to do first is to attempt some generalizations about the impact of different kinds of change upon the major centres of power, and then, since we are in an era of negotiations, to create two models, admittedly very crude, of the different structures of international relations that might be produced by success, failure or compromise in each of them. In conclusion I will attempt to suggest the kinds of policies and attitudes that it seems to me will be required to preserve stability, order and enough justice to preserve order, in an international system that steadily generates fresh, and fresh kinds of, power.

The two developments which have changed the pattern and nature of international politics in recent years, the Sino–Soviet dispute and then the redefinition of American interests, are not yet completed – and the fact that the central balance will continue to alter in character throughout much of the coming decade is one factor of which all countries, and not just the principal actors themselves, will have to take account. Assuming that the Soviet Union and China remain mutually hostile, and I find this the most probable assumption though hopefully not at the present level of armed defiance, it is going to be more difficult for them, and take longer, to achieve a code of peaceful coexistence than it took the United States and the Soviet Union, partly because their ideological rift is that of two Romes of the same faith, partly because they are neither of them content with the status quo, partly because their strategic relationship is more unbalanced than it was between the two old super-powers except in the very early days of the nuclear age. A stable relationship, even an 'adversary partnership', between the mainland powers may lie some distance down our perspective of the next ten years and possibly beyond it, though it is not in the interest of another country to exacerbate the conflict.

Nor are the policy and interests of the United States fully redefined. The Nixon Doctrine, for instance, is by no means an adequate or comprehensive statement of policy for the 1970s. Even her adversarial relationships, to which Nixon and Kissinger have devoted most attention, are still not finally codified and cannot be at least until the outcome of SALT Two and the future of Taiwan are clearer. The development of American relations with her allies to which President Nixon presumably intends to devote much of the rest of his second term now depends not only on the outcome and interaction of several formal negotiations but on the degree of authority the President is himself able to command at home. Because the latter is now diminished, negotiations may move at a slower pace than seemed likely at the beginning of 1973, and it may not now be until the late 1970s that it will be clear whether the Atlantic Alliance or the American–Japanese relationship have a real prospect of enduring through the latter part of the century. This reduction in pace, if it occurs, may be no bad thing for it will give the Community a breathing space in which to settle its own differences and fortify its own structure of authority, and help Japan to clarify her long-term political interests. But whoever leads the internal American debate, and at whatever pace external negotiations proceed, one must assume that the breadth of perspective and generosity of spirit that distinguished much of American post-war foreign policy is a thing of the past. Though circumstances make conceptions like isolationism quite irrelevant, though statesmanship can overcome disillusionment, the United States is in the midst of a period of intense domestic debate, which may well become heightened if problems like inflation or energy remain as severe as when I write, a social process which at the same time absorbs political and intellectual energy and creates new and more complex external interests.

But we can be more specific about the future if we glance back at the problems that have been identified as affecting much of international society in the light of what has been said about the interests of the major actors. For unlike the classical international system where the system itself had a tendency towards equilibrium unless disturbed by the activities of a particular state or empire, we have lived for several generations in a world in which developments in science and technology, economic relationships, changes in social attitudes, can have a disequilibrating effect despite the proclivities of governments.

The main focus of change in the international system which I have attempted to identify in chapter five and elsewhere will not be felt with the same force in, nor have the same effect upon, all the major and significant powers. The United States, it is true, is likely to be directly affected by them all: social change in the sense of a smouldering crisis of confidence in government which may produce administrations that are externally more inflexible because their domestic base is weaker than that of previous ones; transnationalism which the United States has done so much to generate but whose effects she now increasingly feels; changes in the distribution of strategic power with which she will be especially preoccupied; change in the utility of other forms of military power; increasing dependence on external supplies of oil and other raw materials; and a position of only *primus inter pares* in negotiating new trade and monetary relationships.

Japan's policy and position will be affected, perhaps even more sharply than the United States, by social change, by transnationalism, by energy dependence, and by the pressures of her partners for increased access to her markets and a more responsive fiscal policy. But she will be only indirectly affected by changes in the balance of strategic power, since she possesses none herself. She will, however, be considerably affected by the way in which the revolution in maritime interests become codified.

The impact of different kinds of change on the countries of the Community will be uneven, though all will feel the effect of all of them in some degree or other. Britain and France have got plenty of domestic troubles and many internal weaknesses: bad labour relations and antiquated industries; the Ulster problem for Britain; in France a strong Communist party and public alienation from an administrative structure that is still basically that of Richelieu. But both have a tradition of respect for political and intellectual leadership that is weakened and not yet breached. Italian policy is beset by many disruptive social forces, while their incidence in the smaller countries, even if weaker, is leading to introspection of which neutralism could well become the political expression. Germany may be a country of gradually rising social tension, so that its anchorage in the Community which mediates and institutionalizes transnational pressures is becoming even more important to stability in Europe than the Atlantic Alliance which was Germany's original framework. The Community countries will all be directly affected by changes in the strategic balance, for European security is directly related to it. They are all in greater or lesser degree becoming more dependent on imported energy and raw materials, and though a period of tough bargaining with the United States on trade might temporarily promote their unity, a *débacle* in the international monetary system would probably break up the Community itself, especially if it leads to industrial depression.

To what extent can the mainland powers insulate themselves from the more obvious processes of change? China can probably do so rather successfully except on the strategic plane. External trade is in China not a basic foundation of the economy as it has become in that other once autarchic country, the United States. Transnationalism need make little impact on what is now an efficient instead of an inefficient dictatorship. China has other diplomatic instruments at her command than military power. But strategic change could affect her position vitally; now that it has been confirmed that the Soviet Union has developed MIRV, which will greatly increase the weight of any nuclear attack she could mount against China, the invulnerability of the land-based missile force that China is developing becomes open to question. She may therefore have to rely much more on friendship and understanding with the United States than she would prefer until such time, probably fifteen years hence, when she can deploy an effective submarine deterrent.

The Soviet Union can isolate herself much less from all the winds of change than China. Communications and social change, however much suppressed, will have an influence, especially in creating ethnic tensions, and will probably have the effect of making the government more rigid in its dealings with the rest of the world on most forms of transnational activity, more insistent on ideological conformity in Eastern Europe, until a more confident type of leader emerges. Yet such rigidity will conflict with her need for Western technology. On the strategic plane she is herself the prime motive force of change, but an exploitation of both MIRV and numerical superority in missiles could trigger a new arms race with the United States which would undermine many of the gains in power and status she has made over the past few years. She can to a certain extent exploit some of the Western economic tensions. She can attempt to reverse the world's changing attitudes to the legitimacy of great-power military intervention; but she can only wield this traditional attribute of great-power influence as long as her military power remains latent; its actual use, most particularly outside Eastern Europe, would isolate her even more rapidly and decisively than Vietnam isolated the United States, which at the beginning of her active involvement in South East Asia had a large reserve of international goodwill to drawn on, a reserve which the Soviet Union for the most part lacks.

But change in all its aspects presents the Soviet leaders with two kinds of dilemma. One is that they must either accept the logic of the latest phase of the arms race which requires a relationship of intimacy with the United States, in which case both lose some of their influence over international politics (with the added short-term difficulty that Brezhnev becomes, as it were, tarred with Nixon's brush), or they must resume a wholly competitive relationship with the United States, in which case many of the arguments within the Western Alliance system diminish in significance and she is confronted again with a more united group of states who are collectively considerably more powerful and influential than she is. The other dilemma is that the leadership either seeks greater access to Western technology and agricultural products, which is the present policy, in which case Soviet planning decisions are in some aspects dependent on Western decisions, or, by retreating into autarchy again, it disappoints the material expectations of its own people and weakens its own position. The only way they can escape from their two dilemmas is to cultivate special relationships with different parts of the Western alliance system on specific issues and in the process help to break it up, but this is possible only in an atmosphere of steadily declining confidence among the Western powers themselves.

Scylla and Charybdis

I think one can only introduce any precision into one's estimate of how the interactions of states on the different planes where change is forcing them to negotiate may shape the late twentieth-century international system, if one tries to develop models of different outcomes. The fact that there are a number of major actual negotiations impending makes it both realistic and convenient to develop alternative scenarios around them. I have called one model Scylla and the other Charybdis and I suggest that we place ourselves a few years hence, say in 1977 when a new American President comes to power.

Scylla

(1) In SALT Two, a negotiation that was protracted beyond the target date for its completion, the Soviet Union and the United States found it impossible to reach an agreed formula for the restraint of MIRV which was the central focus of negotiation. The Soviet Union pointed to the larger number of warheads the United States deployed in *Minuteman* III and *Poseidon* by reason of its lead in the development of MIRVs; the United States emphasized the much larger number and larger size of launchers the Soviet Union possessed and the superiority she would attain in the weight of attack she could mount against the United States when these had been fitted with multiple warheads. Their negotiations were bedevilled by the difficulties of monitoring any agreement; and they were only able to agree on the phasing out of small numbers of obsolete missiles such as the American *Titan* and *Minuteman* I, the Soviet SS-7 and older types of submarine.

(2) Partly as a consequence of the increased proportion of resources each super-power now felt it necessary to devote to research, development and production of strategic weapons, the MBFR negotiations had by 1976 resulted in agreement in a reduction of one-third of the forces of each super-power stationed outside their borders in the European area: leaving, as far as ground forces were concerned, roughly three American divisions in central Europe and twenty Soviet divisions. No agreement was reached on the reduction of indigenous European forces, although unilateral reductions in their size or the length of military service had been taking place throughout the first half of the 1970s.

(3) By reason of the cloud cast over the CSCE by the failure of Soviet–American negotiations in SALT Two, no agreements of substance were reached except in the political 'basket' that recognized the inviolability of frontiers, the peaceful settlement of disputes and so on. Thus the Warsaw Pact countries did not attain their objective of greater technological assistance from the West; nor the Western countries acceptance of the freer flow of information and personal movements.

(4) In the intra-Western negotiations on trade and money, the conflicts of interest between the major industrial powers proved for the most part irreconcilable. The fact that the American Administration had been given little flexibility by Congress made it impossible to reach agreement on the elimination of industrial tariffs; the Community had failed to find a new basis for its agricultural policy; while together these problems produced an atmosphere in which it was impossible to tackle the difficult questions of quotas and non-tariff barriers.

At the same time, the fact that little headway was being made on the resolution of difficulties in trade barriers, coupled with the fact that floating exchange rates seemed to suit a number of important countries, meant that attempts to re-codify the international monetary system were also stultified. More and more talk was now heard in Europe of strengthening the Community's preferential arrangements in Eurafrica, in Washington of developing stronger bilateral ties with countries like Brazil, Saudi Arabia and Iran, and in Tokyo of developing a politico-economic sphere of influence around the Pacific basin, even if it meant a sharp degree of Japanese rearmament.

(5) Negotiations between OPEC and OECD countries had revealed the same basic disunity among the Western powers. By 1977 long-term bilateral agreements were in process of negotiation between the United States and Saudi Arabia, between Iran and Japan, between Iraq and France, and between Italy and Libya. Britain had nationalized her North Sea concessions.

(6) In the Conference on the Law of the Sea of 1974–6, the principal industrial nations refused to recognize a broader jurisdiction for the other maritime countries over ocean exploration and fishing than the new twelve-mile limit of territorial waters to which they had (reluctantly) agreed. The conference adjourned

without having made progress on the ownership of the ocean bed or the control of narrow waters.

Charybdis
(1) In SALT Two, the two super-powers reached agreement, first to convert the interim agreement of 1972 into treaty form; second, to forego any further deployment of MIRV except for their submarine-launched missiles; third, to begin a gradual process of reducing their inventories of strategic weapons by dismantling all types of missiles of more than ten years old, including medium-range Soviet missiles targeted on western Europe, and not replacing them. The United States agreed to withdraw FBS in Europe, though not on her aircraft carriers elsewhere. The Soviet Union maintained its opposition to ground inspection and it was acknowledged that the agreement could be monitored by 'national means' (i.e. observation satellites) and traditional intelligence methods.

(2) It was agreed to reunite the CSCE and MBFR negotiations, so an agreement to reduce American and Soviet forces in central Europe by one-fifth was embedded in a broader one not only on a code of political behaviour but on mechanisms of crisis management, including a European Commission, of which both super-powers were members, with an undertaking by both that neither would use such a body as a means of interfering in the internal arrangements of the other's alliance, of COMECON or of the Community. This hurdle having been cleared it became possible to negotiate limited agreements in the exchange of technological information and somewhat greater freedom of movements, books and journals.

(3) The Tokyo round of trade negotiations was basically successful in agreeing to the elimination of tariffs among the developed countries, the generalization of preferences given by different ones to developing countries, a reorganization of agricultural policies so that they became an aspect of domestic social, rather than external economic, policy, plus stricter adherence to the rules of GATT on quotas. At broadly the same time it was agreed that, in the interests of stability, it was essential to restore coherence to the international monetary system by reinforcing the authority of the IMF, steadily expanding the volume of SDRs so that the dollar became eventually secondary to them as the basic international

currency. Agreement was reached on the ground rules for the making of parity changes, related to a country's reserve position.

(4) In the 1975 and subsequent negotiations between OPEC and the main oil-importing countries, OECD was used as the means of evolving a common position for the latter, especially as governments rather than companies were the negotiating agents. In view of the prospect that a bilateral OECD–OPEC bargain might prejudice the interests of the developing countries, because the OECD countries have other sources of oil than the OPEC countries, and because the problem of conserving the use of raw materials in general was a matter of increasing public concern, there was growing discussion of creating a new UN agency to monitor and institutionalize all such relationships.

(5) In the Law of the Sea conference, the effect that different technological revolutions have had in altering the whole of men's interests in and relations to the ocean was recognized in a new convention that created international control over the exploitation of the deep ocean, defined the boundaries of a country's continental shelf more clearly, gave countries wider jurisdiction over fishing than their territorial waters, and acknowledged, in view of danger of pollution, that riparian states had a right to closer control of straits and narrow waters provided they did not infringe the right of 'innocent passage'.

I said that these scenarios were crude ones, and the reader may wish to develop his own variations on them: he may, for instance, argue that if super-power negotiations on arms control should fail, the prospects for successful compromise in the Western economic and monetary negotiations are improved, though I think this assumes too mechanistic a relationship between each subject. I offer them largely as a set of building blocks to illustrate the material out of which our choices about the future will be largely made. The world's true course will lie somewhere between these two. The most important variables I would judge to be the SALT negotiations, the trade negotiations, and new oil relationships. But, lest it be thought *Scylla* is simply a pessimistic and *Charybdis* simply an optimistic scenario, it is worth dwelling briefly on the implications of both, for the one contains dangers not only for the West but for the mainland powers as well, while the other has difficult implications for the West as well as for the East.

At first sight *Scylla* implies a major shift in the balance of power in favour of the Soviet Union. Though she might not be able to develop a meaningful strategic superiority over the United States, she would confront a Western alliance system whose component countries were at loggerheads on economic issues and cut-throat in their competition for assured supplies of oil and raw materials. Though China might well be frightened by the prospect of un-limited Soviet deployment of MIRV and might wish for a closer relationship with the United States, she would have little to offer in return, and the prospect of a frustrated Japan, fed up with the behaviour of her Western partners, would complicate China's options, as well as giving the Soviet Union the opportunity to draw Japan into a somewhat closer relationship to herself for economic reasons. The Community, torn by its own divisions, not only on economic and raw-material issues, but by differing views of the implications of the failure of SALT and of the East–West negotia-tions in Europe, might be heading for dissolution, the British and French placing greater emphasis on their own strategic power, Germany either on the necessity for a new national relationship with the East, or else a position of complete autonomy. The United States, now forced to concentrate increased resources on her strategic arsenal and embittered by her dealings with her allies of the post-war era, would feel forced to give overriding priority to her national requirements, protecting her markets and her currency by every means at her disposal while competing every-where with her former partners for markets and raw materials. The dissolution of the Atlantic Alliance and of the American alliance system in general would be in sight.

But would such an anarchic world suit the interests of the Soviet Union, even though she might be able to call the tune in Europe and East Asia? If the next round of the arms race were conducted *à outrance*, her technological base is narrower than that of the United States and the logic of the unlimited exploitation of MIRV is a shift entirely from land-based missiles, for whose deployment the Soviet Union has plenty of empty real estate, to the ocean to which her access is more limited than that of the United States. The partial failure of CSCE would also deny her access to Western technology on which the acceleration of her economy as a whole depends. The internal strains would be con-siderable and to these would be added the acceleration of that multipolar world whose emergence she has tried to avert. The

EPE—L

possibility of a nuclear Japan, the possibility even of a nuclear Germany, the end of real hopes of stabilizing her relationship with China, might be poor compensation for the right to call herself the world's strongest power, or the ability to advance her interests in the developing world.

Charybdis creates its own problems too. The negotiation of mutual restraint on MIRV and the diminution of the strategic arsenals of the super-powers in SALT Two implies, as I have said earlier, a degree of Soviet–American confidence in each other's word and intentions which would carry overtones of condominium. The European NATO powers would feel this especially as the agreement involves the removal of the FBS aircraft and medium-range missiles in Europe which they have come to regard as an essential ingredient of the spectrum of deterrence there. The agreed departure of even a fifth of the American forces in Europe when coupled with the likelihood of further withdrawals for domestic reasons would involve the evolution of a close system of defence cooperation in the Community to which the Soviet Union is opposed (and France is hesitant) so that the maintenance of the kind of comprehensive Europe-wide agreements mentioned in the scenario would be a difficult one. The successful reconciliation of the conflicting economic interests of the Western partners in the Tokyo negotiations would involve in some cases severe internal adjustments on their part, which predicates not only that the negotiations are pervaded by a spirit of compromise but that the major governments have the domestic authority to make such adjustments. China might feel increasingly estranged from a system that implied both super-power confidence on the strategic level and a continuing identity of interest between the major units of the Western world (even though she has little interest in the breakdown in Japanese–American relations) and might become more assertive in developing Asia and elsewhere.

But if the ark which the international family is attempting to navigate through this strait can steer closer to the whirlpool of Charybdis than to the rock of Scylla, then the prospects for stability as the latter part of our decade unfolds seem to me brighter for a number of reasons. Restraint in the strategic arms race would not only diminish the dangers and costs which a new phase of technological innovation has always carried; it would also mean that Soviet and American resources, intellectual as well as material, would be available for better purposes; restraint and reduction is also a particular Western interest in helping to diminish the alienation which a rising generation feels from the continuous modernization or augmentation, at great expense, of weapons which cannot rationally be used. It would also diminish the alienation which the non-nuclear powers feel from the nuclear. The restoration of economic good relations among the Western partners and the avoidance of mercantilism would alleviate the danger that each would pursue its own path to security, even at the expense of the others, that the Community would break up, and Japan lapse into irredentism in much the same way as the Smoot-Hawley Tariff and Imperial Preference encourged or forced her to do in the early 1930s. More generous treatment of the developing world as a whole by liberalization of tariffs and other means, and by making concessions to those that have maritime interests, rather than a hectic scramble for special deals on oil and raw materials by the industrial powers, from which only parts of the developing world would benefit, would not only be equitable but would also avert a growing sense of despair about the relations of the poor countries with the rich, which it would open to the mainland powers to exploit. A ship can survive the skirting of a whirlpool better than the hitting of a rock.

The control of change

What conceptual framework, what code of navigation, do we require to improve the prospect that we shall successfully navigate the rockstrewn and turbulent waters that lie ahead of us? For a framework or a chart we must have: events move too fast, too many countries are affected, public opinion is too articulate, to enable us to rest content with the improvization of a few political leaders, the more so since this is not an age that will be remembered for its towering leadership. False concepts of the future, for instance that a return to traditional calculations of cabinet diplomacy will provide peace and equilibrium, are as misleading as nostalgia for the vanished simplicities of the bipolar world.

Before suggesting any conceptions or propositions that might guide our approach to world order in the coming decade and beyond, let me emphasize a few central points that have been implicit in the analysis I have attempted. The first is that the international system has become more plural, power and initiative of all kinds have become more diffused, than in the post-war era, not simply within the Communist world or the American alliance systems but to many other states of what was once the Third World. The great powers do not dominate the emerging international system to the extent they have dominated earlier ones and their diplomacy is subject to more public scrutiny than in the past. Second, we have reached a point in which political ideology is no longer an overriding motive in the way states behave, but has by no means disappeared. Even if simple conceptions like democracy versus communism or dictatorship present only a partial guide to the lines of stress in international politics, it is still true that there are groups of states who share a common outlook, are more permeable to each other's influence, or can identify a larger range of common interests with each other than with other states. It is these differences of heritage, association or interest which create the balances of power in the world, not simply the tactical manœuvrings of the large states or the existence of formal alliances.

Third, this is a very highly armed world, not only in terms of nuclear weapons but of the armouries that middle and smaller powers maintain. Because this is so, because the post-war era has been strewn with so much armed conflict, and because neither a concert of the great powers nor an international authority in reality exists to keep the peace, all states of any significance are tending to become more prudent in their consideration of the use of force.* This is not the same as saying that the period ahead of us will be one of peaceful change alone, for this assumes that every significant state is prepared to give peace higher priority than any other issue that may arise. It also ignores the relative ease with which terrorism or subversion can be organized. But the disposition of international society is against armed conflict and those who engage in it. This may have the effect of making processes of change slower, but it also probably means that the military power of great states is less impressive or decisive as a form of influence. Fourth, in a world in which the dividing line between external and internal policy is becoming increasingly blurred, in which much of international relations, especially in the developed world, is really concerned with the harmonization of different domestic

* This was written before the Egyptian–Syrian attack in Israel in October 1973. But the fourth Arab–Israel war seems to me the exception that proves the rule; all parties to the dispute have lost much of their freedom of action by reason of it.

policies, the success with which a country tackles its internal problems and faces new challenges at home, is an important factor in
the degree of external influence it exerts. This has always been
true to some extent; the connection becomes more and more
direct all the time, and if major states can be said to be introspective in a way in which they were not in the post-war years, it
is partly from an awareness that their societies are on trial.

In my view there are three fundamental requirements for the
negotiating of the coming decade at the lowest level of tension
that is possible in a period when so many new forces are at work.
First, the maintenance of an organic political and economic
relationship between the United States, Europe and Japan;
second, the encouragement of all promising forms of regional
association while maintaining the accessibility of their component
states, especially in the developing world, to all the major powers;
third, the creation of new forms of international organization to
remove certain new, global problems from the interplay of power
politics. These are not pieties, but, in my view, requirements
which if neglected may create great and perhaps irreparable
damage to order, prosperity and justice.

I do not believe that the European–American or the Japanese–
American relationship contains the seeds of inevitable demise but
I do believe that, by a series of careless actions on all sides, both
relationships could become so hollow that it would only take an
incident to make them seem no longer worth sustaining. I need
not recapitulate the difficulties that exist in both. They are not
identical. The American relationship with Europe is still largely a
multilateral one on every issue except trade, and much of the
American resentment of the Community derives from the fact that
it has failed to develop the coherence or institutions to shoulder
broader burdens while challenging the United States on the plane
of trade itself. The Japanese–American relationship is a bilateral
one in which military considerations play a smaller part, but is
clouded not only by competition but by less easy intercourse. This
does create real difficulties for any Administration, as American
public opinion becomes more materially affected by such competition yet perceives less sharply than Washington, the risks of
breaking up either relationship or converting it into one of hostility. For without her alliance with Japan, American influence in
East Asia, which may diminish in any case, would drop sharply.
If the Atlantic Alliance degenerated or was disbanded not only

would American security interests be directly affected but she would lose all influence over the politics of Europe and thereby much of her political leverage with her fellow super-power. The balance of power, which remains a real concept in the nuclear age, for we have no higher government of the world, would have tilted permanently in favour of the Soviet Union.

There has been one basic inconsistency in the American perception of her relationship with her major allies, and it is hard to see how her alliances can progress on the more equal footing that the rise in the relative power of Europe and Japan necessitate, or how to restore the concept of coalition until it is confronted. In encouraging the economic development and political independence of both Europe and Japan, in telling them that she aimed at a more equal relationship, it was explicit that she did not wish them to acquire strategic power; and this has broadly been accepted. But an implicit assumption has emerged in recent years, namely that the United States can remain the master of all aspects of high policy, particularly in dealing with the mainland powers, even if her moves may conflict with the interests of her allies or undermine their confidence in her, because 'they have nowhere else to go'. While this may have been true in the past it is not necessarily true of the future, in an era of strategic stalemate and of super-power dètente that American and Soviet necessites have brought about. Japan has other options to a continuing association with the United States, even though she is a vulnerable power; though they may be bad ones from the standpoint of international stability, an embittered or distrustful relationship might lead her to consider them. The dissolution of the Atlantic Alliance might, it is true, break up the Community, some countries opting for neutrality, others for a new alliance among themselves; it might be the end of their collective venture, but the individual countries would survive, some perhaps in a rather 'Finlandized' relationship with the Soviet Union, some with more freedom of action. But equally it might galvanize the Community into developing the institutions of a centralized power system, difficult though this undoubtedly would be. In a more plural world, the range of choice increases for states, even vulnerable ones, and even if they are disagreeable choices, the assumption that the United States can play a lone hand simply encourages recalcitrance on the part of her allies, and weakens her own position, since, unlike the Soviet Union, she is not prepared to bring them to heel by force.

If a breakdown of the American alliance systems is to be avoided, then the requirements of converting it into a true system of coalition must be confronted. This is not, so it seems to me, primarily a matter of developing new institutional machinery, for the techniques and institutions of alliance policy making, developed over the past quarter century, are adequate if properly used; it is more a matter of perspective and of practice. It involves candid recognition of the fact that the United States has strategic responsibilities to herself, to her allies and to the Soviet Union which she cannot devolve without risking a serious rise in international tension. But it also involves recognition that strategic relationships and considerations now govern a smaller area of international behaviour than in the post-war era, so that her allies have greater, though by no means unlimited, freedom of action which they have a right to exercise, provided their actions do not jeopardize the interests of the Western community as a whole. It means accepting the fact that there is a link, psychological as well as logical, between their actions towards each other on the different planes of power and activity where their interests intersect, that if they appear to inflict damage on each other in one field of interaction, it becomes more difficult to sustain confidence in others. It means acknowledging the extent to which their societies are interdependent and open to each other's influence and it implies recognition of the fact that the style of one government affects the others; that just as Gaullism was a factor in encouraging American unilateralism, so American Gaullism fosters Japanese nationalism and so on. As Helmut Schmidt has observed what we label conflicts of interest in the West are often plain failures to understand each other's decision-making process. In short, it means acknowledging that a community or commonweath of nations abides by somewhat different rules than the formal codes of diplomacy, that its members accept a higher degree of obligation to consult, to inform, to adjust or harmonize their domestic and external policies, to give each other the benefit of the doubt than states in general are expected to do. That is really what the experiment of the European Community is all about, and one of the challenges of the coming decade is to discover whether the essence of 'community', in a more generalized sense, can be sustained in Western relations as a whole.

I have explained earlier the reasons why I believe that Washington still has to be treated as the main centre of collective decision-making if the Western alliance system is to survive, but I have also tried to warn against thinking of it exclusively as simply a trilateral relationship of Europe, the United States and Japan: Canada, for one, is an important pillar of the Western system, and so for many purposes are the EFTA countries of Europe and so is Australia. Moreover, with the decline of American dominance, older forms of association that straddle the developed and the developing world like the Commonwealth are reviving in value. New forms of association are emerging in the developing world whose coherence it is a Western interest to encourage, although it is also in their interest to resist the creation of any new exclusive spheres of influence by the great powers which, most particularly in Asia, could undermine the prospects of sustaining peace through the coming period of change.

Finally, the prospect of peaceful change depends also on our ability to restore vitality to international institutions and to revive the spirit of internationalism which marked the post-war period but became weakened by the great-power jockeying of recent years. The United States has ceased to place any serious trust in the United Nations and because she has tended to by-pass it so have the other major powers. Yet there are several reasons for questioning whether we dare let the universal organization wither on the vine. For one thing three important states, previously outside it, are now members, China and the two Germanys. Second, the UN does provide a real mechanism for the restraint of conflict even if its achievements as a security organization have not lived up to the expectation of its founders; it is a fact of post-war history that war and intervention have been more successfully restrained in those areas with which it has been consistently associated, such as the Middle East, than in those where its authority has seldom been invoked, such as South East Asia. There remains, moreover, great scope for the kind of 'preventive diplomacy' which is the responsibility of its Secretary General. Third, it is difficult to see how the pressure for social and political introversion in the developed countries and the distaste of the rising generation for 'power politics' can be prevented from degenerating into parochialism if a new spirit of internationalism, of which the UN is one medium, cannot be rekindled; I know that this is not a fashionable view in the governments of today's major powers, but I do not see how the affairs of a more plural world can be managed simply by bargains among them; otherwise the late 1970s may have unpleasant similarities with the 1930s.

There is also need for a more functional kind of internationalism, directed to new and particular problems, if the forces of change are to be prevented from undermining such stability as national policies have achieved, forces that are too broad and complex even for an improved Western spirit of coalition and community to deal with. Environmental and ecological problems have already been accepted as universal in their incidence, as has the future control of the oceans. The solution of trade and monetary conflicts requires the revision of earlier international instruments but also obedience to these codes and the international machinery they provide once revision has been agreed upon. The control of transnational economic activity will require the establishment of a similar code if its threat to political sovereignty is not thought to outweigh its real advantages, and to sow dissension between the developed and the developing world. Problems like the prevention of food shortage in one place and surpluses in another will require a superb international intelligence which the market mechanism alone cannot provide. The growing demands on limited resources of oil and raw materials cannot, as I have argued earlier, be restrained and reconciled simply by processes of bargaining, even between collectivities of producers and consumers. At some point, sooner rather than later, one must hope, the concept of arms control must be extended to the trade in armaments, which could not be done simply by agreements among the major arms producers. All these problems call not necessarily for large new UN agencies, but for conventions and codes that could be serviced and supervised only by the UN because their incidence is universal.

The end of the post-war era has been characterized by a traditional process of structural adjustment among the major states. But the quantitative and qualitative changes in the relations of states and societies have not yet been fully tackled. A plural world, faced with new problems and with many old ones left unsolved, will require the intelligent use of both old and new techniques of adjustment if the hope that it will be less dominated by conflict than the past forty years, is to be given any firm foundation.

A profound responsibility for this process of evolution lies on the shoulders of the West, on the democracies of the Pacific and the Atlantic. It was the West that evolved not only the liberating concept of the sovereign state but also devised the rules of civilized intercourse between them. It has been the West that has been the cradle of political ideas, including Marxism, and seems likely to remain so. However great the power of Russia, however fine and fair the civilization of China or of India, however just the claims of the developing countries, if the springs of political improvisation in the West dry up then the new agenda of world politics will be a barren one.

Tables: Some simple orders of Magnitude

The Political Size of the Major Powers

The Major Powers	GNP ($ billion)	Population (millions)	Military manpower (’000)	Strategic nuclear delivery systems	Exports as a percentage of world exports[1]
1952					
USA	350	157·5	3550	800	20·6
USSR	113[2]	184·8	4600	—	—
China	59[3]	586·9	—	—	—
Britain	44	50·7	890	—	10·4
France	29	42·4	645	—	5·2
Germany	32	48·7	—	—	5·4
Japan	16	85·5	114	—	1·7
1962					
USA	560	186·7	2827	1835	17·4
USSR	229[2]	221·7	3600	865	5·6
China	79[3]	689 (1960)	3000	—	1·2
Britain	81	53·3	445	90	9·1
France	74	47·0	742	—	5·9
Germany	89	54·8	389	—	10·6
EEC	232	173·3	1784	—	27·4
Japan	59	94·9	216	—	3·9
1972					
USA	1152	208·8	2253	2165	12·4
USSR	439[2]	250·5	3425	2830	3·5
China	128[3] (1971)	800·0	2880	150	0·6 (1971)
Britain	151	55·8	352	144	6·1
France	202	51·7	503	92	6·6
Germany	259	61·7	475	—	11·6
EEC[4]	661	191·0	1608	—	31·0
Japan	317	106·0	266	—	7·1

[1] For 1952 the non-market Economies are excluded from the total.
[2] Net Material Product at 0·72 roubles = $1.
[3] In 1970 constant dollars.
[4] Before enlargement.

Aid to developing countries and multilateral agencies ($m)

	1961	*1971*
USA	2943	3324
Britain	457	561
France	903	1088
Germany	366	734
Japan	108	511
EEC	1477	2637

Notes and References

Chapter 1

1. *Time*, 1 January 1972.
2. *Things to Come: Thinking about the 70s and 80s*, by Herman Kahn and B. Bruce-Biggs (New York: Macmillan, 1972) Chapter 3.
3. *The English Constitution*, Preface to the Second Edition, 1872.
4. Quoted in *National Interest*, Joseph Frankel (New York: Praeger; London: Pall Mall, 1970) p. 34.
5. Bertrand de Jouvenel, *The Art of Conjecture* (New York: Basic Books; London: Weidenfeld and Nicolson, 1967). Karl Deutsch, e.g. 'Towards an inventory of basic trends and patterns in comparative and international politics', *America Political Science Review*, LIV, 1960. Herman Kahn, *Things to Come* and *The Year 2000* (Macmillan, 1967).
6. de Jouvenel, *op. cit.*

Chapter 2

1. *The Cold War as History*, p. 46 (New York: Harper and Row; London: Chatto & Windus, 1967).
2. *Present at the Creation*, p. 356 (New York: Norton; London: Hamish Hamilton, 1969).
3. See, for instance, Robert Osgood, *The Entangling Alliance*, chapter 2 (University of Chicago Press, 1962).
4. This dilemma was first clarified publicly in an article by Albert Wohlstetter, 'The Delicate Balance of Terror' in *Foreign Affairs*, January 1959, which was a de-classified version of an earlier study of the RAND Corporation that demonstrated by means of mathematical logic that no increase in the number of bombers

or of dispersal bases could satisfactorily overcome this basic problem of this vulnerability.

5   See *Survey of the Sino-Soviet Dispute 1963–1967*, by John Gittings, pp. 104–5. OUP (London and New York, 1968).

6   See, for instance, Gittings, *op. cit.*, for documents; Zagoria, Donald S., *The Sino–Soviet Conflict 1956–61* (1962); Griffiths, W.E., *The Sino–Soviet Rift* (1964); Mehnert, Klaus, *Peking and Moscow* (1963).

7   I think the most explicit account of this is in my *Crisis Management* (Paris: The Atlantic Institute, 1966).

8   For a comprehensive account, including the discussions within the Administration in Washington, there is no substitute for *The Pentagon Papers* which are best studied in what is known as the Gravel Edition (Boston: The Beacon Press, 4 volumes) especially Volumes III and IV. For an excellent synoptic account based on these papers see 'The United States and Vietnam' by Geoffrey Warner in *International Affairs* (RIIA, London), July and October 1972.

9   'A World Adrift', *Encounter*, February 1972.

10 Quoted in *Status of US Strategic Power:* Report by Preparedness Investigating Sub-Committee of the Senate Armed Services Committee, September 1968.

Chapter 3

1   W.W. Rostow, *The Diffusion of Power* (New York, 1972) p. 410. 'In January 1966 Johnson let Kosygin take the lead as an intermediary between Ayub and Shastri in Tashkent, and he orchestrated American diplomacy in such a way as to ease Kosygin's task. (I heard Johnson several times observe: "I couldn't be seen; but I was at Tashkent.")'

2   Morton Kaplan, *System and Process in International Politics*, pp. 37–43 (New York: Wiley, 1957).

3   For an excellent statement of this case see Kenneth N.Waltz, 'The Stability of a Bipolar World', *Daedalus*, Summer 1964.

4   I have not described the various ups and downs of the SALT negotiations between November 1969 and May 1972 of which there is, in any case, only limited public knowledge. *Strategic Survey* (London, IISS) for 1970 and 1971 gives a clear résumé of such knowledge as was available of the positions of both sides during those years. See also John Newhouse, *Cold Dawn: The*

Story of SALT (New York: Holt, Rinehart and Winston, 1973).

5 *United States Policy for the 1970s*, p. 44.

6 Robert S.McNamara, *One Hundred Countries, Two Billion People*, (New York: Praeger, 1973).

7 *Development Cooperation*, 1972 Review (Paris, OECD), Table 26.

8 *Ibid.* and from *Partners in Development*, 'Report of the Commission on International Development' (The Pearson Commission) (New York: Praeger, London: Pall Mall, 1969).

9 Quoted in 'Are the Rich Countries getting Richer and the Poor Countries Poorer?', by Theodore Caplow in *Foreign Policy*, Summer 1971.

10 *Development Cooperation*, pp. 48–50.

11 McNamara, *op. cit.*, p. 73. In fact the real American figure seems likely to be even lower than this, for the Administration asked for only $1 billion for development, or 0·10 per cent of GNP for 1973–4, and indicated that it will ask for the same figure in subsequent fiscal years.

Chapter 4

1 *The Military Balance 1972–1973*, p. 83 (London, IISS).

2 For two clear analyses of the achievements and omissions of the 1972 agreement see *Strategic Survey 1972* (IISS) and SIPRI Research Reports Nos 5 and 6 (Stockholm International Peace Research Institute).

3 See 'The Decisive Years Ahead' by John W.Tuthill, p. 41, *The Atlantic Papers*, 4, 1972 (Paris: The Atlantic Institute for International Affairs, 1973).

4 The books that give the best sense of the concerns of the early 1960s about nuclear proliferation are: *Stratégie de l'âge Nucléaire* by Pierre Gallois (Paris: Calmann-Levy, 1960): *The Spread of Nuclear Weapons* by Leonard Beaton and John Maddox (London, Chatto and Windus for ISS, 1962) (one of the first scholarly examinations of the problem, of which I am proud to have been the instigator); and *A World of Nuclear Powers* ed. Alastair Buchan (New York: Columbia UP, 1966).

5 See, for instance, *Convergence*, by S.H.Huntington and Z.Brezinski.

6 In the issue of *Time* of 3 January 1972 President Nixon is quoted as follows: 'We must remember the only time in the

history of the world that we have had any extended period of peace is when there has been balance of power. It is when one nation becomes infinitely more powerful in relation to its potential competitor that the danger of war arises. So I believe in a world in which the United States is powerful. I think it will be a safer world and a better world if we have a strong, healthy United States, Europe, Soviet Union, China, Japan, each balancing the other, not playing one against the other, an even balance.'

7 'Central Issues of American Foreign Policy', in *Agenda for the Nation* (Washington: The Brookings Institution, 1968).

Chapter 5

1 'The Bent Twig: A Note on Nationalism', *Foreign Affairs*, October 1972.

2 See S. H. Huntington, 'Transnational Organizations in World Politics', *World Politics*, April 1973, p. 344. This subject has only recently begun to attract the amount of intellectual and analytical attention it deserves. The most comprehensive study so far is *Transnational Relations and World Politics*, edited by Robert O. Keohane and Joseph S. Nye, Jr (Cambridge: Harvard University Press, 1972).

3 Quoted in Huntington, *op. cit.*, p. 363.

4 *Policy Perspectives for International Trade and Economic Relations*. Report by the High Level Group (Paris: OECD, 1972).

5 See Keohane and Nye, *op. cit.*, pp. 396–8.

6 *Op. cit.*, p. 367.

7 *The Energy Outlook*, Table 4. Royal Dutch/Shell Group, September 1972.

8 I am grateful to Robert Mabro of St Antony's College, Oxford, for these figures.

9 Shell, *ibid.*

10 See James A. Akins, 'The Oil Crisis: This Time the Wolf is at the Door', *Foreign Affairs*, April 1973.

11 Akins, *op. cit.*, p. 477.

12 'There is a consensus that it would be difficult for us to offer to any eastern hemisphere market a preferred access to our energy market . . . for this would go against our long established policy of not discriminating in favour of any single eastern hemisphere

EPÉ—L*

supplier nation. We think we should be cautious about negotiating bilateral special energy arrangements.' William E.Simons, Deputy Secretary of the Treasury, before the Senate Foreign Relations Committee, 31 May 1973.

13 See, for instance, 'An Atlantic–Japanese Energy Policy' by Walter J.Levy. Paper prepared for the European–American Conference at Amsterdam, March 1973.

14 Shell, *op. cit.*, Figure 3.

15 *US Energy Outlook*, p. 16, National Petroleum Council. December 1972.

16 *The Limits of Growth* by Donella H.Meadows and others. Report for the Club of Rome (New American Library; London: Earth Island Ltd, 1972).

17 *Resources and Man* (San Francisco: W.H.Freeman, 1969).

18 *Reshaping the International Economic Order*. A Tripartite Report by twelve economists from North America, Japan, and the European Community. (Washington: The Brookings Institution, 1971.)

19 See 'Trade Policy is Foreign Policy' by Richard Cooper in *Foreign Policy*, Winter 1972–3.

20 *Ibid.*

21 *Ibid.*

22 Quoted in Cooper, *op. cit.*

23 *Ibid.*

24 E.g., the trenchant American economist C.Fred Bergsten has advocated an annual increase of at least $4–5 billion of SDR's. 'The New Economics and US Foreign Policy', *Foreign Affairs*, January 1972.

25 *Reshaping the International Economic Order*, p. 6.

26 *On the Use of Military Power in the Nuclear Age*, Chapter 3 (Princeton University Press, 1966).

27 'War and International Order' in *The Bases of International Order* edited by Alan James (London: Oxford University Press, 1973).

28 'Central Issue of American Foreign Policy' in *Agenda for the Nation*, edited by Kermit Gordon (Washington: The Brookings Institution, 1968).

29 'After Containment: The Foundations of the Military Establishment' in *The Annals of the American Academy of Political Science*, Vol. 406 March 1973.

30 *Ibid.*

31 For a clear statement of the factors with which the negotiators

of SALT Two must grapple, see *Strategic Survey* 1972 (London: IISS) pp. 18–19.

32 What follows is largely based on Professor D.P.O'Connell's 'Legal Control of the Sea', *The Round Table*, October 1972. I am also grateful to Mr James Fawcett for his advice.

Chapter 6

1 'Moscow's View of the Balance of Power', *The World Today*, March 1973.
2 Press Conference, San Clemente, 25 June 1973.
3 See *The Economist*, 23 December 1972, p. 31.
4 *Soviet Analyst*, 15 February 1973.
5 *The Economist, op. cit.*
6 *Ibid.*, 7 April 1973, p. 106.
7 One example among many is by Moscow's leading Americanologist, G.A.Arbatov, in *USA*, November 1971.
8 Quoted in *Soviet Analyst*, 26 April 1973.
9 See 'If Mao had come to Washington' by Barbara Tuchman, *Foreign Affairs*, October 1972.
10 *Peking, Moscow and Beyond*, p. 11, by William E.Griffith (Washington: Center for Strategic and International Studies, 1973).
11 Chinese imports and exports with OECD countries are worth about $2·5 billion a year out of an estimated total of $4·5 billion in 1970. Estimates of Chinese GNP vary widely from a 1971 Japanese estimate of $75 billion to Chou En-lai's figure of $120 billion as the gross value of industrial, transport and agricultural production (which is not quite the same as GNP). The percentages I have quoted assume that the true figure is of the order of $100 billion annually but it may be higher, for the growth rate of the Chinese economy is now impressive after the setbacks of the 1960s.
12 'China seeks network of friends' by David Bonavia, *The Times*, 19 June 1973.

Chapter 7

1 William Watts and Lloyd E.Free (eds), *State of the Nation* (New York: Universe Books for Potomac Associates), p. 47.
2 *Op. cit.*, p. 203.

3 *Op. cit.*, p. 35 and p. 201.

4 *Op. cit.*, pp. 220–1 and p. 276.

5 Frank L.Klingberg, 'The Historical Alternation of Moods in American Foreign Policy', *World Politics*, January 1952.

6 Although *State of the Nation* shows that nearly two-thirds (63 per cent) of Americans still believe that the US should cooperate fully with the UN. *Op. cit.*, p. 200.

7 *US Foreign Policy for the 1970s*. The President's Report to the Congress, 3 May 1973, p. 43.

8 *The Rey Report* (OECD), Table 5c.

9 Press Conference on the President's Foreign Policy Report, 3 May 1973. For criticisms of the President's formulation see Stanley Hoffman's and my own articles in *Foreign Affairs*, July 1972.

10 'The US Forces and the Zero Draft'. Adelphi Papers 94 (London: IISS, 1973).

11 Statement in the Senate Foreign Relations Committee, 27 February 1973.

12 'US Foreign Policy', *Foreign Affairs*, July 1973.

13 'A Plea for Energy Independence', *Foreign Affairs*, July 1973.

14 'US Balance of Payments', *Survey of Current Business*, March 1973.

15 Hearings Before the Permanent Sub-Committee, Senate Committee on Government Operations, 17 April 1973.

16 See, for instance, 'Crisis in the Millpond', *The Economist*, 14 July 1973.

17 Robert W.Tucker, *A New Isolationism: Threat or Promise?* (Washington: Potomac Associates, 1972).

18 François Duchene, 'The Strategic Consequences of the European Community', *Survival*, January/February 1973.

19 Address to the Associated Press, New York, 23 April 1973.

20 *Ibid.*

21 *Ibid.*

22 Quoted in Karl Kaiser, *Europe and the United States: the Future of the Relationship* (Washington: Columbia Books Inc., 1973), p. 125.

23 At a conference on *Les Relations Extérieure de la Communauté Européene Enlargie*, Brussels, 29 November–1 December 1972.

24 'The New Atlantic Charter', *The World Today*, June 1973.

25 'Sources of Strain in Transatlantic Relations', *International Affairs*, October 1972.

26 This could, of course, only be done over a period of time, for as Karl Kaiser has put it, 'a policy of transferring responsibilities to a group which cannot assume them simply diminishes the security of everyone', *op. cit.*, p. 97.

27 *Op. cit.*, p. 142.

28 See, for instance, Brezinski, *op. cit.*, *Foreign Affairs*, July 1973.

29 'The Insulation of the Presidency', by H.G.Nicholas in *Government and Opposition*, Spring 1973.

30 *A World Restored* (Boston: Houghton Mifflin, 1957) pp. 326–9.

31 'The White Revolutionary: Reflections on Bismarck', *Daedalus*, Summer 1968, p. 921.

Chapter 8

1   *Europe: Journey to an Unknown Destination*, The 1972 Reith Lectures, p. 37 (London: Pelican, 1973).

2   See for instance, 'Stuck Fast', by John Newhouse; 'Why the Malaise?', by Edward C.Morse, *Foreign Affairs*, January 1973. *The Decisive Years Ahead* by John W.Tuthill, Atlantic Papers 4, 1972, p. 23–5 (Paris: The Atlantic Institute).

3   This case was emphasized by Ralf Dahrendorf in two articles in *Die Zeit* (theoretically anonymous) on 9 and 16 July 1971.

4   Shonfield, *op. cit.*, p. 37.

5   *Ibid.*, p. 88.

6   Various proposals on strengthening the Parliament are usefully summarized in *Europe: the Radical Challenge* by Hugh Thomas (New York: Harper and Row; London: Weidenfeld and Nicolson, 1973), Chapter 3.

7   See 'Europe's Food Balance' by John Marsh and Pierre Uri in *Europe's Tomorrow* (London: Fontana/Collins for Chatham House and PEP, 1972).

8   See *A Future for European Agriculture* by Pierre Uri (Paris: The Atlantic Institute) Atlantic Papers 4, 1971.

9   'A New European Defence' in *Foreign Affairs*, October 1971.

10 *Ibid.*, A similar proposal is contained in my 'The Future of NATO', *International Conciliation*, November 1967.

11 *Shonfield, op. cit.*

12 Congressional Briefing on the SALT agreement, 15 June 1972.

13 *Survival*, May/June 1973.

14 'Atlantic Security in the Seventies', paper presented to the North Atlantic Assembly, September 1971, and in *US Troops in*

Europe by John Newhouse and others (Washington: Brookings Institution, 1971).

15 An unofficial estimate produced by Charles Schultz, *Setting National Priorities in the 1972 Budget* (Washington: Brookings Institution, 1971) produced the much higher figure of $25·4 billion for the American NATO commitment, but this was based on the quite unrealistic assumption that without the NATO commitment the United States could demobilize over nine divisions which would leave her one of the world's minor military powers.

16 Quoted in 'America's Move' by Benjamin S.Rosenthal, *Foreign Affairs*, Spring 1973.

17 See 'The Wasteful Ways of NATO' by Steven L.Canby, *Foreign Policy*, Autumn 1972. Reprinted in *Survival*, January/February 1973.

18 *Ibid*. This article makes a number of other trenchant points which I have not dealt with here.

19 *Ibid*.

20 For the former see Gerda Zellentin in *The World Today*, January 1973; for the latter see a paper by the Oslo International Peace Research Institute quoted in Kaiser, *op. cit.*, p. 65 et seq. For a much earlier sketch along the same lines see my 'The Future of NATO', *International Conciliation*, November 1967 (New York: Carnegie Endowment).

21 Kaiser, *op. cit.*, p. 72.

22 See in particular a speech by William Casey, Under-Secretary of State for Economic Affairs at the University of Georgia Law School, 27 April 1973.

23 Kaiser, *op. cit.*, p. 70.

24 'The Images of Polish, American, German and Chinese Youth', Audience and Public Opinion Department, Radio Free Europe.

25 'Does Europe have a Future?', *Foreign Affairs*, October 1972.

26 See *Reshaping the International Economic Order*, (Washington: Brookings Institute, 1972).

27 See *A Foreign Trade Policy for the EEC* by Dr Theo Peeters, Centre of Economic Studies, Catholic University of Louvain.

Chapter 9

1 See, for instance, *Japanese Society* by Chie Nakane (Berkeley: University of California Press; London: Weidenfeld, 1970).

2 In addition to Miss Nakane's book, I commend *The Fragile Blossom* by Zbgniew Brezinski (New York: Harper & Row, 1972) which is the fruit of a year's sojourn and observation in Japan.

3 *Op. cit.*, p. 23.

4 Brezinski, p. 50, makes the point that Japanese decision-taking in World War Two was slow and indeterminate. The same point emerges from Guy Wint's study (with Peter Calvocoressi) of the Japanese war effort in *Total War* (New York: Pantheon; London: Allen Lane, 1972). Professor Kosaka in his *Options for Japan's Foreign Policy* (London: IISS, Adelphi Paper No. 97) calls it 'a system of mutual irresponsibility'.

5 *Japanese Economic Policies and Security* by Richard Ellingworth (IISS, Adelphi Paper No. 90).

6 Kosaka, *op. cit.* (See Note 4).

7 See statement by Mr Kiichi Aichi, the Finance Minister, on 24 April 1973. Also *The Economist's* survey 'A Special Strength', 31 March 1973, p. 19.

8 Brezinski, *op. cit.*, p. 64.

9 *Yomiuri Shimbun*, May 1970.

10 For a succinct account of why the Japanese distrust the Russians by a Japanese diplomat, see *Japanese Security and the United States* by Kurio Muraoka (London: IISS, Adelphi Paper No. 95)

11 *Op. cit.*, pp. 91 and 117.

12 On 27 February 1973, for instance, Mr Tanisuburo Mashimoto, the influential Secretary General of the LDP, cited as evidence of the denial to Japan of a role commensurate with her power, her lack of a permanent seat on the Security Council and her exclusion from discussions on the rehabilitation of Indo-China.

13 Kosaka, *op. cit.*

14 These figures are derived from polls conducted by *Mainichi Shimbun*, quoted in 'Japan's Role in a New World Order' by Professor Kei Wakaizumi, *Foreign Affairs*, January 1973.

16 Wakaizumi, *op. cit.*

17 Soedjatmoko, 'The End of Bipolarity', *East Asia and the World System* (London: IISS, Adelphi Paper No. 92).

Chapter 10

1 'The Community is Working', *Foreign Affairs*, July 1973.

2 *US Foreign Policy for the 1970s*, 3 May 1973, p. 50.

3 For an excellent analysis of the current Indian–American relationship see 'India and America at Odds' by William J.Barnds, *International Affairs*, July 1973.

4 Repeated in *US Foreign Policy, op. cit.*, p. 40.

5 Robert A.Scalapino, *Asia and the Major Powers* (Stanford: AEI–Hoover Policy Studies, 1972).

6 'Chinese External Policies: Scope and Limitations', in *East Asia and the World System* (London: IISS, Adelphi Paper No. 92).

7 See 'Stability Mechanisms in South East Asia – II' by Philip Darby, *International Affairs*, April 1973. This and his article in the January issue of the same journal provide an excellent analysis of the whole problem.

8 See Scalapino, *op. cit.*, p. 90.

9 In *The Reform of Power* (London: Chatto and Windus, 1972).

10 'The Role of the Major Powers in the Eastern Asia–Pacific Region.' Reprinted in *Survival*, January/February 1972.

Index

312, 318; interests in Asia, 289–290, 300; border dispute, 42–3; diplomacy, 43, 80, 156, 165; and East Africa, 280; and Eastern Europe, 162–3; economic and military position, 42; focuses of change, 305; generational change, 35; and India, 289–90, 294; and Indonesia, 285–6; detente with Japan, 63, 161–2, 262, 271–3; and Latin America, 280; leadership succession, 167; military power, 67, 128; minority groups, 93; new partners?, 161–4; and North Korea, 297; nuclear armaments, 31, 76, 137: and Pakistan, 46, 55; policy objects, 157, 162–4; political size, 322–3; realpolitik, 156–61; a regional power, 166; and social values, 92–3; and South East Asia, 30, 290, 295; and Soviet Union, 4, 6, 21–2, 25, 42–3, 146–7, 154, 158–9, 164–7, 287–90; strategic power, 159–60; trade policy, 20, 162, 163–4, 329; and trilateral balance of influence, 80–1; UN membership, 43, 45; and United States, 25, 30–1, 43–6, 47, 157, 181, 286; and Vietnam settlement, 64

Chou En-lai, 13, 42, 45, 156, 161–2, 164, 209

coal reserves, 102
'cod war', 239
coexistence, 77
cogniscence, 300
Cold War, 3–4, 16–20
Cominform, 19
Comintern, 19
Committee of Twenty, 123
Common Agricultural Policy, 28, 71, 117, 215, 216–19, 254, 256–7
Commonwealth, 19, 46, 148, 217; and EEC, 253; Far East defence agreement, 55; South East Asia defence system, 34
Commonwealth Sugar Agreement, 117

communications, 87; mass media, 89
Communist states, oil consumption, 100; trade, 97, 119–20
company law, EEC policy, 219
computer industry, Europe, 219
Concorde, 10, 219
Congo, 29
Congress (US), increased power, 171
Congress Party (India), 293
Connally, John, 172, 196, 198
Cooper, Richard, 117
Copyright Convention, 145
Cote d'Ivoire, 174
Council of Ministers (EEC), 211–212, 224
Council for Mutual Economic Assistance (COMECON), 70, 250, 309
Croatia, 148
Cuba, 28, 40, 54; missile crisis, 22, 23, 24, 131
Cultural Revolution, 25, 31, 33, 35, 77
currencies, crisis of 1972–3, 125–6; fixed parities, 124–5; floating rates, 126, 215; international, 124; *see also* monetary system
Cyprus, 29, 57, 138
Czechoslovakia, 17, 33, 38, 48, 50, 77, 93, 119, 239, 245, 250; Soviet intervention, 31, 129

Dahrendorf, Dr Ralf, 197
Damansky Island, 42
D'Avignon Committee, 212
de Gaulle, President, 6, 23, 24, 27, 32, 52, 80, 195, 208
Debré, Michel, 223
'Defence Commission' (EEC), 224, 225
Democratic Party (US), 171
Democratic Socialist Party (Japan), 261
Denmark, 52
Denmark Sound, 139
deterrent strategy, 20–1, 142
Deutsch, Karl, 11

Selected Abbreviations

ABM   Anti-Ballistic Missile
CAP   Common Agricultural Policy
CENTO   Central Treaty Organization
COMECON   Council for Mutual Economic Cooperation
CSCE   European Conference on Security and Cooperation (the ordering of initials derives from the French translation)
DDR/GDR   East Germany
ECAFE   Economic Commission for Asia and the Far East
ECSC   European Coal and Steel Community
EDC   European Defence Community
EFTA   European Free Trade Area
FAO   Food and Agricultural Organization
FBS   Forward Based System
GATT   General Agreement on Trade and Tariffs
ICBM   Intercontinental Ballistic Missile
IISS   International Institute for Strategic Studies
IMF   International Monetary Fund
MFBR   Mutual and Balanced Force Reductions (The official title has now been changed to Mutual Force Reductions and Associated Measures)
MIRV   Multiple Independently Targetable Re-entry Vehicle
MRV   Multiple Re-entry Vehicle
OECD   Organization for Economic Cooperation and Development
OPEC   Organization of Petroleum Exporting Countries
PLA   People's Liberation Army
SACEUR   Supreme Allied Commander, Europe
SALT   Strategic Arms Limitation Talks
SDR   Special Drawing Rights
SEATO   South East Asia Treaty Organization
SLBM   Submarine Launched Ballistic Missile
UNCTAD   United Nations Commission on Trade and Development

ALASTAIR BUCHAN was educated at Eton and Oxford and after
World War II became a journalist first for the *Economist* and then
the *Observer* in London. He was Director of the Institute for Strategic Studies in London from 1958 until 1970, and is currently
professor of international relations at Oxford. During 1974-1975,
he will be a fellow at the Smithsonian Institution's Woodrow Wilson
International Center for Scholars in Washington. Professor Buchan
has written or edited nine books.